The Invention
of Taste

SENSORY STUDIES SERIES

Series Editor: David Howes
ISSN: 2052–3092

As the leading publisher of scholarship on the culture of the senses, we are delighted to present this series of cutting-edge case studies, syntheses and translations in the emergent field of sensory studies. Building on the success of the *Sensory Formations* series, this new venture provides an invaluable resource for those involved in researching and teaching courses on the senses as subjects of study and means of inquiry. Embracing the insights of a wide array of humanities and social science disciplines, the field of sensory studies has emerged as the most comprehensive and dynamic framework yet for making sense of human experience. The series offers something for every disciplinary taste and sensory inclination.

Published Titles:

Michael Bull and John P. Mitchell (eds), *Ritual, Performance and the Senses*

François Laplantine, *The Life of the Senses: Introduction to a Modal Anthropology*

Forthcoming Titles:

Rupert Cox, *The Sound of the Sky Being Torn: A Political Ecology of Military Aircraft Noise*

Alex Rhys-Taylor, *Food and Multiculture: A Sensory Ethnography of East London*

The Invention of Taste

A Cultural Account of Desire, Delight and Disgust in Fashion, Food and Art

Luca Vercelloni

Translated by Kate Singleton

Bloomsbury Academic
An imprint of Bloomsbury Publishing Plc

B L O O M S B U R Y
LONDON · OXFORD · NEW YORK · NEW DELHI · SYDNEY

Bloomsbury Academic

An imprint of Bloomsbury Publishing Plc

50 Bedford Square	1385 Broadway
London	New York
WC1B 3DP	NY 10018
UK	USA

www.bloomsbury.com

BLOOMSBURY and the Diana logo are trademarks of Bloomsbury Publishing Plc

First published in Italian in 2005

© Luca Vercelloni, 2005 and 2016

English language translation © Kate Singleton, 2016

Luca Vercelloni has asserted his right under the Copyright, Designs and Patents Act, 1988, to be identified as Author of this work.

British Library Cataloguing-in-Publication Data

A catalogue record for this book is available from the British Library.

ISBN:	HB:	978-1-4742-7360-2
	ePDF:	978-1-4742-7361-9
	ePub:	978-1-4742-7362-6

Library of Congress Cataloging-in-Publication Data

A catalog record for this book is available from the Library of Congress.

Typeset by RefineCatch Limited, Bungay, Suffolk

Printed and bound in Great Britain

CONTENTS

Preface: Accounting for Taste

David Howes

This book is about one of the more fascinating developments in the cultural history of the senses: the invention of "taste." It is written by an interdisciplinary scholar of the first order, a man who moves comfortably across the disciplines of history, philosophy and sociology. The fact that Luca Vercelloni is also a brand expert, and founder of the international consulting firm Brandvoyant, gives him an added insight into contemporary tastes. His account is accordingly a "history of the present," an archeology of the genesis and proliferation of a peculiarly modern sensibility.

To give some historical background to this account, Aristotle identified taste as one of the five senses, but characterized it as "a form of touch," hence lacking autonomy. In the ensuing centuries, as the idea of a hierarchy of the senses was elaborated, taste was grouped with the "lower," "bodily" senses of touch and smell, as opposed to the "higher," "intellectual" senses of sight and hearing. Due to its association with self-indulgent sensuality, it was subject to extensive moral regulation.[1] To be a gourmand—that is, one who revelled in the pleasures of the palate—was to commit the sin of gluttony, one of the seven cardinal sins. With the increasing secularization of society in modernity, gustatory indulgence would lose much of its negative connotation and associations. Vercelloni relates, in one of the many revelations of this book, that a number of former "sins" were in effect recast as "virtues": the sin of vainglory was reconstituted as personal ambition, the sin of sloth was recast as leisure, and the gluttonous delight in fine foods was converted, on the one hand, into gastronomy, and, on the other, metaphorized as the sense of discernment, of beauty. According to Vercelloni, this transformation of vices into virtues was a key element in the coming to be of modern society.

The transformation or bifurcation in the meaning of taste, which appears to have originated in sixteenth-century Italy or seventeenth-century Spain (there is some dispute), unfolded gradually and reached its apogee in the eighteenth century. That century has come down to us under various names: the "Age of Reason" or "Enlightenment," but also the "Age of Sensibility," and, of course, the "Century of Taste." The German philosopher Alexander von Baumgarten played a role in the doubling or reconstitution of taste as the aesthetic sense by introducing the term aesthetic. This term was derived

from the Greek *aisthēsis* (meaning sense perception) to refer to the capacity
to discern the unity in multiplicity of sensible qualities, without recourse to
reason. The new "aesthetic" sense was accorded a variety of names in
English until, thanks to the interventions of Alexander Pope and David
Hume, it became known as taste.[2] However, it is another German philosopher,
Immanuel Kant, to whom we owe the most influential and indeed
transcendental account of this new faculty, as elaborated in the *Critique of
the Power of Judgment*.

   Why taste? Vercelloni asks. Why not refer to this newly-theorized sense
of beauty as a "third eye" or "inner ear"? It would appear that what
commended the metaphor of taste to the thinkers of this period was the
presumed spontaneous and pre-rational as well as subjective character of
this sense. *De gustibus non est disputandum*—"there is no accounting for
taste," as the saying went, with the implication that in this field "to each his
own" applies. This construction agreed with the rising tide of individualism,
the cult of sensibility, and the burgeoning influence of an empiricist mindset
that undermined the Platonic idea of Beauty. Henceforth, the experience of
beauty could only be a matter of perception, not an objective quality.

   It was against this backdrop that the term taste was metaphorized—i.e.,
borrowed from the sphere of the palate and applied to the realm of aesthetics.
In the course of this transposition it was also severed from sensory pleasure.
The purification of taste was the work of Immanuel Kant. Vercelloni
emphasizes that the puritanical and totalitarian, though resolutely
egalitarian, account of taste as based in "disinterestedness" proposed by
Kant was but one construction among others, even if it would prove the
most enduring. There was also the more hedonistic and conciliatory though
distinctly élitist account proposed by Hume, which centred on the sensibility
of the educated gentleman or "Man of Taste." For Kant, however, the
judgment of taste—as related particularly to the fine arts—had to be
disinterested, universal, necessary and pure, which is to say impermeable to
pleasure and need. Hence the famous line: "whoever declares something to
be beautiful wishes that everyone should approve of the object in question."[3]
In this way, beauty (or the experience of "spiritual" pleasure which derives
from it) was isolated, sealed off from the body, and what is merely agreeable
or useful, and came to center on the elevation of the mind. In a new variation
of the religious strictures on sensuality, everything turned on the "continence
of desire" or taming of inclinations, the "snuffing of sensuality," as Vercelloni
puts it, in the cause of intellectual refinement.

   The elevation of sensibility decreed by Kant was motivated by ideology.
It was tied to the Enlightenment dream of a society based on the principle of
universal rights and mutual respect in which each subject "gives the law" to
him- or herself voluntarily. On this account, taste (aesthetic taste, that is)
promotes upward integration and the edification of the subject, in contrast
to the *ancien régime*, where taste was the preserve of an élite, modeled on
the unrestricted gratifications of the aristocracy. However, there was a
contradiction embedded in this construction. On the surface it appeared to

be open to every man, and held out the possibility of consensus, the emergence of a shared sensibility. But this construction obscured the underside of the judgment of taste, which entailed the rejection of all that is facile, childish, vulgar or "primitive." Viewed from this angle, taste can also be seen as a force for discrimination downwards. To have taste, a certain *savoir vivre*, as the bourgeoisie would come to define it, could serve as a source of "cultural capital,"[4] which was the very antithesis of disinterestedness as conceived by Kant.

Vercelloni is adept at exposing the contradictions embedded in the Kantian doctrine of "pure" taste, with its emphasis on controlling (or sublimating) desire "for the betterment of sensibility and manners." But he does not stop there. Rather, he plunges into an exploration of various "lesser" manifestations of taste, which developed as the term spread to encompass discernment in other domains besides the fine arts—most notably food and fashion—on its way to becoming the most ubiquitous disposition of the nascent consumer culture. The taste of the palate and taste in clothing were dismissed or belittled by Kant on account of their seemingly ephemeral and whimsical character—their lack of continence and consistency. But these "impure" tastes, with their accent on frivolity or excess (i.e. distance from necessity) would win out over the aesthetics of solemnity and distance championed by Kant on account of their link to the post-Enlightenment penchant for self-fashioning and privileging of personal identity over social equality.

To understand this shift entails delving into the other meaning of the adage *De gustibus non est disputandum*, which is hidden from us today because of our ignorance of the premodern cosmology on which it was based. Vercelloni's archeology of gustatory perception indicates that the reason there could be no disputing taste was due to medieval dietetics. The latter regimen was informed by humoral theory, which held that the temperament of each individual was determined by the balance of humors in the body, which, in turn, was often assigned an astrological basis. The task of the cook was to blend the hot or cold, wet or dry qualities of the food served up to match or modulate the temperament of his patron. In this view, there was nothing temperamental (in a modern sense) or fickle about taste. Individual tastes were cosmologically conditioned, hence given in the order of things, intrinsically incommensurable, and therefore impervious to disputation.

Of note in this connection was the curious phenomenon of the "silence of taste"[5] in the first cooking manuals and recipe books (dating from the mid-seventeenth century) which contained the seeds of the discourse of gastronomy. The authors of these books did not rationalize their concoctions in terms of the pleasures they afforded (that would have been immoral), but referred instead to the Providence of the Creator, or the therapeutic benefits of different foodstuffs. Taste (gustatory taste, that is) was muted, and, aside from providing recipes, the food writing of the period dwelt mainly on the rules of comportment (table manners) and the visual order or architecture of the banquet, as if the repasts concerned were intended more as feasts for the eyes than the palate. It was not until the latter half of the eighteenth century that the cult of good food and elegant dining, with Versailles as its epicentre, became established, and the thoroughly modern figure of the gourmet or gastronome arrived on the scene.

The role of the gastronome, as the name implies, is "to rule over the appetites of others." Unlike the seventeenth-century authors of cookery books, who often wrote in the third person, the gastronome writes in the first person. He uses his personal taste to sample and pronounce judgments, which can then be followed by others (i.e. status seekers). The whole point of the gastronome's existence is to make an exception of himself, to "show off his unparalleled sensory refinement."[6] His is a discourse that eschews universality, being founded on the pleasures of diversity, and goes to great length in the pursuit of detail. Gastronomic writing evoked "voluptuous experience, titillating the tastebuds and promoting lubricious salivation." Kant—as well as the Church Fathers—would have been aghast.

The literature of gastronomy never amounted to more than a minor literary genre, disdained by philosophers, but its "appetising eloquence" proved disarming—and charming. Most importantly, according to Vercelloni, it was addressed to an audience "desirous of discovering exactly what it should experience, prefer and appreciate," and provided "a way of enclosing individual sensibility." This function was particularly important in the heady days after the Revolution of 1789 when restaurants sprang up all over Paris, manned by the chefs who had been put out of work by the execution of their patrons. Middle-class restaurants provided the bourgeoisie with an institutional context for self-fashioning, and the gastronome provided them with a compass and language for their desires. Another key supplier of the means of individuation that arose during this period was the fashion house.[7] Like the restaurant, it provided its clients with a range of options from which each could choose. In this way, *haute cuisine* and *haute couture*, which were both inspired by and derived from court society, were commercialized and rendered respectable diversions as "vehicles for the principle of personal style." From this perspective, the most salient outcome of the revolutionary period was thus not so much the right to equality as the "right to desire," to pursue happiness. The "arts of pleasing"—gastronomy and fashion—now vied with the fine arts as avenues for the discovery and refinement of individual sensibility.

This brings us to the final chapter of Vercelloni's book, "The Economy of Taste in Consumer Society," which covers the period from the beginning of the nineteenth century down to the present. In the section on "Bewitching Commodities," Vercelloni traces the trajectory from the first *magasins de nouveautés* and arcades to the *grands magasins*, such as the Bon Marché department store, and universal exhibitions that served as sites for the "democratization of luxury" and idealization of commodities. This period witnessed the transformation of capitalism from a mode of production predicated on self-discipline and sensory restriction into a mode of presentation-seduction (e.g. window displays, advertising) and consumption, premised on self-indulgence and sensory enticement.

In "Ease and Progress," Vercelloni describes how the shock that came in the wake of the democratization of luxury and the onslaught of commodities, the proliferation of tastes, and the rise of mass taste provoked a rearguard action. This came in the form of the Modernist Movement. The proponents of Modernism denigrated ornament, denounced the spread of "feminine taste" (on account of its alleged frivolity and excess), and decried anything that was easy, or comfortable. They spoke in the name of rationality, progress and efficiency with such slogans as "form follows function" and "less is more." Kant would have approved. The "enlightened" ascetic aesthetic of contemplation and distance reasserted itself —as can be seen in the linear purity and grey predictability of the modern office tower, or the home designed as a "machine for living." Then Modernism lost its hold, became just one style among others, and was even outstripped by the style of streamlining (e.g. the tailfins of a 1950s Chevrolet, which had as much to do with ornamentation as function).

In a section entitled "The Gallery of Iconoclasm," Vercelloni relates how modern art (the art of the avant garde) was born with "the explicit intention of *not pleasing*." Divorced from aesthetics (as conventionally understood), it became an outlet for "the spirit of desecration" and scandal. This in turn is exemplified by Marcel Duchamp's submission of "Fountain," which consisted of a urinal turned on its side, as an exhibition for the Salon of Independent Artists in New York in 1917. By taking the lowliest of everyday objects (a readymade at that) and promoting it as art, Duchamp upset and made a mockery of the established norms of art. (While rejected at the time, Duchamp's gesture has been growing in stature ever since.) Art after Duchamp would emphasize individual genius (or self-referentiality) over beauty and skill. As for taste, "Taste is no longer the faculty for recognizing an abstract ideal, a shared goal to which all ages in history were supposed to draw closer. [Instead, it] is Style that commands, the prototype of all individual predilections: gratuitous, revocable, and yet at the same time irresistible and inexplicably contagious."

In "Tattooed Man," Vercelloni delves deeper into the election of style as a dominant ideal of taste in the twentieth century as exemplified by the figure of the fashion designer. The fashion designer "lays down the laws of vanity": his or her signature helps people in their choice of what to wear by canonizing (a particular) taste or style. Designers such as Christian Dior and Pierre Cardin have also drawn up a vast range of previously unrelated commodities—"from garments to cosmetics, chocolate, furniture and appliances"—into the realm of fashion, under the system of brand licensing, investing them "with their personal charisma to further their commercial success." The exponential growth of the style trade, which centres on "the metamorphosis of brands into the symbols and mirages of lifestyles," can no longer be explained in terms of competition between social classes, "trickle-down" effects, and the like, because designers now increasingly take their inspiration from the streets (e.g., grunge, hiphop). Rather, the "irresistibility of fashion lies in its ability to foment desires and encourage the compulsion for luxury, or at least what is superfluous, in the name of self-realization." Sadly, being a follower of fashion is no guarantee of happiness or "material grace." It just as often issues in disappointment and depression, "the empty chimera of unfulfilled promise."

In the final section of Chapter 5, Vercelloni turns his attention to the "nutritional prosperity" that the industrialization of the food chain and globalization have wrought. Ours is an age of overabundance that holds out the promise of unlimited freedom of choice. It is no longer the case that you are what you eat; instead you eat (or at least try to eat) what you would like to be. Food choice is no longer conditioned by cultural background and family habit, but rather by self-affirmation and body-image. However, this ostensible gastro-utopia has created more hunger, not less, and instituted an ever-growing rift between control and indulgence, between the duties involved in looking after one's health and giving in to temptation. Whence the proliferation of diets promising nutritional salvation and longevity, and all the new gastronomies of pleasure beginning with the *nouvelle cuisine* of the 1970s, which heralded a return to "nature," the primacy of ingredients over processing, and "lighter," "simpler" fare (in contrast to the monumental, pompous dishes of *haute cuisine*). Also of note in this connection is the phenomenon of "gastronomic restoration"—the counter-revolution in taste that has put pasta and olive oil (essential ingredients of the Mediterranean diet), daily doses of red wine (the French elixir) and "gastronomic treasures" (the "typical" products of a given *terroir*) back on the "High Table of Comestibles." Of course, these time-honored traditions are no less invented than the latest food fad, but we delight in the reassurance they provide just the same.

Summing up, Vercelloni writes: "Impure, changeable and concupiscent though it may be, taste is the true engine of consumer society, the organ of individual preferences and the tool with which people build up their personalities. Spurned by educated aesthetics, it has its revenge in ratifying an inalienable right: the search for human happiness; in other words the right to desire."

In this account, I have provided only the briefest sketch of the many twists and turns of Vercelloni's own account of the "odyssey" of taste. The map he provides is vital reading for anyone—taste-maker, cultural historian or ordinary consumer—interested in understanding how tastes are invented and diffused in today's society. He gives us access, in a way which is rare in contemporary cultural history, to the big picture, in all its eclectic detail. When this work was first published in Italian in 2005, it attracted much critical acclaim. Vercelloni nevertheless revised it extensively for this English edition. He was fortunate to find Kate Singleton to translate his work, for she has succeeded magnificently at transposing the author's many subtle, and deeply perspicacious, turns of phrase into their English equivalents.

Just as the history of sight is not synonymous with that of painting, and the history of smell must needs depart from that of perfume, so the history of taste could never be confined to the history of cuisine. The extent to which taste has spread since its metaphorization, and become the ground for so many struggles (between classes, between sexes) in so many domains (fashion, food, art, architecture, design), across so many senses (there is taste in music as well as food), the paradoxical way in which taste has been universally adopted as a means for *individual* expression and gratification and serves as the engine of consumer society—point to the necessity for a *cultural* account of taste. It is such an account that is provided in this book, giving the lie to the still commonplace expression *De gustibus non est disputandum*.

Notes

1   For excellent accounts of the moral regulation of the senses in the early modern period see W. de Boer, "The Counter-Reformation of the Senses," in A. Bamji, G. Jansen and M. Laven (eds), *The Ashgate Research Companion to the Counter Reformation*, Ashgate Publishing, Farnham, Surrey, 2013, pp. 243-60; and C. Classen, *The Deepest Sense: A Cultural History of Touch*, University of Illinois Press, Champaign, 2012.

2   Other terms for this new faculty included the "inner sense," the "seventh sense" and the "sense of beauty." The invention—or, discrimination—of new senses in the eighteenth century is a fascinating topic, which calls out for more investigations like the present one. See D. Howes, "Introduction," in D. Howes (ed.), *The Sixth Sense Reader*, Berg, Oxford, 2009.

3   I. Kant, *Critique of the Power of Judgment*, Cambridge University Press, Cambridge, 2000, p. 121.

4   P. Bourdieu, *Distinction: A Social Critique of the Judgement of Taste*, Harvard University Press, Cambridge, MA, 1984.

5   V. von Hoffman, *Goûter le monde: Une histoire culturelle du goût à l'époque moderne*, Peter Lang, Brussels, 2013.

6   Kant did not approve of people making exceptions of themselves in aesthetics—or in ethics. See G. Grant, *English-Speaking Justice*, House of Anansi Press, Toronto, 1985.

7   Vercelloni quotes Lipovetsky regarding how the rise (and volatility) of fashion is related to "the awareness of being an individual with a specific destiny, the desire to express an original identity and the cultural celebration of personal identity." For Vercelloni himself, however, the matter is not just one of individuation but also one of feminization—the feminization of taste, "the predominance of the female sensibility." See especially his discussion of the Great Sacrifice and the Great Revenge.

References

Boer, Wietse de, "The Counter-Reformation of the Senses," in Alexandra Bamji, Geert Jansen and Mary Laven (eds), *The Ashgate Research Companion to the Counter Reformation*, Ashgate Publishing, Farnham, Surrey, 2013, pp. 243-60.

Bourdieu, Pierre, *Distinction: A Social Critique of the Judgement of Taste*, Harvard University Press, Cambridge, MA, 1984.

Classen, Constance, *The Deepest Sense: A Cultural History of Touch*, University of Illinois Press, Champaign, 2012.

Grant, George, *English-Speaking Justice*, House of Anansi Press, Toronto, 1985.

Hoffman, Viktoria von, *Goûter le monde: Une histoire culturelle du goût à l'époque moderne*, Peter Lang, Brussels, 2013.

Howes, David, "Introduction," in David Howes (ed.), *The Sixth Sense Reader*, Berg, Oxford, 2009, pp. 1-52.

Kant, Immanuel, *Critique of the Power of Judgment*, Cambridge University Press, Cambridge, 2000.

David Howes
Series Editor
30 September 2015

Acknowledgments

Though this book aims to trace a cultural history of taste through different ages, conceptually it starts from the end: from my own empirical observations of consumer behavior, attitudes and aspirations over a period of three decades and in around forty countries. During my research it became increasingly evident that geography, age, gender, social background and education influence and shape people's varied lifestyles and preferences, dreams and desires. Culture is the yardstick and engine of the apparently volatile kaleidoscope of human tastes.

When culture is freed from the artificial confines of academic debate and is extended to embrace material and social phenomena, it also provides the only reliable standpoint for appraisal of the evolution of taste as a social fact.

Several important books have been written about taste, and of course I am indebted to Bourdieu, Croce, Dorfles, Elias, Simmel, Sombart, Tatarkiewicz and many other eminent scholars who have dealt with the topic. But I always I felt that something was missing. The subject required a comprehensive overview that could explain the outwardly irrational manifestations and whimsical practices of taste within the fields of arts, fashion, cuisine, and entertainment. And, above all, why all these fields are subject to the same concept—taste. Analysis of a huge quantity of facts and figures persuaded me that individual taste represents a cultural construct, an implicit self-portrait that relates our identity to that of others in an ongoing process of emulation and differentiation, sense of belonging and aspiration to change. Such are the guidelines that I have used in my exploration of the different stages of the history of taste.

I spent five years writing the first Italian edition of the book, and another five revising and enriching the text for the present English edition. I am particularly grateful to my friend Sebastiano Cossia Castiglioni, a connoisseur of fine arts, wine and cuisine, who encouraged me to accomplish this double effort and provided me with precious advice. I am also very grateful to Kate Singleton who patiently and skillfully accomplished the polished and impeccable English translation of the text. Special thanks also go to Serena Feloj who helped me with a meticulous bibliographic revision. Lastly, I am beholden to Jennifer Schmidt of Bloomsbury, who first acknowledged the value of the manuscript, and I especially am grateful to professor David Howes for his enthusiastic support of the publication and for agreeing to write the insightful preface.

Introduction

The history of successful ideas is full of discontinuity and metamorphosis. And that of taste is no exception. For such twists and turns actually help promote what is new, widening its relevance and sphere of acceptance, changing habits and modifying representative images.

The odyssey of taste is swathed in enigma and paradox, starting with the original meaning of the word. As one of the five senses, taste is a natural faculty, an integral part of our biological constitution. However, it is also acquired, and thus not entirely natural: an expression of habit, tradition and the civilizing process no less than of corporeity. Taste is stimulated by hunger and the instinct for survival, but also by the seduction of value and privilege. It captures and reveals human pleasure, starting with the primordial need to satiate hunger and thirst. It is adaptable, variable and subject to influence, in relation to the variety and availability of food and drink. The sense of beauty that guides visual taste presents much the same problem, in that it is spontaneous and unintentional, and yet at the same time susceptible to improvement, refinement and education. Though it tends to conform to models imposed by society, it can also vary according to culture and historic period. Thus both gastronomic and aesthetic taste are characterized by the same basic ambivalence.

This essential contradiction is part and parcel of the history of taste, perceived as an expression of a sensibility that can be communicated, learned and perfected. On this account taste can also claim to be an uncontestable form of knowledge, however partial, imperfect and elusive it may appear to be.

Another feature intrinsic to the idea is the stratification of meanings and spheres of experience inherent in its development. Taste comes across as pooled knowledge, as an accumulation that absorbs and reshapes earlier conceptions rather than erasing them. When the term is used to refer to something immaterial, the original sensorial meaning acts as an analogy that supports and divulges the new semantic content. Even when taste invests an exclusively spiritual sphere, its relationship to the palate remains, by way of difference and contrast.

When knowledge and experience are stratified, they inevitably interweave and do so with many other threads of history. In particular, with the history of art and its contemplative function, which both have a great deal to do with taste as a metaphor. But also with the history of costume and fashion, whose evolution mirrors the loosening of moral constraints; with the invention of good manners; with the development of luxury; with the stylization of vanity and appearance—all of which are an integral part of the metaphor in its widest acceptance. As for the history of ideas and ideology, it engages taste within the overall perspective of modern subject's spiritual prerogatives. Lastly there is the history of cuisine and gastronomy, which tends towards the refinement of the palate and the portrayal of taste as a manifestation of privilege and cultural accomplishment.

At this point it is clear that only an "eclectic" reconstruction of the history of taste can throw light on the points of contact, mutual influence and fusion that have characterized its parallel lives. Such an approach has the advantage of transcending the disciplinary confines and interpretative constraints typical of the specialist perspective. Its originality lies in its ability to cross borders and provide new insights.

The first of the five chapters of this book is devoted to the invention of the metaphor that transformed a bodily sense into a faculty of the mind. Scholars of the past have posited a number of explanations for this phenomenon, but most of them leave many questions unanswered. Why exactly did taste become a metaphor? What counter-effects did this semantic development have on artistic perception? What were the conditions that made this side-step possible? As we shall see, the famous medieval adage *de gustibus non est disputandum* helped mediate the transition, but acquired a whole new meaning in the process.

Chapter 2 reconstructs the main stages in the "moral history" of taste. Starting with the manifestations of "weakness" criticized by ancient Greek and Roman commentators, it traces the secularization of the capital sins to focus on the birth of sumptuous cuisine and the necessary refinement of appetites. In so doing, it throws light on how the spread and acceptance of an idea paved the way for the expression of predilection, and thus the evolution of customs and the development of self-awareness.

In Chapter 3, thoughts are centered on the main theories of taste propounded by philosophers once the phenomenon had spread from the sphere of the body to that of the mind. Though many authors have argued that the whole process was both natural and intrinsically excellent, it is our opinion that the Kantian divide between palate and mind is anything but the objective fruit of theoretical endeavor. To the contrary, it is the necessary corollary of Enlightenment equalitarianism.

Chapter 4 takes a look at two "lesser" manifestations of taste: gastronomy and fashion, which continue to exercise considerable influence despite Kant's evident disapproval. Until recently, in fact, academic study spurned these two spheres of activity, which were deemed extraneous to serious literature. The chapter also proposes possible explanations for just why this should have been so.

Finally, Chapter 5 deals with the various different manifestations of taste in contemporary society, where the term implies "good taste" and is thus a measure of social distinction. This in itself means redefining the phenomenon and establishing a new framework for its applications. The commercialization of taste, the aesthetic straitjacket imposed by architecture and design, the rejection of common criteria for appreciating modern art, and the wide range of identities offered by ubiquitous fashion all relate to the paradoxes of taste during the twentieth century. The chapter then examines taste relating to the palate in an age when such sensorial perception has been irreversibly remodeled and transformed by ideological and conceptual constraints. The chapter ends by providing an account of the triumph of pleasure in consumer society, with its power to manipulate the development of taste, from its first appearance as a metaphor through to the present day.

1

The Success of a Metaphor

The figurative use of the term "taste" to refer to the human faculty for discerning between what is beautiful and what is ugly is a relatively recent cultural acquisition. It implies being in possession of measure, refinement and skill (in dressing, self-expression, and the appraisal of other people's accomplishments); but also the enjoyment of products intended for contemplation, and indeed the ability to describe a cultural context and the stylistic features characteristic of a given period, nation or artistic circle.

Taste, as a word, has become so common in everyday language that nowadays it would be impossible to contain it within the sphere of its original meaning: the sensation of the palate, or the perception of the flavor of a given food or delicacy. Taste has definitively come to embrace the universe that derives from that sensorial Ur-experience, in other words, the experience of what is beautiful.

Yet, for a good thousand years, Western civilization was perfectly able to cope without this extended meaning, despite people's evident interest in the availability of precious products. Luxury and opulence, elegant attire and coiffure, fine tapestries, paintings and sculptures all held sway well before the word taste was introduced to signify discernment. Those who could, read poetry, listened to music and went to the theater. They talked long and deep about the sublime, and even spent fortunes on the purchase of particular foods and spices. And they did so without feeling the need to establish a link or similitude between the perception of beauty and the sense that pertains to the palate.

The Sense of Discernment

The figurative use of the term taste thus brings about a neologism, which is believed to have spread between the sixteenth and seventeenth centuries, leaving its mark on manners of speech and thought.

That said, however, scholars do not agree over what exactly came when. Benedetto Croce,[1] among others, argued that the origin of the metaphor is to be found in the stirring of arts and ideas that centered on Renaissance Italy. Initially interchangeable with "judgment," a word it was later to replace, taste in this case was the organ of aesthetic sensibility: that special faculty that eludes reason, but allows communication between the artist and his or her public. In other words, between two characters who play different roles with respect to the past. The artist is no longer the skilled craftsman who submits to the desires of the patron or client, but an individual moved by inspiration and endowed with charismatic talent who expresses his creative genius in his work. Those who are able to grasp and appreciate the brilliance and originality of style above and beyond meaning or intent constitute the artist's public. And it is taste that creates the link between the two.

Other scholars, including Schümmer[2] and Franckowiak,[3] were more inclined to attribute the paternity of the taste metaphor to Spanish authors on morality, especially Baltasar Gracián, for whom taste was not so much an expression of the recognition of beauty as a person's ability to choose and pursue whatever suits his or her nature and contributes to the sensation of happiness. It was thus conceived as an inclination that is both natural and cultivated, in so far as it is part of human society and only in this instance acquires relevance and value. Within this perspective, Gracián speaks of *good taste*, which he deemed a precious gift in social life. Indeed, he related it to *tact*, which is another sense that has extended its original range of significance to embrace discretion and composure.

Regardless of where the extended meaning of taste may first have originated, the cultural roots underlying the success of the metaphor are somewhat different. While both aim at explaining the newly acquired importance of sensibility within the hierarchy of human faculties, one pertains to the world of art and the awareness of beauty, and the other to the refinement and stylization of behavior. The taste metaphor is thus an expression of the new culture that is both a product and an image of Europe, but one that is based on an essential ambiguity, shaped by growing social awareness and therefore subject to continual change.

Benedetto Croce hesitated initially, but ultimately ascribed the paternity of the metaphor to Italy. Later Robert Klein followed suit, but with greater conviction. In their view, it was Italy that nurtured the modern conception of taste into being.

According to Klein, the gestation of the taste concept as an expression of aesthetic sensibility came about during the sixteenth century, under the influence of natural philosophy, especially in the disciplines relating to the soul: astrology, the theory of temperaments, magic and their most subtle, worldly manifestations, particularly the theory of love, of female beauty, of persuasion, of musical modes and of melancholic genius.[4]

Klein identified in the treatises on art of the period a progressive replacement of the term "judgment" with that of "taste," and argued that this lexical mutation both accompanied and to some extent promoted a cultural hiatus. For while "judgment" still bears witness to a certain intellectual approach and assumes the existence of ideal rules, the taste metaphor suggests something more akin to an instinctive faculty relating to the appetites, a sphere in which judgment (or its quasi synonym, "discretion") introduces a further, decisive acknowledgment: the discovery of artistic individuality.

The success of the metaphor is thus the epilogue of an age in the history of aesthetics: the doctrine of *mimesis*, which had prevailed for several thousand years, gives way to the exaltation of individual genius as the source and inspiration of artistic creation, a wellspring of energy that transcends the established order and stands in opposition to tradition. As Hauser has pointed out, this conception was entirely alien to the Middle Ages, which did not attribute value to originality and to creative spontaneity, but rather urged artists to imitate, and indeed copy, their masters.[5] No longer tied to ideal canons and established rules, the painter heeded only his own inner desire to "paint himself." In other words, a concept of taste that was tantamount to *style* or *manner* brought about an "involuntary self-portrait" on the part of the artist, which in its turn ushered in newfound glory, reputation and market value.

The inevitable counterpart to artistic celebrity was the parallel refinement of critical acumen among those in a position to appreciate and appraise works of art. Indeed, it was taste that acted as the commercial platform linking artist and potential customer. And it is worth pointing out that the phenomenon of collecting that came about during the Renaissance coincided chronologically with the perception of the artist as a creative spirit that was not anchored to the desires of the patron or customer.

Up until the fifteenth century, the art market had been shaped by demand. Each work was created as the fruit of a commission, which implied exact awareness of where it was to be displayed: an altarpiece for a chapel with which the painter was familiar, for instance, or a devotional painting for a particular room, or indeed the portrait of a family member for a certain wall.[6] Since many different arts, which included what we would now call crafts as well as painting and sculpture, were practiced in the same workshop, they tend to blend in with each other. Only during the following century, when art was accorded a degree of autonomy, did the creative spirit acquire independence from practical goals in a manner that placed art on a totally different footing to crafts. At this point the artist was free to give full rein to his creative inspiration, with little regard for the desires of the patron or client. And this, in its turn, gave rise to a new generation of buyers: experts, connoisseurs, who no longer made their purchases as part of celebratory or commemorative obligations, but as an expression of their desire to possess the works of famous artists of that period, or indeed of the past. Little wonder, then, the market for antiquities also came into being during the same age.

Essential to this development was the fact that the experts and connoisseurs were necessarily "*huomini di gusto*," or men of taste, who attributed value to works of art regardless of their practical purpose. So just as taste became a metaphor, it also evolved to imply *good taste*—even if the term itself was still to be coined. This meant that right from the outset, the concept of taste was able to exercise a sort of cultural monopoly: "what we call Renaissance was the patrimony of ideas, jealously guarded and exclusive, of an élite imbued with Latin culture. The most meaningful works of art were created for this circle. The world at large knew nothing about them whatsoever. This gave rise to the distance between the cultured minority and the uncultured majority that was to prove insuperable and decisive for all future developments, though it was practically unheard of in earlier ages. No one ever decided (as they did later) to create a culture that was deliberately reserved for an élite, and from which the majority was to be excluded."[7]

If good taste is the ultimate arbiter in appraising works of art, the attention of the public inevitably slips from content to form, from interpretation to impression, from understanding to contemplation. Art at this point claims its own right to exist, freeing itself of the subordinate role it had played in an earlier age, when it had necessarily contained a message, albeit in allegorical terms. Formal perfection and immediate impact were certainly required to capture the attention of the viewer, but only as a way of achieving a higher goal: that of communicating a moral, religious or social message. In this sense, art worked along the same lines as fables, which in medieval times turned to elegance and style not for the sake of beauty, but in order to be rhetorically effective.

From the Renaissance on, the importance of the communicative functions of a work of art diminished as the accent on visual impact became more marked. Moreover, the contemplation of beauty brought with it conscious admiration of the creative genius of the artist. If medieval art was largely bent on education, the primary focus of that of the Renaissance was the principle of *delectatio*, or experiencing delight. This was a radical break with the past.

A great many books have been written in praise of the autonomy acquired by art. Very few, on the other hand, have taken a more critical approach to the subject. Yet to appreciate fully the degree of change that came about, the cultural shock that it produced, and the concomitant disarray in artistic perception, it would probably be more instructive to listen to the lament of the defeated rather than the panegyrics of the victors—and not only because modernity has learned to turn a deaf ear to the ensuing confusion. To formulate the question in more immediate terms, if an orthodox Schoolman of the Middle Ages were catapulted into the twentieth century (or even the nineteenth, for that matter) and could obtain an overall view of the history of art during the past five centuries, what would be his reaction?

Confronted by the despotic supremacy of form over content, he might well surmise that "the current approach (to works of art) may be compared to that of a traveler who, when he finds a signpost, proceeds to admire its elegance, to ask who made it, and finally cuts it down to use as a mantelpiece ornament."[8]

To our hypothetical time traveler, not only the emphasis on form would appear to be incomprehensible, but also the aesthetic foundations of modern art: "The Greek original of the word 'aesthetic' means perception by the senses. Aesthetic experience is a faculty that we shared with animals and vegetables, and is irrational. The 'aesthetic soul' is that part of a psychic makeup that 'senses' things and reacts to them: in other words, the 'sentimental' part of us. To identify our approach to art with the pursuit of these reactions is not to make art 'fine,' but to apply it only to the life of pleasure."[9] So to claim that the aesthetic can be assimilated with art is simply misguided: "Aesthetic experience is of the skin you love to touch, or the fruit you love to taste. (To speak of) 'disinterested aesthetic contemplation' is a contradiction in terms and a pure non-sense."[10]

At this point the astonished Schoolman would be bound to express his complete disapproval of what he had seen. If art fails to communicate ideas, aiming at no higher good than the promise of pleasure, if its only goal is to tickle our emotional sphere, then the chances are that feelings alone will claim to be the arbiter of beauty, and all judgment will be a question of taste. In other words, all aesthetic appraisals will be entirely subjective. If this is the case, then art would be not just a question of opinion, but also the subject of moral reproof: "The purpose of art it to give pleasure, the work of art as a source of pleasure is its own end; (. . .) our conception of beauty is literally skin-deep; (. . .) the work of art is then a luxury, an accessory to the life of pleasure."[11] Furthermore, "to equate love of art with love of fine sensation is to make of works of art a kind of aphrodisiac":[12] today we "prostitute its thesis to an aesthesis; and this is the sin of luxury."[13]

To think that the taste metaphor could lead to so much!

As Croce pointed out, the expression was coined as a result of the new ideas and disquisitions on art. With respect to Klein's reconstruction, however, Croce moved the birth of the metaphor forward to the seventeenth century, when "several new words emerged, or new meanings for existing words, such as: genius, taste, imagination or fantasy, sentiment and other similar terms."[14] Amid such lexical fervor, the word *taste* took on a number of figurative meanings. In Italy and Spain, the term *gusto*, borrowed directly from the sphere of the palate and applied to the spirit—or indeed to entertainment—was equivalent to *pleasure* or *delight*. Another meaning that was equally common in Italy, as Klein also appreciated, was *judgment* (*giudizio*), applied to "any literary, scientific or artistic matter."[15] For Croce, however, there were only two anticipations of what taste, "the special faculty or attitude of the soul," would mean in modern times. He initially believed that Spain and France were the source of this semantic development. In the mid-1600s, Spain adopted what Croce described as an expression of "concise eloquence: good taste," meaning a form of behavior based on *discretion* or *tact*, whereas France, during the last quarter of the same century, started using the term in its aesthetic sense.[16] Later, however, Croce reviewed his original attribution, distinguishing between the words themselves and the ideas for which they stood, and arriving at the conclusion that Italy had played a fundamental role in the ensuing extension of meaning. "It was the Italians . . . who posited a special aesthetic power or faculty that was able to judge without logical arguments, as clearly defined by Zuccolo in 1623."[17]

The fact remains, however, that the Italian and French dictionaries of the period fail to include the new meaning of the term. Yet while the early editions of the *Vocabolario degli Accademici della Crusca* are entirely reticent on the subject,[18] the *Dictionnaire de l'Académie Française* (1694) does at least prepare the ground for change, listing and clarifying in considerable detail most of the modern interpretations of taste. Alongside expressions that were evidently already in use, such as "good taste, delicate taste, exquisite or depraved taste," we also come across the following distinctions:

a. the sense that presumably originated in Spain, suggesting "discernment, fine judgment, sensitivity";

b. the more Hedonistic, sensual meaning that implies "pleasurable or enjoyable feelings regarding a given object";

c. the more formal, style-oriented use of the word that communicates the idea of "the way in which something is made or done, or the particular character of a work";

d. the historical, critical extension of the term that is applied to the "character of an author, a painter, a sculptor, or the general character of a century."

Clearly these partial definitions of taste still fail to tally with the modern conception of the term that so obsessed the philosophers and moralists of the following century. What is missing is the meaning whose origins Croce attributed to Italy: the idea of a "superior power" of eye and ear (without which "even horses and dogs would have the same taste for painting or music that we enjoy") that combines with the senses "to create judgment, which increases in relation to the gifts of nature and the skills of art, *yet without requiring rational discourse.*"[19]

Before this conception of taste could become part of the idiomatic expressions of learned speech it had to be freed of the audaciously pictorial metaphor, which took several decades. The international success of the metaphor was certainly enormous, as an entry written in 1778 by Voltaire for the *Encyclopédie* made explicit. Without bothering to outline the birth and development of the concept, he simply declared that "this sense, this gift for distinguishing our foods has produced in all known languages the metaphor that uses the word taste to express sensitivity to the beauty and defects of all arts."[20]

To differentiate itself from the past and make its intent more intelligible, the change in aesthetic sensibility clearly called for new terminology. To be precise, what was required was a word that could stand for the special faculty of judgment; a form of mixed metaphor, or catachresis, as it is known in rhetoric.[21] But just why was taste the chosen term, especially in view of the fact that since ancient times this particular sense had been deemed the most abject and wretched of faculties? Why seek a paragon with the palate, rather than suggesting a third eye, or an inner ear, to follow Zuccolo's line of argument, or indeed the heart itself, given that the elusive faculty was so full of sentiment?

Evidently because the taste option was more effective and better suited to expressing the anti-dogmatic questions in hand. Underlying its superior suitability were two essential and decisive aspects of the future debate on taste and its manifold manifestations: one concerned pleasure, and the other spontaneity (as opposed to reasoning).

As far as the former is concerned, it would be tempting to explain that taste was able to gain ground as a metaphor for artistic discernment because, of all the senses, it is arguably the most universal and instinctive vehicle of pleasure. In actual fact, however, the question is rather less straightforward. If direct comparison with appraisal of the palate is to work, then we must deal with the moral and aesthetic question of how to distinguish between the two levels of pleasure. Voltaire claimed that the taste of the palate related to the taste of the spirit rather as the gourmet related to the connoisseur;[22] indeed, he believed that even in questions of culinary preference it was legitimate to speak of bad or depraved taste. "Just as physical bad taste consists of being stimulated by sauces that are too spicy and refined, so bad taste in the arts lies in the appreciation of contrived ornamentation rather than in that of beautiful nature. Depraved taste in food is choosing what other people find disgusting: it is a sort of sickness. Depravation of taste in the arts is finding pleasure in those subjects which appall refined minds, is preferring burlesque to noble, choosing what is affected and artificial over what is simple and natural: it is a sickness of the spirit."[23]

The parallels end here. While taste of the palate is innate, universal and related to genetic makeup, that of the spirit is not a feature of all men, or indeed of all peoples. It requires protracted cultural training to achieve refinement, and favorable social and political conditions to gain ground. So when "one says that there is no disputing taste, this is true if we're talking about taste as a sense, that is about the disgust certain foods provoke and the preference some people have for others: there is no disputing such reactions because you cannot correct a physical defect."

But the question is different when talking of art. In this case, the defects of the mind (in other words, the inability to recognize beauty) can be corrected, that is refined. Likewise, according to Montesquieu, if it is true that taste is "the measure of pleasure," then there are acquired pleasures, and others that are entirely spiritual, in other words detached from the senses and "founded on the inclinations and prejudices that certain institutions, customs and habits" have imposed upon the human spirit.[24]

More complex still is the second aspect of the metaphor, which pertains to the pre-rational or spontaneous character of taste. Ever since the sixteenth century, all treatises on the subject have underlined the impulsive nature of taste in contrast to the labored nature of reason. The former concerns "immediate discernment, like that of the tongue and the palate, and, like this, comes before reflection."[25] Some authors even posited a "sixth sense," against which "concepts and disputes are of no avail," since no argument could convince us "to believe the opposite of what we perceive."[26]

During the Renaissance, this insistence on the instinctive nature of taste became the backbone of the metaphor, the true antidote to intellectualism brandished to assert the emancipation of art and the exaltation of individuality. Once it had become an established creed, however, it unleashed a host of contradictions: if taste does not heed reason, is it truly arbitrary? And if this is the case, why do people busy themselves with "producing works of art, costly and elegant edifices, fine gardens and other such labors"?[27] If the saying "each to his/her own" is true, then how can we speak of "good taste"? And if taste is instinctive, how can it be refined? Lastly, if it is vain to account for taste, how come so much time is spent discussing it?

De gustibus non est disputandum: in essence the famous medieval adage embraces the entire history of taste. Its gradual loss of verisimilitude and the repertory of confutations that so engaged innumerable thinkers (including some of the greatest minds of the Enlightenment) are part of the tangled web that this book hopes to unravel and explain.

Changing Meaning of an Adage

To this end, we must position the question sociologically. In premodern society generally, including tribal communities and imperial cities, according to Alain Laurent, the social order tended to be "rigidly hierarchical and coherent, where the whole held complete sway over the parts, or individuals. People's behavior was entirely established by group membership, by the unthinking submission to its laws and by the practice of largely unchanging traditions. No individual could claim autonomy of choice regarding values and rules of conduct, but rather acted as an interdependent fragment of a collective awareness."[28] It is obvious that in such conditions there was little scope for the urge to establish and express individual predilections. Such volubility would imply excess, and when the consumption of food was subordinated to the unreliable, strenuous availability of the raw material, filling the stomach preceded the pleasures of the palate. Of course the finest morsels were the prerogative of chiefs and kings, and always had been, but the fact that food reflected the social pyramid was not enough to explain the system of personal preferences and idiosyncrasies that were later to resemble taste, as we conceive of it today.

The second stage in our inquiry revolves around the invention of the taste adage. The anonymous Schoolman who thought it up was unquestionably referring to the realms of physical taste, to the palate. As for the *disputatio*, it was simply a discussion technique used for teaching in medieval universities. Its goal was to clarify dubious, badly formulated or contradictory statements by means of interrelated, serried argument. Presumably the conclusion that there should be no disputing the taste of the palate was simply the fruit of an unresolved *disputatio*. This laconic outcome merely signified that it was impossible to establish a scale of values within the sphere of oral sensations: no taste was better than any other because they all pertain (in other words, are produced by) individual temperaments. Clearly this shifted the discussion from the realm of culture to that of nature, which in its turn implied a change in specialization: taste was not the prerogative of metaphysics and logic, but of medicine and dietetics.

The outstanding feature of the third stage lies in the way the debate concerning taste and beauty during the Renaissance was accompanied by the adaptation of the finer points of the discussion to the wider world of their application. When the word taste is used figuratively, is it still true that it cannot be disputed? If the metaphor is basically valid, this is thanks to the fact that artistic appreciation, no less than appraisal by the palate, represents final judgments that are not open to appeal. It would thus seem that there is no disputing taste here either: no right or wrong against which to measure a particular perception. As in the case of the predilection of the palate, there are no true or false, good or bad tastes in relation to artistic products: all tastes, however erratic, are equally legitimate. Clearly the whole matter of disputing—or otherwise—depends on the authority of the relative argument. However, this is precisely where the taste debate reveals its weakness, since it is based on the repetition of a pleasurable experience produced by a given stimulus. That said, it is not true that all tastes are equally valid: unlike the sphere of fashion, the fine arts are not governed by whim and deliberate oddity. Moreover, there may be no irrefutable proof of the existence of beauty in a particular situation, but by and large some general agreement does exist. Lastly, although the *delectatio* aroused by a masterpiece cannot be explained by logical reasoning, within a given cultural milieu there generally tends to be a certain amount of concurrence.

Paradoxical though it may seem, taste is thus both one's own and that of many others, changeable and constant, innate and acquired, good and bad, refined and vulgar. Moreover, the history of taste is inevitably interwoven with these ambiguities. Philosophers of the past recognized the enigma, did all they could to resolve it, and ultimately agreed that taste was a sort of elevation of the mind similar in various respects to a particular form of knowledge. They thus concurred that there was no point in disputing taste through rational argument, but that discussing it was reasonable enough. Since then, though the discussions have abounded and true disputations have failed,[29] it is hard to imagine that the approach to the matter will change much in times to come.

And this in itself leads to further reflection. Indifferent to questions of principle and legitimacy, taste began to contaminate a growing number of individuals and subjects, spreading beyond the field of art to involve the values and destinies of individuals. Those touched by it were no longer just inspired artists, voyeur patrons or sophisticated humanist thinkers, but also hordes of sensitive beings who started visiting museums and art galleries with great enthusiasm. Later came the snobs and dandies who adopted taste as a *raison d'être*, a mainstay and point of honor. To say nothing of the gastronomes (etymologically speaking, the "governors of the stomach"), who elevated the function of digestion to the ineffable realms of palatal orgasm.

In the kaleidoscope of fashions and desires for luxury, the saying "each to his/her own" seems particularly well suited to the contemporary age. Individual taste relates to style a bit like one of those water pumps that sucks in at one end and spews it out at the other. To maintain that taste is never divisive is clearly ridiculous, even in times of cultural relativism and epistemological bric-a-brac.

Gallery owners and art critics, fashion and product designers, food writers, advertising gurus and spin doctors have all made a specialization out of taste, for which they are often handsomely rewarded. Granted, in such cases the *disputatio* side of rational argument has played a practically non-existent role, because the principle of authority, founded on fame and individual reputation, has tended to hold sway. But then hasn't much the same thing happened in other fields of the human sciences?

Taste today has become a question of capital importance, literally speaking, in view of its direct influence on company assets. And not just in the food industry, but also in sectors pertaining to tobacco, alcohol, perfumery and—to go beyond the domain of taste buds and smell—clothes and accessories, furniture and cars, music and entertainment, tourism and leisure pursuits. In other words, in practically every "mature" sector taste represents the main spur for competition and the true elixir of commercial success. In this case it is the market that approves or rejects the enticements of taste: when basic needs are met, it is the logic of desire that takes over, and here the last word lies with the consumer, who expresses his or her individual taste, albeit along with the rest of a vast collectivity.

Bearing all this in mind, the aim of this book is to reveal to what extent the history of taste goes well beyond the history of a metaphor (and the parallel decline of an adage).

To this end, it hopes to illustrate how:

1 The invention of taste in the figurative sense acts as a divide between two ages: not only as regards the history of art, since taste soon transcended this particular sector, but also as regards its role in the history of Western culture, where taste will shape the developmental and emulative process.

2 As taste spread and became more democratic, it managed to preserve its original hedonistic value, but in time lost its primal spontaneity to become a tool of mediated preference, in other words of socially and commercially conditioned choice.

3 The success of the metaphor was ultimately to lead to the retroactive redefinition of the original meaning of the term (taste as the sense of the palate), absorbing it into the extended meaning, and thereby projecting it into the fickle realm of luxury.

4 The "ideological success" of taste propeled it into contemporary consumer society like an ineluctable overdose, spreading progressively though the system of predilection and aspiration so as to shape our desires and our perception of reality.

To reach this epilogue, however, we must first take a close look at how taste was perceived and practiced before the concept itself was discovered and extended.

2

Pleasures and Morals

Notes on the Archeology of Taste

There are three major transformations in society that sum up the birth of
what we generally refer to as taste: the unseating of content by form;
the exaltation of self-proclaimed artistic demigods; and the sensual fusion
that has come to underlie the perception of art work. That said, however,
art is not the only sphere in which taste has informed the way people
think and what they desire. Taste does not relate so much to hunger as to
an appetite for something specific, and the metaphoric use of the term
transcends the relationship between artist and public, influencing a range of
experiences that have more to do with general rules than with individual
exceptions. No matter how refined the habits and customs of everyday life
may appear to be, they do not accommodate the outré touch of creative
genius (at least not until the invention of *haute couture*), or the ecstatic gaze
of the onlooker.

The experience of beauty embodies different sorts and degrees of intensity
and tone, starting from the elevated realm of the major arts (those that are
defined as *fine arts*) and embracing in descending order lesser forms of
creativity described as *decorative* or *applied* arts, where the aesthetic factor
works as a sort of surplus in relation to the object's primary function.
Regardless of the value of the materials used, or the exquisite craftsmanship
involved, a piece of furniture or an ornamental object is first and foremost
simply that: an item of furnishing that has no claim to the sort of
contemplation reserved for the figurative arts. The distinction between art
and crafts consists in the fact that the former implies a unique product that
embodies the artist's personality, whereas the latter is a multiple that
conforms to the style of a tradition or school. Regardless of the degree of
cultural prestige and the difference in viewing conditions, however, to some
extent art and crafts do actually share a certain objective: that of showing
themselves off, of enhancing or beautifying something (a church, a square, a
public building, a private home), or eliciting admiration on the part of
viewers, or stimulating their aesthetic appreciation. Moreover, personal
ornament and attire, including jewelry, headgear, coiffure, makeup and
perfume, as well as uniform, arms and armor, follow pretty much the same

rules: in other words, they represent the initial vehicle of elegance and opulence.

The way in which we adorn, embellish and enhance our bodies cannot claim to operate on the same lofty sphere as the arts, be they figurative or decorative. Yet our choices in this sense certainly define an extremely stringent and pervasive aesthetic realm precisely because they establish the roles that we play on the social stage. Refinement in terms of clothing, ornament and look, along with sophistication in what we eat (where the cultural perception of good taste transcends the more material taste for food, or indeed the taste of the food itself), are not just conventions pertaining to good manners, but stage props essential to the whole theatrical performance. Competing cultural models, together with the symbols of admiration and infatuation, all come under the jurisdiction of taste.

Yet behavior bent on ostentation, on extremes of refinement, or indeed waste, was widespread in ancient times, to the extent that such habits became almost synonymous with the fortunes of a particular city or civilization. The history of Western society alone provides plentiful examples of the taste for luxury, from Sybaritic voluptuary to the magnificence of imperial Rome. The desire for splendor was expressed not only in lavish dwellings and legions of servants, but also in the acquisition of sumptuous commodities, those frivolous, short-lived objects that often end up by undermining wealth.

This in itself brings to the fore some interesting questions concerning the nature of taste in antiquity. It would seem that the phenomenon itself predates the historic etymology of the term and its use as a metaphor. In other words, the origins of taste can be traced back to well before the word itself became part of everyday parlance. Granted, this claim depends on the definition of *taste* as an analogy, and on the appropriateness of applying it retrospectively to the behavior of past civilizations.

One factor pertaining to our current perception of taste is its role in the projection of esteem. Taste is seen as the subjective ability to discern things intuitively, a gut reaction to an external stimulus, be this beautiful or ugly, sophisticated or obvious, refined or vulgar, authentic or fake. Taste, or rather *good taste*, is the compass that directs our perceptive apparatus on the high seas of sensation. Refinement of taste is what allows a person to become a connoisseur, to rise above blind, emotional reaction and the innate tendency that guides it. Perceptions thus involve an infinite range of subtle distinctions.

This was all abundantly clear in Antiquity. Suffice it to recall the figure of Gaius Petronius Arbiter, the refined *viveur* who practically invented dandyism and whose name alone suggests his role as a judge of all forms of elegance.[1] That said, the information that has come down to us about Petronius is extremely patchy so, rather than studying the author himself, for a better understanding of the manifestations of taste in early times we should turn to Trimalchio, his alter ego in the *Satyricon*. A freedman who has acquired enormous wealth through maritime trade, Trimalchio is a parvenu who uses grotesque extravagance to gain prestige and merit with the true notables, in other words with those who lived off the income from their estates. He is a sociological caricature, portrayed in pitilessly realistic terms.

Hostility towards merchants who managed to accumulate great fortunes in a short space of time was a constant feature of ancient Greek and Roman society. The process of social competition that they were able to unleash was seen as a threat, to be met with moral disapproval and aesthetic disdain: "Inherited wealth defended itself against upstart merchants by imputing to them every conceivable vice: merchants are rootless, greedy, the source of all evil; they promote luxury and weakness; they distort nature by traveling to far-off lands, violating the natural barrier of the seas and bringing back what nature will not permit to grow at home."[2]

In this sense, Satyricon can be seen as a chapter in the unending battle between bad and good taste, between the material ostentation of wealth and waste and the cultural heritage of refinement and good judgment. It also reveals how the ancient Romans believed that these latter traits could not be acquired, but only nurtured and handed down. The banquet, which was the most tangible and widely practiced expression of munificence, was also the quintessential opportunity for carousing and revelry, to the extent that it naturally became a prime target for satire.

Although the love of food and fine cuisine met with contempt and scorn on the part of men of letters and philosophers, in Antiquity such passions became one of the most sophisticated manifestations of connoisseurship. "In imperial Rome, gourmets made a point of showing off their discernment as regards the origins of what they ate, rather as today's wine buffs do concerning what's in their glass. Juvenal refers to a certain Montano, who could tell from the first taste whether an oyster came from the Circeo, or from the rocky Lucrino area, or from the seabed of Rutupia. Likewise, at a mere glance he could identify the provenance of a sea-urchin. Often such appraisals went to exaggerated lengths. When judging a food of animal or vegetable origin, even the time of capture or harvest was taken into consideration."[3] Certainly, the pleasures of the table were held in high esteem well before Lucullus and Apicius described them. In the golden age of the Sybarites, half a millennium earlier, cooks were granted a sort of copyright for their culinary creations that lasted for one year. Twenty-five centuries later, the stars of Nouvelle Cuisine had prepared the ground for similar claims on the part of the chefs propriétaires. Plato himself referred to the Sicilian Miteco as "the Phidias of cooks," which clearly means that in his own times a cook could become a pan-Hellenic celebrity with the prestige of an artist.

It goes without saying that the gourmets of the past did more than simply devote themselves to heightening their senses and indulging in the pleasures of the table. When taste transcends mere refinement, the positive image created extends to embrace desire, including the flame of passion that can end up as a mania. This is where excess and abandon coincide with the

Dionysiac dimension, which was very much part of classical civilization, and as such continually criticized by moralists of various doctrines.

There is no need to turn to the taste for sensual license and the ensuing repertoire of sexual fantasy and distraction to find examples of voluptuary consumption in Antiquity. The food rituals and gastronomic frenzies that were fashionable at the time comprised plentiful examples of *opsophagia*, a form of *gourmandise* typical of Athenian culture involving an absolute passion for relishes, in other words the tasty accompaniment to the staple dish. For the Greeks, this was fish, which was a luxury item for private consumption, unlike various meats, which could be part of a sacrificial or social ritual.[4] To say nothing of the ancient Roman custom of self-induced vomiting as a way of extending the pleasures of the palate beyond the limits of the human metabolism: the gastronomic frenzy of Lucullus and the other Roman gluttons.

Aesthetic ecstasy, which is the sublimated and socially acceptable version of taste as desire, is another form of behavior that can be traced back to Antiquity. From Aristotelian catharsis to the experience of the sublime theorized by Pseudo-Longinus, the shuddering of the soul brought about by a work of art is the thread that links up the aesthetic conceptions of the past.

A further aspect of the question lies in the vast range of customs and behavior. Showing off luxury and opulence, the manifestations of distinction and emulation, ostentation and exhibitionism are all part of the picture. Here again, the past provides us with plentiful examples.

It was not just a question of reclining on magnificent couches around the banqueting table, or going to great lengths to acquire the rarest of fine foods, or breeding fish in special seawater pools on private estates whose owners were mockingly described as *piscinarii* by Cicero. There was also the attitude of men wishing to make an impact, to cut a swathe in the public eye. Horace made fun of such pretentions, rather as modern-day critics do of people showing off on motorbikes or in sports cars. "They paraded through the city in carriages that were taller than the usual ones," he declared, "or they raced through at great speed drawn by horses."[5] And of course there were equivalent jibes for the female contingent, who had no compunction about turning themselves into "itinerant jewelry stores," so bedecked were they with rings, "buckles, hair pins, ornate golden hair ribbons enhanced with gemstones, earrings, bracelets, necklaces; to say nothing of the necklaces and the huge ankle rings."[6]

As for artifice in the form of cosmetics, back at the time of Pericles women often dyed their hair "to make it blonde, the eternally favourite colour: wigs and false switches were also common. Furthermore women shaved or plucked superfluous hair, as well as using beauty creams, all sorts of perfumes and make-up. Courtesans not only employed white-lead ceruse and alkanet rouge, but also emphasized their eyes and eyebrows with black or brown liners, and were well acquainted with the use of *strophion*, or brassiere."[7]

One of the most interesting aspects of the whole question of taste is the underlying social and political dimension. In Antiquity, this largely took the form of dissuasion, enacted through moral censure and legislative deterrents.

Much attention has been devoted to the cases of sumptuary laws promulgated in ancient Rome in order to rein in excesses in luxury and manifestations of decadence. The *Lex Oppia* of 215 BC prohibited women from possessing more than a certain amount of gold jewelry and precious ornaments, from wearing colored garments (especially purple cloths), and from traveling by carriage in the city. The *Lex Orchia* of 182 BC established how many guests could be invited to a private banquet, and later even the expenditure for hospitality and the menu were subject to constraints. Then in 161 BC the *Lex Fannia* obliged citizens to take a solemn oath whereby they promised to keep their sumptuous purchases within certain limits, defined with a differentiation for feast days. To say nothing of the *Lex Aemilia*, passed in 76 BC, which prohibited the consumption of imported shellfish and fowl.[8] Such countermeasures, which largely turned out to be ineffective, do at least provide us with an idea of how extreme indulgence in the dictates of taste was perceived as potentially destructive for the established social order.

During the Stoic period, and later at the dawn of Christianity, self-control and the ability to rein in the appetites fired a form of moral superiority that was typical of those who saw themselves as free of the slavery of vice and self-indulgence. Such restraint was seen as admirable, a point of reference in the education of the offspring of the aristocracy. Yet, from Veblen to Bourdieu, the distance from need as such, the symbolic sublimation of desire and the perception of pleasure as innocent have long been recognized as the distinctive trait of the leisured classes. As for sumptuary laws, they have reappeared from time to time right up to the present, largely as forms of taxation on the added value of luxury goods or commodities that are imported from abroad.

Not even the idea that taste should be accessible to a wider circle is really a prerogative of modernity. And nor is the ensuing multiplication of the sources by means of which desires can be gratified. Imperial Rome was a clear example of a society based on entertainment. And even if such pursuits had little to do with aesthetic discernment, they remained intimately linked to the personal sphere of pleasure and predilection that established the success—or otherwise—of a given event or participant. The circus and the arena, fights and naval battles, games and races, music and dance, pantomimes and comedies were all pleasures to be enjoyed socially. They could delight or disappoint, but their aim was always to entertain the audience. As such, events of this sort fell within the sphere of taste. Indeed, often within that of *bad taste*, since the intellectuals of the time rarely failed to denounce them as manifestations of decadence and vulgarity.

Along with baths, wine and sex (which, as a Roman proverb declared, may have shortened life, but was actually "true life" itself), the system of collective entertainment belonged to the realms of universal pleasures, pursued and enjoyed by a society that was intimately given to a frenzy of hedonism. Of the gratifications available to Roman citizens, only the games and spectacular events were spared by the political establishment, precisely because such sumptuous entertainments had very widespread appeal. By contrast, other manifestations of excess in taste, especially those relating to effeminacy or ostentatious dissipation and expenditure, were condemned as undermining the established social order.

Current historical interpretation tends to reduce Roman entertainment to a deliberate *panem et circenses* control mechanism aimed at diminishing social tensions and fostering political consensus. However, this does not explain what was really the first large-scale experiment with *mass culture*; a phenomenon whose impact and influence were unequaled in antiquity. The fun and entertainment device was, at best, a secondary expression of magnificence, a form of collective self-indulgence that had little to do with shaping personal quirks and preferences. Only the ostentatious splendors of modern-day Hollywood and Las Vegas come anywhere near the scale of the mega events of Imperial Rome.

That said, the suggestion that history repeats itself, that everything has already been tried out in past ages, is actually misleading. Modern taste differs from that of Antiquity in various ways, as we shall see.

Part of the previous chapter was devoted to the relationship between aesthetic perception and the way this can be shaped by the ongoing process of individualism in art. The fact that modern taste largely derives from this cultural imprinting is also significant as regards its "lesser" manifestations. Taste can be intended as the manner in which a work of art is selected and perceived. Yet taste also shapes behavior and the way people present themselves. In both cases it is culture that helps form perception. Assimilation of the predominant culture is essential to the education of the latter-day gentleman, not least because both forms of taste play a part in the overall image.

In other words, the self-determination of aesthetic judgment with all its hedonistic overtones reveals, and perhaps introduces, a wider form of autonomy based on the discovery of subjectivity. This is evident in many different sectors, from politics to morals, fashion to food. The wide range of spheres in which taste now lays down the law involves a deep-rooted labyrinth of social, economic and ideological ramifications whose further implications are beyond the scope of this book. Suffice it to point out that the ensuing centrality of the individual redefines the role of each person within his or her social context, thereby reshaping the very essence of Western sensitivity.

It was the stylization of behavior in court society that originally gave impetus to the process, both chronologically and culturally. Granted, other civilizations and epochs have witnessed a similar refinement of manners. But with the formation of nation states and the intermixing of church and aristocracy that began in the sixteenth century, for the first time the phenomenon acquired social prestige in the form of ideological support. In this way behavior trickled down from the establishment and was progressively absorbed by the common man, in time becoming a form of spontaneous action, a cultural blueprint. The outcome amounts to "the production of a fundamentally new economy of the psyche, whereby a particular culture, opposed to that of the 'savages,' sets out on a triumphal march with a claim to being exclusive. While this is a spectacle for Europe, it is also a global discipline for its followers. With varying degrees of efficacy, in relation to the groups and periods involved, it suppresses the direct expression of passions and bodily functions."[9]

The civilizing process, reconstructed by Norbert Elias to explain the change in customs that began in the early Middle Ages,[10] redefined the threshold of modesty and repugnance relating to what was socially acceptable and what was perceived as disgusting. In other words, it turned sensitivity into a cultural phenomenon. The world of appearances, the sphere of what was ephemeral, the battle of tastes became criteria for mutual recognition and the principles of social stratification. The emulation of glorified court behavior implied a community of images and desires, a repertory of conventional acts, words, pleasures and novelties. By the same token, however, this shared perception encouraged the social élite to further disparage and exclude the world of those who were not part of their lofty rank.

This is the historic context in which taste came into its own, helping to define both the despot and the underdog, the judge and the condemned, the upholder of orthodoxy and the heretic. As consumption and behavior grew in sophistication, multiplying their applications and appearance, taste became an integral part of a socio-cultural process, injecting its development with new impetus.

The role played by luxury within the evolution of capitalism revolved around the perception and gratification of desires, which in their turn implied consumption and investment. Such were the elements that shaped modern taste. When the exhibition of luxury became an expression of aristocratic and bourgeois decorum (in other words, when certain hitherto unknown commodities were suddenly perceived as necessary by a given generation), taste became part of everyday life, which it shaped in its own image, thereby playing a major role in individual self-esteem and gratification.

At this point it is easier to grasp the difference between modern taste and that of the phenomenon *ante litteram*. Modern taste revolves around the individual, whose skittish but constant desires fire its development. Central to the whole system is the thirst for excess, for the superfluous, that manifests itself in the passion for novelty, refinement and comfort: all those totally unnecessary things that we think we might like to have and that suddenly become an essential part of our lives. The appearance on the scene of the individual desirous of novelty is an integral part of the construction of modernity.

In this sense, taste represents much more than a simple cog in the wheel of history. It acts as a lubricant, indeed as a fuel. All things considered, taste has been the principle vehicle of the new mentality, an invitingly intuitive tool that allows the individual to understand, share and partake in select novelty. Clearly the aim is not so much to redefine sensibilities, but to make inroads into the realm of values. The outcome is a seductively non-conformist take on behavior that undermines the traditional view of things to such an extent that it rocks the very foundations of established perceptions of vice and virtue.

The Development of a Lay Morality

Like a mirror image of the cardinal virtues, the seven deadly sins represented a concentrated version of the precepts, fears and prejudices that were rooted in Greek Stoicism, permeated Ancient Roman culture and were formalized in the Middle Ages, where they spoke for the prevailing vision of the world.

The soul at its most wretched and the shortcomings of personality were early forms of vice that could lead to the transgression of divine teachings. When this early form of vice was followed by action, the outcome was sin, in other words misdeeds perpetrated against the established order of society. Four of these vices pertained to the rejection of a given condition or position within the community, and the obligations that derived therefrom: *vainglory* amounted to excessive ambition; *acedia* was the lack of attachment to duty; *wrath* was the loss of self-control; *envy* arose from inappropriate comparison with another person's condition. The latter was also a form of destructive desire, like the remaining three vices: *avarice*, or lust for money; *gluttony*, or yearning for food; and *lechery*, meaning an excessive sexual appetite.

These sins were considered "capital" because they generated other vices and sins:

> vainglory ushers in disobedience, an overbearing sense of superiority, hypocrisy, quarrelsomeness, obstinacy, discord and constant demands for novelty. Envy gives rise to hate, insinuation, gossip, delight in other people's affliction and sufferance when things go well for them. Wrath leads to quarrels, the swollen chin, insults, shouting, indignation and cussing. Melancholy is accompanied by nastiness, rancor, cowardice, desperation, laxity in adhering to rules, a wandering mind attracted by forbidden subjects. Betrayal, fraud, cheating, false promises, restlessness, violence and hardness of heart are born of avarice. Next come loose-tongued talk, ribaldry, smuttiness, verbosity, the dulling of the senses. Lechery leads to mental blindness, inconsiderateness, inconstancy, giving in, self-love, hate of God, attachment to the world, horror or desperation for future destiny.[11]

In inverse correspondence to the deadly sins there were seven cardinal virtues, four of which derived from Stoicism (prudence, diligence, temperance, justice), while the remaining three (faith, hope, charity) were of Christian origin. In the *psychomachia* between vice and virtue that provided the following six centuries with the parameters for moral inhibition and incentive, there was no space for desire. What was deemed appropriate behavior was far removed from anything of the sort: bodily yearning was repressed, pleasure was equated with guilt, personal desires were banished in the name of ideals and interests that transcended the individual sphere: "overeating, drinking without measure, indulging in the pleasures of the flesh betray the body's ability to prevaricate over reason, the rejection of the organs of social submission (the nervous system) to the advantage of those of radical subjectivity (the rest). Mortification, penitence, meditation on the terrible consequences that derive from veneration of the pleasures of the palate: by renouncing the energies that permeate the body, man contributes to the establishment of social order, promoting the structure and efficiency of the fabric of civilization."[12]

Hate of novelty, fear of sexuality and the dulling of passions all revealed the desire to limit and subdue individual free will. In other words, to eradicate the sin of pride, which was the first of all vices, a spur for the most potentially insidious foolish aspirations: "what is condemned is the mere possibility of dissatisfaction concerning one's lot in life, the very idea that the individual might desire a different place, a different destiny; indeed might act to bring such things about. Rebellion against the state of things, desire for a different world, the pride implicit in the attempt to create a more pleasant condition: these, in the eyes of the moralists, are characteristics of the person overly desirous of expanding his control of self and surroundings."[13]

On the other hand, when desire is reined in by the principle of the inviolable nature of what already exists, repressing subjectivity and imagination, taste is clearly deprived of all content: without the palate there would be no gastronomy, without pride the arts and elegance would not be cultivated, without envy there would be no fashions to follow or models to emulate, and without lust all jewelry, cosmetics and other manifestations of narcissism and seduction would be pointless.

This brings us to an obvious conclusion: a civilization of taste that revolves around subjective pleasure and desire can only prosper if the remains of traditional moral precepts are dismantled and replaced by a bulwark defending new values and convictions. To present-day sensibilities, what was accepted as a rule in a past era now appears to be a sort of caricature, something grotesque, like a deforming mirror. The deadly sins are turned completely upside down, to the extent that they become absolute needs, individual requirements, the object of social approval and therapeutic support, the essence of commercial seduction, a spur to consumption, a means of self-affirmation, an irresistible leisure pursuit.

As we moderns see it, the satisfaction of these needs is not just an inviolable right, but rather the main source of life's gratifications and the only criterion with which to measure the quality of life in concrete terms. The gluttony that once meant greed now signifies the cult of the table, a consolatory rite, a worthy form of pleasure. By the same token, pride becomes self-esteem, initiative, the desire for self-improvement, while sloth justifies spare time and leisure. As for the thirst for wealth, clearly it is nothing more than the legitimate desire to raise social standing and living conditions. Likewise, envy drives forward the consumer economy, and lust is essential *to joie de vivre* and the elixir of eternal youth. Anger lends itself to the development of ideals, political engagement, social indignation and rebellion, a passion for sport. If anything, those who are excluded from such earthly pleasures are considered social outcasts or pathological cases. In the here-and-now paradise of total self-indulgence and universal eudemonia, all that remains of the constraints of bygone ages is a sort of peripheral inferno, perceived as an unfortunate but inevitable "malaise of civilization." Within this perspective, uncontroled gluttony can lead to bulimia, alcoholism, addiction to cigarettes or drugs. But fear not: for each of these sins of lack of restraint, the new religion of wellbeing offers specialized purgatories equipped with the most modern forms of expiation. In relation to the gravity and nature of the problem, the guilty can opt for gyms, beauty farms, diets for losing weight, anorectic pills, artificial sweeteners, antidepressants, psychoanalytical sessions, plastic surgery . . .

Greater detail is hardly necessary. For our present purposes the main objective is to observe the moment of transition when vices turn into virtues. This crumbling of identities was already evident in court society and in the early manifestations of capitalism, especially where the new social contexts interacted with the dynamics of taste.

What do alchemists, the discoverers of philosopher's stones, petty thieves, freebooters, diviners, treasure hunters, tricksters, usurers, gamblers, speculators, *donneurs d'avis* and *brasseurs d'affaires* have in common? All these and the many other illustrious forerunners of the modern entrepreneurial spirit clearly share an urgent desire to get rich (greed), to rise above their current social rank (envy), to perceive themselves as the arbiters of their own destiny (pride), and to aspire to a life of pleasure, waste and refinement (gluttony, lust, sloth).[14] According to the medieval classification of vice, they should all be banished to the dark underworld of the fraudulent.

Not that life at court, despite its appeal for the ranks of would-be nobility, provided a more edifying picture. In the career of a courtier, arrogance and envy were the guidelines for dressing up and behavior, in what Norbert Elias described as a deliberate strategic plan aimed at gaining or losing opportunities for prestige and status, within the incessant competition for power.[15]

As for avarice, it also played a role, though in the shape of an extreme version of its opposite. The bourgeois ethic recommended caution in the handling of the family budget, to the extent that expenditure should be less than income, so that the difference can be reinvested, to the benefit of the family patrimony. By contrast, the court ethic promoted dissipation, in other words the acquisition of prestige through ostentatious display. Thus greed for money was transformed into an insatiable appetite for glory and honor, and the desire for gain into ambition at court, such that a person who tended to be tight-fisted could become a spendthrift. Little wonder that the figures of the miser and of the squanderer appear to be practically interchangeable, relegated to the same circle of vice in medieval iconography.

By the same token, gluttony and lust were equally active. Cooking became cuisine, in other words a refined art, for the delight of princely palates in a period in which the dining table was turned into a sort of gastronomic theater. Within the same context, a new female figure came to the fore to exercise her charms on the male members of the select society around her, occupying a position somewhere between "*la femme honnête*" and "*la putaine.*" As Sombart pointed out, Romance languages have come up with a colorful range of epithets to describe this particular female genre: courtesan, concubine, *maitresse, grande amoureuse, grande cocotte*, kept woman, and so on.[16]

Yet it is luxury that best embodies and exemplifies the new morality based on what is ephemeral. Luxury is the magnet that attracts the urge towards social prestige, and to some extent actually manages to satisfy it, at least for a short time. It is luxury that promotes and forges the desire for refinement, creating the conditions for the development of commerce. And it is luxury that swells the ranks and aspirations of social climbers, providing a justification for vice and laxity.

It is interesting to note that in Latin, lust and luxury were "a single word (*luxuria*) and which consisted in denying oneself nothing and believing that 'anything goes'."[17] Little wonder, then, that manifestations of luxury also helped shape the ways in which the passions could go beyond the confines of morality and decency. Whether this took the form of self-indulgence (gluttony and lust), of avarice (redirecting wealth from patronage to the private sphere), or personal ambition (vainglory), it was still a case of uncontroled desire.

Change came about when luxury was no longer merely a sign of eccentricity and moral decadence, but asserted itself at the pinnacle of the social pyramid, putting on a show for the admiration of those clinging onto the rung just below. Life at court was a device for magnificence, a showcase for sumptuousness, a propagator of extravagance, the yeast of discretionary consumption, providing daily performances of luxury at its most visible.

As Norbert Elias pointed out, "in a society in which everything to do with an individual stands for something in social terms, expenditure on the part of those who occupy the higher echelons of society is an absolute necessity: a way of achieving social affirmation, especially if—and this is indeed common in current society—there is constant competition on the part of the members of the society to establish and maintain status and prestige. A duke must have a house built that immediately shows that he is a duke and not a baronet, and the same applies for his entire public persona."[18]

Luxury thus becomes the main criterion for the certification of social eminence. The display of luxury is not merely a symbolic manifestation of reality, but rather reality itself: "the way social prestige and success depend directly on how much is spent on maintaining the household and on consumption has also been described by Werner Sombart. As the German author revealed, a person whose appearance falls short of his rank soon loses respect in his given society. In the continual race for status and prestige, he will be overtaken by other competitors, and will run the risk of being ruined, sidestepped or ousted from the group or rank to which he originally belonged."[19]

Expenditure for representation included the costs of courtesans, a discretionary commodity that called for some very expensive maintenance. Before achieving acceptance on the part of the spouse, new fashions in clothing usually featured in the wardrobe of the mistress, whose public appearances tended to anticipate what would later become à la mode, rather as those of modern-day fashion models do. A woman's attire thus took on an erotic charge that reflected the growing sensuality of taste. It was a widespread cultural assumption that women like what makes them attractive, in other words whatever enhances their appearance and appeals to their vanity. What was new in this case was that they were finally able to give free rein to their inclinations and predilections. Repressed, censured and denigrated since the times of Cato and Tertullian, the female genius was at last able to make claims of its own.

According to Sombart, the boom in luxury commodities that characterized the seventeenth and eighteenth centuries was largely attributable to women— or rather the power that they began to wield at court. Women became the high priestesses of luxury, in the sense that they both enjoyed and distributed discretionary consumption, establishing in the public arena exactly what was and was not in fashion.

Radical transformations in how luxury was perceived and used gave rise to a growth in consumption that entirely pertained to the female sphere. During the Middle Ages, luxury was essentially a public phenomenon that involved shows, jousting, processions and banquets. In the hands of women, it underwent a form of *privatization*, becoming domestic and less ephemeral. This brought about a decrease in expenditure for servants in relation to what was spent on durable goods such as clothing, jewelry and furnishings, which in its turn ushered in forms of sensuality and refinement that are closer to female tastes.[20] This explains the increasing role of applied arts in domestic furnishings, the supremacy of rococo over baroque, and the growing impact of intricate pastries and desserts in the overall universe of refined cuisine.

The focus on what was private, objective, refined and sensual helped shape perceptions and appraisals of luxury: in other words, taste. Moreover, as luxury expanded, its accentuation in feminine terms was to influence the future history of Western sensibilities, and not always in positive terms. Since then, in fact, the realms of taste have moved from artistic statement to decorative seduction, from the flair of artists to that of couturiers and designers, from the contemplation of what is beautiful to indulgence in the showmanship of short-lived delights.

This constitutes the first step in the direction of turning what is a daily occurrence into an aesthetic experience. As Sombart was to declare, the transformation was largely effected by women and involved focusing on cushions covered in Lyons silk rather than ornamental colonnades, on pale blue underwear rather than pale blue silk bed covers with white tulle canopies, on grey silken hosiery, satin dresses, on the obvious seduction of gowns decorated with swan or ostrich feathers and Flanders lace.[21] The outcome was a noisy, showy "salon symphony" that was to continue, with all due variations, until the dawn of the twentieth century. Only when the Modernist Movement upturned established norms and spoke out against decoration in starkly virile terms was the female monopoly of the domestic scene called to account and contrasted.

As taste underwent feminization it also became more subject to change. Despite the efforts of Enlightenment philosophers and aesthetes to position it on a universal pedestal, at the dawn of the modern age taste proved to be increasingly prone to whim, which in its turn made it culturally datable. In the Middle Ages, the great multi-generational workshops and building sites were conceived as properties to be handed down to future generations. By contrast, the modern conception and production of luxury commodities as goods for individual enjoyment brought about an acceleration of supply, which was accompanied by a multiplication of styles and interests. Little wonder, then, that taste soon came to mirror the short-lived whims of fashion, embracing and provoking sudden change: to whit, the complete turnarounds in taste that have become a common occurrence in the space of a lifetime.

This helps explain why the multiplication of luxury has been interpreted as the economic spur of capitalism. Because the proliferation of private consumption brought about elevated levels of commodity obsolescence, consumer behavior became somewhat unpredictable, requiring a more proactive approach to supply. During the seventeenth century, the silk and lace industries, the manufacture of mirrors, china, glass, the wool industry and sugar production all grew at an extraordinary rate to meet the increasing demand for such commodities. These sectors all took on a basically capitalist structure because this was better suited to the new conditions of the market. In their turn, they also influenced the other luxury industries, which adopted the same model. Clearly only those who could avail themselves of plenty of investment capital were able to purchase rare, expensive raw materials. Furthermore, expanding production called for a higher degree of specialization, because customers were becoming increasingly sophisticated and demanding. In other words, the entrepreneur required overall vision and a farsighted approach that allowed him to predict the oscillations of demand. Handling the complexity of the market called for greater organizational skills. To add to which, since many of the new entrepreneurs were actually foreigners, they also had to have the clout to overcome the various protectionist constraints erected by the local artisan guilds. The mechanized production of artifacts that came about with technological progress is generally held to be responsible for this phenomenon, whereas in fact it only came about at a slightly later stage.[22]

At this point, it is clear that there was no going back once luxury became a rule for behavior, providing social hierarchies with order. At this point, economists and philosophers stopped criticizing and began praising the virtues that increased the prosperity of the state and the wellbeing of nations:[23] luxury was spurring competition and the thirst for novelty, percolating down from the realms of the aristocracy to the more pedestrian spheres of tradesmen intent on learning to show off and be fashionable like the best of them. The desire for discretionary goods thus fomented markets and promoted social mobility. A new morality had pervaded the mentality of the leisured classes, and those who aspired to join their ranks. It was a virtuous circle linking exhibition, aspiration and the dynamics of consumption.

In this way taste not only fueled luxury and furthered feminine vanity, but also gave rise to the socio-economic development that was to usher in the modern era, *quod erat demonstrandum*. Even the Ur-faculty intrinsic to the palate, the form of perception that happens to bear the same name, had also undergone indelible change.

Refining Appetites and Mouthing Euphemisms

Of all vices, the one that seems most difficult to cure is gluttony. Any effort to contain or contrast it has to come to terms with the fact that it is necessarily related to an essential instinct for survival: "With eating, pleasure is mixed with necessity; we are not able to discern what is required by necessity and what is claimed by pleasure."[24] By contrast, the sin of lust is easier to cast aside, because it is possible to live an entirely chaste life, along the lines of true monks and saints. Transposition of such conduct to the sphere of food leads to ascetic fasting and the luckless anorexic maidens venerated in the Middle Ages, however, and this does not appear to be an edifying model for Western culture.

So gluttony is more a question of measure than any other moral precept. Thus, while it is natural and legitimate to derive pleasure from sustenance, it is unwise and thus wrong to go beyond the confines of need. Indeed, a tendency to indulge this inclination is wont to lead to weakness with regard to other, more insidious temptations. Not only those that have to do with the sin of lust, which is related to gluttony on account of its being a sin of the flesh (in other words, a bodily sin that seeks bodily satisfaction), but also those forms of behavior that derive directly from gluttony and express themselves in conviviality: binging, scurrility, grossness, garrulity and mental torpor.[25] As for drunkenness, though it may prove to be more of a social nuisance than over-indulgence in food, it is in fact simply the liquid version of the same thing.[26] Thomas Aquinas provides some inventive etymology in defense of his conviction that drinking beyond measure is a form of gluttony, in other words an excess of a pleasure that is otherwise legitimate. "The term sobriety derives from a measure: as if the expression were *servans-briam*" (in other words, "able to keep to the measure of one mug"). Thus even in the case of inebriating drinks, "keeping to one measure is extremely admirable: moderate consumption is greatly helpful, whereas the smallest excess hinders the use of reason much more than an excess of food."[27]

Gluttony is thus the unregulated desire to eat and drink. That said, of course, it is not easy to establish the criteria that distinguish the norm from what is abnormal, need from whim, delight from depravation. And once found, are these criteria the same for everyone, or do they vary from one individual to the next? And if they do vary, has this to do with age, or state of health, or the balance of humors, or what exactly? The moral and social problem of gluttony is entirely contained within these questions.

During the Middle Ages, it was theology and morality that addressed matters of principle, while medicine and diet dealt with matters of fact. Only once the various verdicts came under the heading of good manners and gastronomy could gluttony acquire gentility and become part of the rituals of a life of refinement.

The process requires a degree of reflection, however. Just when exactly does appetite exceed need and as a result become a sin of gluttony? According to Gregorius Magnus, the author of one of the earliest analyses of capital and venial sins, we are already guilty of vice when our appetite makes us "eat earlier than we really need to; seek out rare foods; prepare them with refinement; go beyond the limits of quantity needed; give in to insatiable desires."[28] To put it briefly—too early, too much, too refined, too rich, too greedily. Later on, these five declinations of the vice were reduced to a basic dichotomy that finally cleared the ground in which the subject of gastronomy was able to germinate beyond the reach of moral censure: on the one hand the manifestations of gluttony (that could be reduced to quantity and manner); and on the other the expressions of *refinement* (*natural* refinement, that resided in the value of the ingredients, or *artificial* refinement, that was due to culinary skill). Both were affected by the process of the stylization of behavior and used as a measure of social distinction, but with a fundamental difference: the former became part of a form of self-discipline, with its concomitant aura of modesty and disgust; while the latter were exhibited as manifestations of *good taste*, with the ensuing implications of cultural aspiration and social emulation.

In the Middle Ages, nevertheless, the distinction scarcely came to the fore. This explains why Thomas Aquinas may initially appear to recognize, at least in theory, the autonomy of taste as a means for reining in gastronomic pleasure, even though he ultimately concludes that it pertains to gluttony, and is therefore a sin. In his theory of vice, a particular yearning for food, rather than the desire to eat as such, can manifest itself in two situations: "with respect to the substance, the search for costly foods, in other words luxury; with respect to the quality, the desire for foods prepared with excessive care, in other words refinement."[29] Moreover, both "appear to concern the goodness of flavor, which is the essence of taste."[30] This is, of course, a dialectical nicety that the author himself then denies in the solution of the dispute. Evidently the time was not yet ripe for recognizing the flamboyant stereotype of the gourmet. Largely extraneous to the customs and mentality of the Middle Ages, this figure was at the most a reprehensible guzzler, a man given to binging. "Foods that are precious or prepared with refined skill do not elicit pleasure in the glutton on account of their savor, as wines do for those that taste them, because this regards the realms of taste. The folly of this kind of pleasure lies in the fact that it pertains more to curiosity than to the palate. The glutton, on the other hand, finds delight in the very ingestion of precious and refined foods, and this act has more to do with touch." In other words, with the sense that perceives the filling up of the stomach rather than taste as such, which would be content with stimulating the palate.[31]

At this point everything would seem to depend on the exact location in the human body of the organ whose job it is to relieve the intemperance of the palate. If this is in the mouth, and consists of whetting the taste buds before food is actually swallowed, then the sense is clearly taste, which is stimulated by curiosity. This is what happens with gourmands, if and when they are considered to be the gastronomic equivalents of the wine tasters already mentioned.[32] If on the other hand the organ is located in the stomach and advises the guzzler of the fulfillment that comes with satiety following the swallowing of food, then the sense in question is touch, at least according to Thomas Aquinas. What is more, there are significant analogies between this sphere and that of lust. Indeed, in sexual behavior touching, licking, rubbing and seminal fluids derive from contact between bodies, and thus pertain to tactile stimulation. As a corollary of this anatomical reconstruction of gluttony, it is also worth noting that the organs pertaining to these two sins of the flesh—stomach and genitals—also share a degree of proximity to the belly.

In so far as acts of gluttony are considered travesties of moderation, deciding just how much is the right amount is a task for dietary science. "Eating and drinking should be regulated in relation to the requirements of bodily health. Often what is a moderate quantity of food and drink for a healthy man can be excessive for a sick man, and the contrary may also be true, that is, what may be too much for a healthy person could be the right amount for someone who is sick, and has been ordered by his physician to eat enough to provoke vomiting."[33]

This is certainly the case as far as quantity is concerned. But what about quality? If there are fine foods and delectable delicacies just as there are excellent wines selected from casks by skilled tasters, this is thanks to the discernment of merchants and cooks who are sensitive to the inclinations of "taste as such." But this is largely beside the point, in the sense that it cannot be reduced to universal principles because tastes vary from one person to another, just as the right quantity is also an individual factor. Thus the study of variety and difference within the overall sphere of taste pertains to the realms of dietary matters.

In early modern times, dietary precepts were part of a discipline based on respected dogmas whose ancient origins can be traced back to pre-Socratic cosmogony. According to the Sicilian physician Empedocles of Agrigento (fifth century BC), the universe was based on four original elements: air, water, earth and fire. To adapt these to the study of biology, Philistion of

Locri (fourth century BC) transformed them into primary powers or qualities, with paired opposites (wet–dry and hot–cold) that provided the universal coordinates underlying, in varying compositions, all material, organic and inorganic substances. It was Polybus, a contemporary of Philistion and son-in-law of Hypocrates of Cos, who applied this theory to medicine. Polybus believed that the combinations of primary qualities corresponded to the same number of organic fluids, or "humors," that were fundamental components of the human metabolism: blood, which was hot–wet; phlegm, which was cold–wet; yellow bile, which was hot–dry; and black bile, which was dry–cold. Five centuries later, when he was going through the observations of Hypocrates, Galen of Pergamon, who had been the gladiators' physician, came to the conclusion that these were the main principles of a psychosomatic typology. In his view, the humors corresponded to "temperaments"—sanguine, phlegmatic, bilious or choleric, melancholic—which revealed the predominance of one of these primary qualities over the others. When evenly balanced, the primary qualities would produce a perfectly balanced temperament (*eukrasia*), which would be a rare occurrence. In reality, there is usually a dominant humor, and this was believed to account for the individual character and physiognomy of each person. The search for anthropologically constant features fitted in with this overall view by creating a symbiotic correspondence between macro and microcosm. Thus temperaments were held to be influenced both by endogenous factors such as sex, age, consanguinity, and by exogenous factors such as the seasons and the climate. By the same token, the temperament was thought to condition and shape the psychological profile of the individual.[34]

Nutritional needs were also perceived as depending on temperament. If all material substances are a mixture of primary qualities, then food itself is composed of the same elements, and once ingested will produce certain effects on the person's temperament. According to Galen, the human metabolism is naturally attracted by whatever promotes the balance of humors: in other words, the relationship between an individual and food is based on a compensation mechanism controled by intake and elimination, such that the human body, like all other living organisms, "attracts what it requires and eliminates what is extraneous to it."

The opposing humors thus tend to balance each other out. For example, the choleric temperament with its characteristic hot, dry complexion will be inclined to ingest cold, wet substances such as fruit, whereas the phlegmatic temperament, which is cold and wet, will be drawn by hot, dry substances, such as red wine, roasted meats and bread. The best way to stay healthy is to keep to a "natural" diet, in other words a diet that is appropriate for the individual temperament. By the same token, a person who ingests foods with the same composition of humors present in the body is likely to provoke imbalance (*diskrasia*), which will undermine health. "The temperament of the young is hot and rich in blood, whereas that of the old is poor in blood and cold, which means that it is useful for old people to drink wine, because it aids the recovery of the right degree of heat and cold for that age, whereas wine is very damaging for those who are growing. During youth nature is very hot and extremely agitated: wine would provoke over-heating and uncontroled, violent action."[35]

In the dietetics of antiquity, taste was thus the manifestation of the faculty of appetite entrusted with regulating the relationship between requirement and food, in other words between desire and health. The word "idiosyncrasy" was adopted to refer to intolerance for certain substances, either in medicine or nutrition. So Galen used, and presumably introduced, the literal meaning of the words *idios* (particular) and *synkrasia* (mixture—of humors in this case) to refer to the natural (symptomatic) manifestation of revulsion and disgust.

The individual complexion was perceived as deriving from the sex and age of the person, the surrounding environmental conditions, habits formed and adopted, and the influence of the stars and the seasons. In relation to this, taste was the genetically determined somatic trait that, like character and physiognomy, cannot be corrected or reshaped at will. For this very reason, there is no accounting for taste: *de gustibus non est disputandum*.

The cook's task was thus not to appease the desires of the palate or belly, and certainly not to stimulate a capricious inclination for guzzling, which would inevitably undermine health. Instead the cook was supposed to further temperance in taste as a means for achieving correct sustenance for the body. This required skilled knowledge of the "physics" of cooking, which meant "knowing exactly the complexion of the guests, the physical environment and the constitution of the foods, so as to achieve in all cases the right amounts for maintaining the correct balance of humors. (. . .) Thus for every ingredient it is essential to establish the exact composition— *natura*—and its influence on the organism—*vis, facultas*."[36]

This explains the structure of medieval recipes, which not only provided advice on the preservation and preparation of different foods, but also took into account their effect on health. For example, "dry" meats such as beef or venison were best prepared in a stew, whose wetness re-established the balance of humors. Vice-versa, "wet" meats such as goose or lamb were better roasted, because this re-introduced the dry element. Mixtures, sauces, condiments and serving different foods together were subject to the same principles, at least in theory. Apart from modifying the nature of foods as they appear in nature so that they become more digestible, culinary skills were also useful for making dishes tastier, in other words, better suited to the body from the sensorial point of view. Luxury in medieval banquets was not only a question of lavish table settings and complex dishes. It also found expression in the widespread mania for spices, which were originally introduced into Europe—like sugar itself—for their medicinal virtues.

An important exponent of this school of thought was Platina, the fifteenth-century author of a treatise on cooking that met with widespread acclaim. Within the framework of medieval dietetics, with all its moralizing magic, he managed to rescue the activity of the cook from the smoking spit and elevate it to the realms of learning. Starting with the title, *De honesta voluptate et valetudine* (1475), his aim was not to condone revelry and debauchery, but to show men of discernment how best to enjoy life. He viewed good health as the essential moral and dietetic condition for the enjoyment of food and pleasures of the palate. "Not all foods are suited to all men, but there should be a sufficient variety of foods to respond to the different basic principles, to man's different desires in relation to the humors, and to the different tastes, so that each person can have what is good for him, what he likes and what is nutritional for him."[37] The Epicurism that Platina proclaimed to be philologically correct: far from being a justification of luxury and dissoluteness, it was an ideal aimed at the form of self-control essential to true happiness.

Cooking was thus still far from being emancipated from dietetics, and had yet to give in to hedonism or become a freely inventive form of food production entirely dependent on the palate. The idea that taste in its own right could be a worthy goal, free of moral and dietary constraints, could only come about once economic and social transformation had paved the way for ideological change. At this point the statutes and practices of taste could follow individual predilection, undergoing a process of civilization to become a *chimaera disputationum*.[38]

Freed of its earlier obligations, taste could then become a mirror of social differentiation, a catalyst in the civilizing process that was to invest behavior in relation to the new historical and political conditions. As such, taste was thus also able to influence aesthetics and formality, expressing the culture of the church and promoting new models of behavior. Little wonder, then, that it ultimately also came to define gastronomy and refine appetites, ushering in the foundation of *haute cuisine* in the second half of the seventeenth century.

It took a long time for taste to become independent. As Norbert Elias has pointed out,[39] the first stage in the process was slow and pervasive, reflecting the ideology essential to the spread of good manners. Premonitory signs of this development were already visible in the Middle Ages, at the time of the Carolingian renaissance. During this period,

all due attention was paid to "noble behavior" and to everything that was deemed a necessary accessory to food: a fine table with beautiful linens and crockery; good company and pleasant conversation; music and entertainments; elegant behavior. Such was the birth of "good manners," of convivial rites founded on elegance rather than strength; on forms rather than on substance (from the dietary point of view). In court circles of the twelfth to thirteenth centuries these "manners" began to take shape, acting as a measure of social differentiation based less on quantity than on quality, and on precisely how these products were consumed. The new aristocratic culture invested not only the convivial dimension of food, however, but also the products themselves, which had to be more refined and elegant in their tastes, smells and colors. A correct initiation into courtly life was not just a question of appetite (which remained an essential attribute of the nobility), but also of discernment, the ability to select, to distinguish between good and bad foods.[40]

The ritualization of good manners and refinement led to the redefinition of food requirements and appetites. The explanation of variety and difference increasingly revolved around social context, including rank, education and culture, rather than innate traits, climate and season. While the precept of the ancients, according to which food should suit the "quality of the person," still prevailed, individual taste was justified in terms of social rank, which also accounted for the related norms pertaining to precisely how food should be consumed: "the perspective began to change as the idea that the "quality of a person" was largely a social matter gained ground. This in its turn increasingly coincided with the social status of the individual, his or her rank, wealth and power. (. . .) Eating certain things (prepared and cooked in a particular way) was no longer exclusively due to habit or choice. It was becoming a sign of social identity based on an established hierarchy whose preservation called for due observation and respect. (. . .) Fine, elaborate and sophisticated foods of the sort power and wealth could buy and display were suited to the stomach of gentlemen, whereas common, rough foods were the right thing for the stomach of peasants."[41]

The dining tables of Europe required new stages, sets and choreography, and the diners themselves became the actors in the ensuing plays. Where once exterior show, formality and the display of magnificence had held sway, the focus grew more personal, stimulating an *ésprit de finesse* that could educate sensual perception, thereby investing something learned with spontaneity. Taste was undergoing the influence of style, based on the idea that what appeals is not necessarily good, whereas what is good should be appealing. In other words, what is deemed delectable within aristocratic circles is entirely conditioned by convention. Just who shaped the convention depended on social prestige, and those endowed with it became models for behavior and mentors of refinement. The ancient monastic precept (continue to pray and faith will come of its own accord) was thus adapted to suit etiquette: repetition, social acceptance and the spirit of emulation could all act as remedial exercises for refining the appetites.

Far from being the natural expression of subjectivity, taste thus came to be shaped by culture. In this way the space occupied by individual fancy and whim was enclosed within the walls of basic uniformity. To have taste meant to have absorbed the dictates of refinement. This transcended the mere search for rarity, for what was precious and for over-abundance. And in so doing it proved that taste had changed, was no longer a question of exhibiting luxury or laxity, as it had been in ancient civilizations. In the modern mentality that was taking shape, taste had to be *good*: the addition of this attribute, intended as a synonym for "cultivated," "fine" and "natural," was an evident way of excluding those who lacked it. As such it was a fundamental innovation. To have "good taste" implied the ability to learn and appreciate (in other words, to have digested) certain expressions belonging to the sphere of what was considered worthy of appreciation. And these perceptual milestones, taken all together, were what defined "style." Thus good taste was the mastery of a conventional repertoire of tastes, acts and words; submission to an initiatory ceremonial established for the recognition and celebration of a particular social sphere. In this sense, there is no good taste at the table without concomitant rules for manners. "Courtly fashion moved towards the proliferation of small, delicate and costly dishes; knowledgeability and a sense of delicacy in matters of food became something of a mark of the courtier. Now a sense of delicacy implies a degree of restraint too, in so far as it involves discrimination and selection, the rejection as well as the acceptance of certain foods or combination of foods."[42]

The stylization of tastes was to manifest itself in a number of different ways: in the transition from abundance to refinement in culinary preparation as a display of self-control and sophistication in gastronomic enjoyment; in the rhetoric of delicacy,[43] as the criterion for the exclusion of vulgarity in the pleasures of the palate; the spiral of refinement that raised the expectation of pleasure from one banquet to the next; and the invention of the *connoisseur* as a practitioner of ritual *gourmandise* elevated to the highest degree of perfection.

As taste gained autonomy, the gastronomic dimension as such proved to be the final outcome of the social and cultural processes described earlier. It is no coincidence that it should represent the last stage of this evolution, because what had gone before effectively prepared the ground for and nurtured the last stage of the development.

There is, however, a persistent misunderstanding regarding the genealogy of luxury cuisine. It is either perceived to be one of the manifestations of courtly civilization, an embodiment of the transformation "from quantitative display to qualitative elaboration"[44] that marked the breach with the Middle Ages and began with the Italian Renaissance; or it is explained in terms of the emancipation of taste as a culinary art that no longer had anything to do with dietetics and morals, which transfers the focus to the French court during the following century. As far as chronology and place are concerned, the point to bear in mind is that taste changed during its evolution. Through the process of civilization, it underwent domestication, refinement, cultivation and ritualization. In other words, it took centuries of testing and improving before taste could settle down and establish its own identity.

Published in 1651, La Varenne's *Cuisinier François* is commonly held to be the first "irrefutable literary evidence of the birth of a specifically French culinary style."[45] Clearly it is not a subversive manifesto written by an isolated visionary, which means that in all likelihood it represents the first expression to appear in print of new inclinations that were spreading through the kitchens of the French aristocracy of the time.

In other words, the aim of this book is not to establish which country came first in the history of grand cuisine. To do so would simply reduce the history of gastronomy to a collection of anecdotes. This, alas, was a common occurrence until a decade or so ago, though worse still were the various passionate but blinkered efforts to proclaim one particular person as the sole author of the development of fine cuisine. By contrast, what is required is a careful reconstruction of how the various schools of cooking came about, what their particular characteristics were and why they came to the fore in a given period.

Jean-François Revel argued that *haute cuisine* owed nothing to "the specter of the Medici" and that the only contribution of Italians to fine gastronomy was as confectioners.[46] With all due respect to the French, however, the birth of the culinary arts did not depend on the invention of the rich creamy sauces that for three centuries contributed to the dyspepsia of half of Europe. What accounted for the rise of French cuisine above all others (not only Italian, but also Catalan, which was widely acclaimed during the sixteenth century) was the predominance of a particular style that spoke eloquently for the thirst for power and the desire to celebrate Gallic grandeur. In other words, the French school responded with greater gastronomic, aesthetic and rhetorical efficiency to the demand for luxury, refinement and novelty expressed by a civilization that had turned waste into the art of abundance.

Had they lived during the dark ages, La Varenne, Menon, Carême and the Troisgros brothers would never have gained recognition as the founders of a school. While they might have run a successful hostelry or even been appointed to prepare food for the table of pope or king, it is unlikely that they could have revolutionized cooking or reinvented gastronomy because the demand for such actions was lacking: an audience receptive to their creative vein had still to come about.

A totally different situation prevailed with the burgeoning of modern French cuisine. Once aristocratic bellies were so full that there was no room left for further indulgence, and when the inclination for refinement could no longer be satisfied by profusion, then the only way taste could go forward was by demanding sophistication in the way food was prepared. This was—and still is—a sphere in which there is no theoretical or natural limit to the search for perfection in its various successive manifestations. Indeed, the pursuit of perfection was what gave rise to virtuoso techniques and stylistic refinement; that is, to competition among chefs. Variety alone was able to elicit desire. An appreciation of inventiveness, the search for novelty and delight in what is unusual all came to the fore as signs of the new culinary taste.

From this point of view, the most effective interpreter of the new realm of the gastronome chef, architect of taste and high priest of cooking, was not so much La Varenne as the anonymous author of the *Art de bien traiter* (1675), who signed his treatise with the initials L.S.R.

In his polemical desire to excel, to claim the superiority of his own style, and thereby to denigrate anything his contemporaries might try to achieve, L.S.R. repudiated tradition, which he considered a primitive—and thus despicable—stage in culinary art, and instead pursued a double objective: "first and foremost, to make a certain taste, relative to a particular time and place, THE TASTE: absolute, final, possibly even of divine origin and right. And in the second place, to present himself as one of its greatest exponents and at the same time as its sole depositary, thereby becoming the supreme and sublime arbiter of elegance."[47]

It was not so much taste as such as the spirit behind it that marked the advent of the new developments in cooking. Aware of their excellence and originality, the French proclaimed themselves the proprietors of taste. In this perspective, taste was raised to the highest degree of perfection and, like the fine arts, was invested with a degree of elevation that allowed for a supercilious perception of what went on down below, among those wretched creatures forbidden such enjoyment by rank and history. Taste had lost its earlier plurality to become supreme, universal and absolute.[48]

This is precisely how French cuisine managed to impose the ideological supremacy that led to what was perceived as its technical and stylistic superiority with respect to Italian cuisine, which still revealed the sweet/sour element of the medieval tradition. In Sarah Peterson's view,[49] the new perspective was fully established, both symbolically and gastronomically, when the sugary element was removed from the main dishes and repositioned at the end of the meal. The ubiquity of the salt/acid pair that took over from the sweet/sour combination became a sort of taste paradigm that fitted in with the dictates of refined cuisine, which had to whet the appetite and delay the sense of satiety. "The French took the salad—that is, food seasoned with salt and acid—as the framework of the new stimulating cuisine. They derived the notion of extending the salad throughout the meal—from the ancients and the Renaissance Italians, both of whom had served salads at various points during their banquets."[50]

Acid and salted foods were in fact served as hors d'oeuvres as early as ancient Greek and Roman times, with the aim of stimulating the appetite. The Italians expanded the practice, using salads as side dishes that could act as an enticing contrast of tastes with the main dishes, where sweetness still tended to prevail. The French went one step further, transforming the menu into an unending succession of salted dishes. "The entire meal outside the dessert served the function of a salad."[51]

At this point a new liturgy of dining had come into being, one that was to spread throughout Europe: "the French conceived of a salt–sweet divide. They sundered the meal into an extended salad and dessert. For the first time in the West salty and sweet dishes were strictly separated. The French marshaled sugared items at the end, where their supposed power to extinguish the appetite would shut down any further desire to eat and bring on a feeling of satiation."[52]

Unlike Renaissance cuisine, which was still permeated with magic and health claims, French cuisine had become totally secular in the service of frivolity and hedonism. Where the dietary precepts of earlier times had preached temperance and health, the new culinary art exalted taste and stimulated the appetites. Gone were the dishes based on the juxtaposition and mixture of ingredients. In their place came recipes that tended to concentrate flavors and particular aromas. Humors and their interrelations were a thing of the past. This was the age of the mastery of culinary essence.

The many other innovations that were to characterize French cuisine adhered to a similar stylistic register and tended to express the same ideological inspiration. Spices were banned because they were seen as too obvious and immediate. Instead of exalting the natural taste of foods they smothered them. To add to which they were no longer fashionable, enticing, or even particularly rare and costly. By contrast, the "Arcadian" rediscovery of aromatic herbs underlined the element of freshness and spontaneity in majestically structured recipes. What was evidently artificial was also rejected: roasted fowl that were presented with the feathers stuck back on, for instance. Even browning was deemed a form of sham to be avoided. Instead culinary preparation had to be subtle and sophisticated: therein lay its attraction. Fatty sauces also underwent a transformation, in keeping with the general principle that contrast should be attenuated and flavors should blend together. The language of gastronomy gained new terms such as *bisque*, *feuilleté*, *julienne* and *ragout*, which emphasized refinement of preparation and perfection of technique.

One major question remains to be answered, however: Why did all this happen precisely in France, and in France alone? In one of the best books ever written on the history of taste, Stephen Mennell analyzes the parallel rise of *haute cuisine* in France and its coeval failure in England.[53] Could it be just a matter of difference in taste, with the French inclination for what is more sophisticated and overstated, and the English preference for what is quieter and more understated? After all, gardening, which is another form of pleasure derived from shaping nature, reveals similar differences in the two countries. To some extent this is indeed true, because the social implications in the two countries were also very different. The displays of magnificence typical of the French court provided forms of representation and social cohesion that would never have worked in England. And something analogous takes place when the subject is food. Culinary refinement came about in France because the surrounding context was that of the court, where the appurtenances of prestige reflected the absolutist monarchy.

The process could only achieve completion with the civilizing of behavior, the stylization of sensibility and the refinement of appetites. Once freed of moral constraints and dietary precepts, taste was able to focus on the pursuit of happiness, gradually becoming the regulating principle behind Western habits at the outset of the modern age.

Recognizing the pleasures of the table as expressions of *savoir vivre* brought a different focus to the problem: as fornication of the belly was transformed into titillation of the palate, frenetic dining became an expression of good taste. In other words, taste could claim to be a sphere of sensibility analogous to that of appreciation of fine arts. And so it remained— at least until the philosophers persuaded their readers that the pleasures of the mind should be divorced from those of the body.

3

The Birth of Aesthetics and the Bifurcation of Tastes

The twentieth century provided observers with a remarkable range of oddities that claimed to have aesthetic value. They included Dadaism, Cubism, abstract art, monochrome painting, Op and Pop Art, body and land art, to say nothing of artists' excrement, torn canvases, burnt wood, patched bags, mute concerts and exhibitions without pictures. Little wonder, then, that the plurality and ephemeral nature of aesthetic expression have become part and parcel of present-day cultural sensibility.

Contemporary art has focused more on provocation, on shocking the middle classes, than on delivering an edifying message by means of accepted symbols. The idea that art has anything to do with shared perceptions and understanding is something of the past. Instead society has opted for emphasis on individual taste and the multiplication of aesthetic canons, none of which aims at transcending the limited sphere of immediate gratification. One of the outcomes of this change is the pervasive presence of "minor genres" that are excluded from the élite circles of art galleries, literary circles and concert halls, despite the fact they attract numerous aficionados and a wide public, and in so doing act as opportunities for symbolic exchange and social encounter. Apart from the mass cult for *memorabilia* (in other words, for what most people deem the only "true art," to be exhibited in museums, preserved in churches and performed in theaters), such expressions of taste also include popular fiction, film, pop music, gardening, photography and tourism (the latter two having become a form of voyeurism in which images mediate between the individual and contact with reality). In other words, forms of leisure activity in which the attractions of form are interwoven with the need for fun or enjoyment, unleashing what Kant would have called the "free play of the imagination."

As for taste in the physiological sense, worldwide competition has spurred contemporary gastronomy and enology on to a previously unthinkable degree of technical perfection, creating a platform for shared opinions and parameters that are rather more grounded and measurable than those pertaining to the realms of contemporary artistic trends.

Today it is abundantly clear that a passion for art is only one of many potential pastimes, and not the most desirable or the most widespread of leisure pursuits. Moreover, it is also evident that the ephemeral nature of our current aesthetic labyrinth, replete with built-in obsolescence, is simply a reflection of our times. In other words, artistic creation is inextricably interwoven with cultural context, which in its turn is made up of the circle of people who invest such products with value.

Enlightenment Tastes: Perceptions, Contradictions and Aversions

Though this may now seem so obvious that it is hardly worthy of comment, things were very different during the 1700s, also known as "the century of taste"[1] in view of the intense debate that revolved around two aspects of the problem. The first was essentially *political*, in that it pertained to the possibility of making the pleasures of taste accessible to a wider sphere, not least because the extension of the rights of social citizenship implied shared symbolic and cultural privileges. By contrast, the second was *theoretical*, and involved restoring a degree of certainty to aesthetic experience following years in which the evolution of individual tastes had undermined its authority and accentuated the subjective, idiosyncratic nature of artistic expression and perception.

While the Renaissance and Baroque periods had insisted on the authority of the individual over the world, the age of the Enlightenment adopted a very different approach based on continual dissection and analysis. To this end, aesthetic taste was invested with an unconditional existence of its own, free of the need to fit in with the sensorial analogy pertaining to the palate. Buried beneath the many idiomatic expressions of everyday language, the taste metaphor lost its spontaneous, revelatory character once and for all. Reference to the pleasures of food as a way of understanding the perception of beauty no longer had any efficacy or charm. Aesthetic sensibility had acquired a dignity of its own whereby the prosaic gratifications of food and drink could no longer be used as a simile to describe the discernment of modern man and his cultural ambience. What is interesting, however, is the way the attribution of autonomy to the taste for beauty led to the proliferation of contradictions and paradoxes.

When moralists and philosophers did their best to disprove the relativity of taste and its fickle, ephemeral character, they generally referred to taste as a cultural rather than a natural phenomenon, despite the fact that historic experience suggested that art was indeed an elusive, provisional matter. Like the thinkers of earlier times, no one disagreed with the adage that *gustibus non est disputandum*, which spoke for the conviction that taste was influenced by temperament. If taste was to be understood as an "organic" phenomenon, that is, as an expression of a natural trait, clearly it did not lend itself to correction or cultivation. Criticism or reproof were thus entirely out of place.

The disparity of views only came to the fore when taste was considered a form of civilization, akin to and alongside manifestations of urbanity, courtesy and cultivated demeanor. In such situations, the term revealed a marked affinity with the other sense that can be used figuratively, that of touch, or tact.[2] Likewise, when it was deemed a form of superior instinct for beauty, in its own way a link between pleasure of the senses and spiritual elevation.

The original meaning of taste was thus gradually marginalized and subjected to mockery, to the extent that when the culinary simile did come to the surface, it was only in negative terms, to underline the differences between taste for food and aesthetic taste. When this latter began to resemble the former, as it often did when the focus was on habits (for instance, the Scottish predilection for the bagpipes and the Italian preference for the mandolin, or the German habit for starting dinner with a soup, as opposed to the English habit for beginning with a cold dish), the sense of beauty lost its autonomy and standing, slipping into the purgatory of what was random and gratuitous.

Yet what elicited discussion was not the extravagance and oddities of taste, but the degree to which it could claim to be a shared experience. Once the sphere of reference transcended local custom and credence to embrace the lasting masterpieces of literature and art, it was no longer possible to insist that taste was exclusively subjective, and recalcitrant to communication. Common experience clearly showed that the taste for beauty implied a certain amount of agreement, at least within a given period and among a particular social milieu.

Granted, explaining the reasons for this agreement was altogether more complicated, since mere statistical criteria were clearly not enough. It is one thing to verify a shared conviction *a posteriori*, and quite another to postulate *a priori* the existence of a necessary universal faculty that precedes all experience. In other words, the taste enigma resides within the extreme parameters of subjectivity on the one hand, and universality on the other. The paradox naturally gave rise to two very different solutions: either accept the evidence that taste is socially and culturally formed (an approach that belongs to the relativist, sensualist perspective); or postulate a "limbo" in which the vicissitudes of history and culture are removed to leave the field free for aesthetic contemplation in the dogmatic, puritan sense.

The first of these two currents of thought considers taste as the outcome of the process of civilization of customs, culture and the arts; in other words, the expression of the highest state of evolution achieved by a given civilization, which is how the thinkers of the Enlightenment would have described their own period (Voltaire was convinced that earthly paradise corresponded to the Paris of his time, in polemical contrast with those who favored a return to nature).[3] From this point of view, taste inevitably became *good taste*, the ultimate goal of an evolutionary process collectively shaped, refined and perfected by the entire history of humanity. That said, however, setting aside the teleological assessment that attributes primacy in moral and civil progress to contemporary society, it is evident that good taste, as a form of *savoir vivre* by means of which people find the world they live in as agreeable as possible, is in fact a question of empirical experience that is not only short-lived and contingent, but also completely lacking in any formal justification or *raison d'être*.

The second solution to the taste enigma aims at establishing a more solid, universal and necessary foundation for the phenomenon, capable of transcending the historic and social relativism that has beleaguered the concept discussed above. Before taste can be said to be good or bad, refined or vulgar, it exists as a transcendental fact; in other words it precedes all empirical events and underlies the perception of beauty that can be experienced by all human beings, at least theoretically. As such, it represents an essential faculty, part and parcel of the original makeup of humankind.

Clearly this claim to universality gains ground when taste is considered as a metaphor, as opposed to being merely a sense. According to Galen's theory of temperaments, within a properly balanced disposition the constraints of the bodily sphere—in this case the appetite for food—preclude perception of the highest manifestations of culture and nature, which pertain to the spirit. Enlightenment ideology conceived of the sense of beauty in a similar fashion, attributing it to all men of discernment.

Various thinkers of the past embraced the former of these two approaches: Feijóo, Dubos, Voltaire, Burke and Hume, for example. They all perceived taste referred to the palate as the appropriate term of comparison, with common experience acting as a support and tool of persuasion. The confines of likelihood to which they subscribed did not rely entirely on the fact that the subject itself was still relatively new and unexplored. They could also count on a fairly wide and varied audience little versed in the sophisms of language and intellectual abstraction.

The recourse to everyday experience not only encouraged philosophers to embrace the manifestations of custom—including those pertaining to eating habits—within their sphere of enquiry. It also promoted the tendency to view the spirit of the time, which embraced the phenomenon of art, within a given historical context. At the time, even this seemed exposed to the fever of whim and volubility: "the ideal rules of the baroque period were abandoned, and replaced by other rules, based on an idealization that emphasized the 'perceptible' features of reality. Among other traits, sumptuous surfaces, texture, wealth of colors and the charm of gentle curves came to the fore as characteristic of rococo. Moreover, these traits were accompanied by a more frivolous, and possibly more superficial conception of works of art, whereby their decorative, hedonistic nature gained ground at the expense of their seriousness."[4]

If beauty "consists in the absence of regularity, in vitality, picturesqueness and fullness, as well as in the expression of emotions, which have little to do with proportion,"[5] then it must necessarily be considered a form of subjective impression and a byproduct of experience, rather than a manifestation of "nature" or an intrinsic quality of things. This implies that "all beauty is subjective, relative and conventional."[6] Moreover, the flaring up of fashions and the volatility of tastes have in fact infected the fine arts. Taste may not seem to be an irrational, arbitrary phenomenon, but it certainly appears to be contingent and fickle.

In his efforts to confute the axiom forbidding the disputation of tastes, the Benedictine scholar Benito Jerónimo Feijóo[7] distinguished between tastes that are innate and those that are acquired: if the former derive from temperament, the latter are the product of habit and opinion, which means that they are motivated by "apprehension," as Feijóo called it. In the preferences instigated by the unconscious and governed by the mechanisms that shape fashions, reinforce prejudice and forge habits, the primary cause behind the establishment of taste is social convention. It is thus perfectly legitimate to discuss and change opinions pertaining to rarity, fashion and reputation. In fact replacing one convention (an opinion, an infatuation, a desire) with another is a common enough occurrence.

In situations where tastes compete with each other, the "winning contender" does not necessarily stand for value judgments subject to an evolutionist perception of the civilizing process, as various eighteenth-century writers maintained. Feijóo's own cultural relativism was so extreme that it practically disallowed the concept of good and bad taste. If the job of taste as a faculty is to recognize what is pleasurable, "it can never commit errors" for the simple reason that "if it deems something pleasurable, then it reveals a taste for it, finding real pleasure therein." In other words, if taste entirely coincides with pleasure, it cannot be said to be bad. Nowadays, of course, discussions concerning the relativity of tastes appear almost obvious: "the inhabitants of Africa find the greatest possible pleasure in the song of crickets. The Tartars eat horse meat and the Arabs eat that of camels. In certain parts of Africa they eat crocodiles and snakes." So if such sounds and flavors procure pleasure to those who listen to or savor them, then taste has fulfilled its objective and cannot be deemed bad.

So in precisely what way can tastes be subject to disputation? In the sense that they can be "accounted for." This implies that it is possible to discover what governs them, which in its turn suggests they can be suppressed or influenced by means of discussion and persuasion. As we have seen, Feijóo proposed two explanations for the phenomenon: temperament, and apprehension. Temperament is simply the individual nature of a person, according to Galen's remarkably long-lived paradigm. Half a century later, Kant was to return to the same theories in his anthropological dissertations: "A given temperament brings with it particular inclinations: *Mores sequuntur temperamentum*, and these inclinations are accompanied by taste, or rather the pleasure found in gratifying them: in this way the variety of temperaments gives rise to the diversity of inclinations and tastes."[8]

The second explanation regards apprehension, in other words the immediate, intuitive faculty for perceiving, which governs the predisposition of the subject towards the object of pleasure. In this regard, Feijóo mentions two recurrent phenomena: the initiation to what is unusual, and the obsolescence of what is already familiar. It is a common experience to find pleasure in (that is, to gratify the taste for) something that once provoked feelings of disgust or indifference. And by the same token, something that was once considered highly desirable can later be eschewed as uninteresting. This happens because the apprehension or the predisposition of taste can change. Both cases underline how taste is an adaptable, impressionable faculty that is ineluctably subject to social and cultural conditioning: "many have no taste for a certain food at the outset, and yet develop a taste for it later because they hear that it is fashionable, or regularly served at the table of affluent gentlemen; others are drawn by the fact that it comes from distant lands, or is sold at high prices. By the same token, but in reverse, although at the outset they may find it to their taste, this predilection begins to wane when they hear that it is a food for yokels, or common fare among savage, barbarous people. Such information brings about a change in appreciation and reflection that shapes taste. The same thing happens with respect to all other kinds of pleasurable objects perceived by the other senses."[9]

Feijóo's "sociological approach" thus lucidly grasps the mechanisms that shape and spread modern taste, especially in relation to the budding consumer culture. Even more farsighted is his recognition of the way the exercise of taste can contaminate the psychological image. The only form of taste that resides in a bodily organ is that of temperament. The taste of apprehension, on the other hand, is anchored exclusively to "the psychological image, which can be gratified or irritated, according to the impression made on it by what the senses perceive."[10] This explains the distaste for something that was previously considered to be of great worth. When the Jews in the desert began to scorn Manna, Feijóo argues, the source of their scorn did not reside in the palate or in sight, but in the psychological image.

In view of its role within social dynamics and symbolic representation, such variables thus help explain the enigma of the overlapping subjectivity of taste. The confutation of the "taste axiom" thus implies two corollaries: Where the question revolves around temperament and humors, it is clear that there is no disputing taste: "whatever is natural and inevitable cannot be confuted through argument, and likewise there is no reason for considering it plausible or praiseworthy."[11] When on the other hand taste depends on perception, since "the vices of apprehension can be corrected by means of reason," the discussion is not only epistemologically grounded, but also relatively easy to conclude satisfactorily: "if someone beholds with disdain a given food, either because is it not used in his country or because it is very cheap, it is easy to persuade that person through reason that such disdain is ill founded."[12]

In the introduction to his dissertation on beauty and the sublime, even Edmund Burke was ready to recognize the social conditioning that shapes and establishes acquired tastes. If in the elementary stages of taste there is an overall agreement that sweet tastes are pleasant and bitter ones unpleasant, then these inclinations will evolve naturally, modifying individual predilections and multiplying sources of pleasure: "a man frequently comes to prefer the taste of tobacco to that of sugar, and the flavor of vinegar to that of milk; but this makes no confusion in tastes, whilst he is sensible that the tobacco and vinegar are not sweet, and whilst he knows that habit alone has reconciled his palate to these alien pleasures."[13]

Thus Burke too viewed taste as a phenomenon that transcended the sphere of the senses to interfere with the labyrinth of opinions and customs that shape the access to pleasure. The enigma of taste, in his opinion, consisted in its hedonistic bent rather than in its sensorial essence. Though all may agree that we like what is good, it is less easy to identify the reasons behind such a judgment.

Certain case histories can be enlightening. Often something that is first introduced as functional in some way will be ultimately deemed pleasant if it becomes a habit, for such is the "opiate" nature of acquiring tastes:

> thus opium is pleasing to Turks, on account of the agreeable delirium it produces. Tobacco is the delight of Dutchmen, as it diffuses a torpor and pleasing stupefaction. Fermented spirits please our common people, because they banish care, and all consideration of future or present evils. All of these would lie absolutely neglected if their properties had originally gone no further than the taste; but all these together, with tea and coffee, and some other things, have passed from the apothecary's shop to our tables, and were taken for health long before they were thought of for pleasure. *The effect of the drug has made us use it frequently; and frequent use, combined with the agreeable effect, has made the taste itself at last agreeable.*[14]

Moreover, it is evident that if we are really to dispute tastes (that is, argue in favor of the superiority of one over another), the discussion cannot be waylaid in absolute relativism, because that would inevitably end up by reinstating the principle of their unchallengeable nature, albeit extended to the collective dimension. In effect, it is not sufficient to clarify the social premises and the vacuity of the justifications supporting this or that predilection to convince someone that said taste concerns something that is beautiful or ugly, good or bad, as Feijóo would seem to think. Nor is it enough to bring Burke's theory of frequent use into play. The question is too complex and important to accept that the song of a cricket can be equated to the music of Handel, as the Enlightenment philosopher implied. The renewal of the arts and their constantly expanding public, along with the general tendency towards the civilization of behavior, are uncontestable facts, no less than the national and historic diversity of customs and predilections. Good taste becomes a subject for philosophers both as an empirical fact, and as a reflection of social attitude. As such, it calls for a theoretical explanation, which is what has led to the search for a principle of authority, or at least a logical reason to justify the superiority of one point of view over another.

In other words, all efforts are directed towards establishing criteria for the segmentation of the demand for refinement, one that tallies materially and ideologically with the historical process that has been accompanied by the expansion of the platform of consumers. In actual fact, the eighteenth century debate on taste largely revolved around the access to, or exclusion from luxury, especially in England. Thus the consumers themselves became the sole measure of the common ground for taste and its communication. Those able to exercise a *comparative taste* coincided not with an idealized version of the human being, or a subject of the United Kingdom, but more precisely with the select circle of those able to count on a special, refined sense of beauty. In other words, those with the experience to express judgment values. Such is the essence of what is known as "good taste," which is a faculty distributed unevenly among humankind.

The relevance of this faculty as part of the cultural baggage expected of the modern gentleman went beyond the mere experience of beauty: from Gracián and Shaftesbury on, that is from the late 1600s to early 1700s, the question involved "a way of being and acting, a style of thought and behavior, in other words something that invested every aspect—private and public, moral, social and political, and only thereafter aesthetic—of the life of an accomplished man."[15] Only later was the meaning of good taste gradually circumscribed to the ability to recognize the beautiful and the sublime in nature and art.

Since good taste could in no way be considered an innate faculty (a natural disposition may favor it, but it cannot form it), to gain refinement it must necessarily be *learned* (by means of suitable education), *shared* (that is, belong to a particular milieu that prescribes the rules for use), and *desired* (to possess and develop it must coincide with the person's aspirations). Thus from all points of view, good taste is a cultivated faculty, one that is shaped culturally to fit in socially.

So the real question at this point is to decide at precisely what level of the social pyramid it should be located. Once this is established, inter-subjectivity finally looms into shape. In this way Shaftesbury was able to claim that the universal canon of taste was laid down by the authors of antiquity, who represented a shared cultural model. In other words, by defining a rule and appointing an *auctoritas*, good taste was finally able to banish the concept of relativity of tastes. The *de gustibus* argument could no longer apply to good taste, because this latter was the fruit of an unambiguous definition, which allowed it to establish the norms to which it adhered and by means of which it claimed "universality."

At the same time, good taste also laid down the social confines of what could be shared and communicated: "if during the sixteenth and seventeenth centuries taste had been the prerogative of the court, with Shaftesbury it became the prerogative of the gentleman, who was still an aristocrat, but did not gravitate around the court. A gentleman who cultivates public as well as private virtues and, like a philosopher—who is the apotheosis of the gentleman—'aims at excellence, aspires to proper taste, and never loses sight of what is beautiful and dignified.' The gentleman-philosopher is thus the very incarnation of the standard of taste, and as such presents himself as a paradigm for all other men (of his class)."[16] A little later, access to this cultivated sensibility was to become less selective, and the admission procedures more "democratic." When Addison defined good taste as the supreme perception of a well-educated man, his chosen audience "was not the aristocracy, but a well-to-do middle class that aspired to being socially recognized and legitimized as belonging to the sphere of people of quality. Now, access to this class could not just be purchased through money (although this did frequently occur), but through merit, which implied the acquisition of culture and (good) taste. These constituted a form of 'nobility' that differed from that founded on rank and blood. Only thus could a man become a gentleman: by taking on the 'qualities' that had hitherto been the prerogative of the élite, as Shaftesbury still assumed."[17]

Laying down the rules for sensibility meant elevating the contemplation of beauty to the summit of the taste experience, making it the culmination of the process of the refinement and civilization of customs that was to favor the internalization of good manners. This was a sort of symbolic gentrification imbued with its own criterion for social discrimination. As a result, taste was to become a matter of aesthetics that provided the spiritual guidelines for appropriate behavior shared by the élite and by those who aspired to belong to such elevated spheres. At the same time, however, the process also supplied the "instructions" necessary for educating the spectator, that is the person geared to the reception of the work of art as a contemplative pastime.

This state of necessity was ratified by the fact that, well before aesthetics became a specialized discipline in its own right, treatises on beauty moved their main focus from rhetoric and poetics (in other words, the analysis of composition) to the emotional anatomy of the perceiver, that is to the conditions that make an aesthetic experience accessible and sharable. The contemplation of beauty implies the existence of a potential viewer who is able to derive pleasure from the simple act of looking: "this circular causal relationship, which coincides with the one that governs the relationship between faith and the sacred, is a characteristic of all institutions that can only work in so far as they are founded on the objectivity of social exchange, and at the same time relate to the subjective disposition for taking part and getting involved in it."[18]

Recognition of the existence of good taste is, of course, a cultivated variant of the spontaneous faculty for experiencing beauty, and this inherently implies its double: the *bad taste*, whether crude or corrupted, that elicits in the refined observer a sense of disgust and contempt that is as intense as the feeling of wonder experienced before "true" beauty. If we admit the existence of the counterfeit coin that is bad taste, then there is no place for Feijóo's argument, according to which taste cannot be forced into being, and for this very reason is always infallible and intrinsically free of all discussion and disapproval. The very fact of naming bad taste presupposes a value judgment and a form of punishment: that of being expeled from the circle of people who share the privilege of experiencing pleasure before the same external stimulus.

It is thus possible to talk about taste, though perhaps not to dispute it. Clearly it is something that can be communicated and shared, in that it is something felt by a number of people. As a result, recognition of the existence of good taste does actually resolve the problem of the relativity of tastes, though it may not be able to define the terms on which this solution is based. And it is precisely this aspect of the problem that divides the two schools that address the enigma.

For the first of these two approaches, good taste is simply one of a range of worldly pleasures, a view that mirrors something of the intellectual agility of the eighteenth century. Before being freed from the austere precepts of strict puritanical aesthetics, the *voyeur* is first and foremost a *viveur*, who projects his *joie de vivre on* the objects that surround him: "*everything* can become (= be) beautiful if the idea of it is connected with the idea of *something else* that, for *whatever* reason, is (or has been) a source of pleasure."[19] So beauty is not an *objet trouvé*, an intentional experience that makes the world of things, and thus existence itself, more pleasurable: "the agitation of the passions (= the emotions) is in itself a source of pleasure, in so far as it diverts the mind from the state of 'ennui' or boredom that is the worst thing that can happen to us in everyday life."[20]

Before being imprisoned by the liturgy of ecstatic contemplation, aesthetics remains within the realms of the emotions, within the sphere of the imagination that incorporates some of the privileges of leisure and some of the conveniences of entertainment. So what exactly differentiates this type of experience from the pleasures of the banquet or the whims of fashion? Why should art be something more than "the Sunday of life, mere evasion or, at best, a *divertissement*"?[21]

David Hume was the last major philosopher who dared propose a hedonistic, conciliatory solution to this enigma; one that pertained to the social role of pleasure and the need for providing labels.

One of his aims was to confute the conviction, common to many people as well as to the skeptic philosophers, that "all sentiment is right; because sentiment has a reference to nothing beyond itself, and is always real, wherever a man is conscious of it."[22] Although he agreed that all tastes, both bodily and spiritual, are an essentially subjective experience, Hume was actually trying to establish a norm that could help resolve the contentious question regarding the plurality of tastes, so that one could be said to be right and the other wrong. A simple mental experiment was sufficient to prove that this was not a chimera: the comparison between two immeasurable aesthetic entities (two works, two authors, two periods or civilizations), which are generally recognized as being out of proportion one to the other: "whoever would assert an equality of genius and elegance between Ogilby and Milton, or Bunyan and Addison, would be thought to defend no less an extravagance, than if he had maintained a mole-hill to be as high as Teneriffe, or a pond as extensive as the ocean."[23]

In Hume's view, any so-called critic with the foolish audacity to prefer Ogilby to Milton, or Bunyan to Addison, could clearly never be taken seriously. Instead he would be deemed out of his mind, ridiculous, or at best extravagant. The *consensum gentium* thus invalidates the principle of the equality of tastes: it is not true that all tastes are equal because certain of them are statistically more equal than others, especially those that transcend national borders and the sieve of history. Any deviation from the norm, on the other hand, is tantamount to a loss of credibility.

The established criterion of empirical regularity is not enough, however. A more sophisticated approach implies a finer palate, which in its turn calls for a comparison that transcends the obvious and embraces the smallest detail. The Don Quixote parable can shed light on the matter. Take the episode in which two men tasting wine from the same barrel came to different conclusions, one noting a slight hint of leather, and the other of iron: it shows how the superiority of opinion of experts is not based entirely on an act of faith, but on certain basic facts that derive from the progressive refinement of the senses, from the ability to perceive what escapes the layman, from what Hume defined as the "exquisiteness of taste."

As Sancho himself put it, "on emptying the hogshead, there was found at the bottom an old key with a leathern thong tied to it,"[24] which revealed how the keenness of taste of the two men in the anecdote could be proved empirically; in other words, it was possible to convince those who originally mocked them that their claim to superior discernment was actually well founded. There is clearly an analogy between this "emptying the hogshead" and the realm of the fine arts: it lies in the patient, methodical work of the critic, and the discovery and classification of the essential principles underlying "what has been universally found to please in all countries and in all ages,"[25] identifiable through a comparative study of the works and masterpieces of the past and present. Where such information is not available, different levels of subtlety and perfection in taste would of course continue to exist, but without the rule which makes them recognizable and subject to hierarchical organization according their prestige.

So in actual fact it is not only possible, but also advisable, to dispute tastes, since the very operation contributes to the collective refinement of arts and customs. Critics can avail themselves of principles and examples with which they can *convince* those who are less educated and articulate of the fallacy of their points of view, or indeed the vulgarity of their aesthetic perceptions. This naturally leads to recognition of the fact that "the fault lies in himself, and that he wants the delicacy, which is requisite to make him sensible of every beauty and every blemish,"[26] a gift that justifies the superiority of the expert, who at this point can help the mere amateur widen his horizons and refine his perceptions.

At this point the culinary comparison can be seen to work as a sort of paradigm. Although the skills pertaining to refinement are part of what "practice gives to the execution of any work,"[27] Hume does not simply take the similarity between the art critic in relation to aesthetic taste and the wine taster or the gourmet in relation to the palate as proof of the importance of experience and comparison in the process of improving taste and acquiring discernment.

When all is said and done, the fact is that they are one and the same thing. If, as Kant was later to denounce, we maintain that "a taste judgment must be held to be right solely because several people happen to agree with it, and not on account of any *a priori* principle, but (*as in the case of taste referred to the palate*) because a number of subjects happen to react in the same way,"[28] then there is no substantial difference with respect to other sources of pleasure, as long as they also meet with public acclaim: in other words, "beauty is reduced to pleasure, and art to cuisine."[29]

In actual fact what Hume proposes is rather more subtle than a principle of uniformity, according to whichever beauty is what most people like. By invoking the criterion of *consensum gentium*, he is not just tautologically validating the legitimacy of dominant taste. When you get down to it, what experience teaches us is that only a limited circle of individuals is generally thought to have superior abilities of aesthetic judgment. This mandate invests the figure of the critic with authority. It elevates the critic to the rank of arbiter of taste, along with other members of the learned community, thereby providing a solution to the problem of the reciprocally subjective nature of tastes and confirming the norm that we set out to establish.

Essential to this assertion is the demonstration that the fame underlying the authority of the critic is not arbitrary, but culturally and physiologically justified. To paraphrase Ferry, if beauty is simply what people like, what fits in with the inner, almost biological structure of human beings, then the criterion must be shaped by the *most essentially human constitution*, that is by that of the *foremost experts*, which should possess a certain universality, at least in theory, since it purports to be that of all men.[30]

That said, with hindsight Hume's portrait of the ideal critic ("a penetrating sense, together with delicacy of sense refined by practice, trained through comparison and free of all prejudice") today seems more appropriate for a methodical wine taster like Jancis Robinson than for a fashionable art dealer such as Larry Gagosian.

Moreover, the credit enjoyed by critics among an educated, refined élite attuned to the canons of taste is essentially based on the voluntary acceptance of a principle of authority, such that tastes follow pre-established models. Clearly the underlying parameters for these models are not fixed in time, given that they are the empirical outcome of the persuasive powers of opinion leaders and taste makers. And nor does the system leave much space for judgment of the judges, or criticism of the critics, in the case of authoritative but contrasting opinions.

Hume addresses the problem by simply pointing out that aesthetic consensus can claim greater longevity in the course of time than metaphysics and science: "theories of abstract philosophy, systems of profound theology, have prevailed during one age: In a successive period, these have been universally exploded: Their absurdity has been detected: Other theories and systems have supplied their place, which again gave place to their successors:

And nothing has proved more liable to the revolutions of chance and fashion than these pretended decisions of science. *The case is not the same with the beauties of eloquence and poetry.* Just expressions of passion and nature are sure, after a little time, to gain public applause, which they maintain for ever."[31]

It is the degree of unanimity of judgment concerning artistic masterpieces that suggests there might be a common predisposition among sentient subjects. Perhaps the "inner factory" that is our neocortical structure works in the same way for all human beings, in keeping with a recondite, and indeed indemonstrable, predetermined harmony. The taste for beauty would thus appear to be part of our perceptive faculties, a sort of "sixth sense," as it was often called in the past.[32]

Certain incongruities nevertheless remain: individual humors and local customs, for a start. It is not altogether surprising that people should prefer Ovid when they are young, Horace during their maturity, and Tacitus in old age, for such predilections are "innocent and inevitable." By the same token, different ages and nations can express particular inclinations. So the perspicacity of the critic lies in his or her ability to sympathize with an extraneous cultural context, and identify therein what really underlies aesthetic value. In any case, a certain degree of variability would appear to be inevitable when it comes to taste. This is why Hume distinguishes between aesthetic "consideration" and "predilection": only the former is subject to dispute, in other words to criticism. By contrast, the latter, when exercised within a culturally accepted framework, can provide degrees of gratification that vary from one person to another. When all is said and done, is this not the intimate and ultimate meaning of taste as a spontaneous, subjective experience?

Once again, "the problem is that of reconciling the freedom and autonomy of the individual and his private realm (and what could seem more private, free, and autonomous than taste) with the contrasting need for some objective authoritative notion of right (commanding conformity to a more than personal norm and thus some negation of personal freedom) so as to insure that individual freedom and autonomy would not degenerate to chaos and anomie."[33]

To some extent the title of Hume's essay already implies this dilemma: talking about a "standard (social, constraining) of taste (personal, free)"[34] seems more of an oxymoron than an area of research that has run aground.

In actual fact, the true grounds for cultural cohesion in the sphere of taste pertain to the realms of ideology and politics, involving the function of art in general more than they do the individual work of art. In other words, what really counts is the relevance of the concept of beauty as a "luxury item" and the conditions that define its accessibility. Essential to this approach is the vindication of luxury typical of Whig ideology: the gratification of pleasure does not simply involve the happiness of the fortunate few, but also the progress of nations, in other words the growth of productivity and wealth: "in times when industry and the arts flourish, men are kept in perpetual occupation, and enjoy, as their reward, the occupation itself, as well as those pleasures which are the fruit of their labor [. . .] The increase and consumption of all the commodities, which serve to the ornament and pleasure of life, are advantageous to society; because, at the same time that they multiply those innocent gratifications to individuals, they are a kind of *storehouse* of labor, which, in the exigencies of state, may be turned to the public service. In a nation, where there is no demand for such superfluities, men sink into indolence, lose all enjoyment of life, and are useless to the public."[35]

In contrast to what Kant was later to maintain, Hume was also convinced that while taste is arguably a *domesticated* expression of the passions, it is certainly not an *impartial* one. When Hume claims that "convenience is a beauty," and insists that the same principle applies not only to private homes, but also to "tables, chairs, escritoires, chimneys, coaches, saddles, ploughs, and indeed to every work of art; it being an universal rule, that *their beauty is chiefly derived from their utility*, and from their fitness for that purpose, to which they are destined,"[36] he is not just reaffirming the conception of art typical of antiquity, according to which the term designated any product made with skill according to shared rules.

Though Hume's conception of art does indeed embrace the neoclassical ideal, it also transcends it in a vision that paves the way for utilitarianism, whereby the maximization of yield is in itself a source of pleasure. Middle-class comfort, with its delight in possession, in the tangibly reassuring solidity of things, also reveals a world proud of its industriousness and confident in its own sense of the concrete:

> where any object has a tendency to produce pleasure in its possessor, it is always regarded as beautiful [. . .]. Thus the convenience of a house, the fertility of a field, the strength of a horse, the capacity, security, and swift-sailing of a vessel, form the principal beauty of these several objects. Here the object, which is denominated beautiful, pleases only by its tendency to produce a certain effect. That effect is the pleasure or advantage of some other person [. . .] Most of the works of art are esteemed beautiful, in proportion to their fitness for the use of man, and even many of the productions of nature derive their beauty from that source. Handsome and beautiful, on most occasions, is not an absolute but a relative quality, and pleases us by nothing but its tendency to produce an end that is agreeable.[37]

Once the validation has been demonstrated and the implications explained, what could be wrong with a final explanation of the mutual subjectivity of taste within an ideological, political or utilitarian framework? Nothing, in fact—apart from the irritation and disdain that such contamination arouses in those who uphold an exaggerated form of purism: "because Hume is unable to insist on the question of right and instead remains ensnared within the confines of fact, surely his theory risks prolonging the muddle between so-called 'human nature' and the ultimately banal reality of middle class Scottish society in the eighteenth century?"[38]

Was the Kantian debate really that much more interesting?

Kantian Ascetics

"Aesthetics," along with "taste," "art" and "beauty," is one of those words that languished for many decades in a state of lexical neglect. In relatively recent times, however, they have acquired new meaning, energy and purpose that has rescued them from the realms of the obvious and brought them back to center stage. As Nietzsche pointed out in relation to words pertaining to morality, when such terms regain lost ground they often shape events and initiate developments.

The revival of the term "aesthetic" within philosophical debate and its progressive diffusion in common speech has led to an important change in the history of taste: on the one hand, the word pertains to a specialist discipline largely devoted to the experience of beauty via sight and hearing, thereby excluding other senses and passions; on the other, it has been adopted by non-specialists who contribute to the way it is used to describe a discerning, shared experience of pleasure that transcends what otherwise risks appearing to be chilly formality and detachment. Both developments are somewhat surprising, given the fact that the etymology of the word does not include "references to beauty, art or pleasure,"[39] in other words to the concepts that delimit its sphere of application.

The Greek word *aisthetikos* means "sensitive," in the "perceptible" sense, as opposed to *noetikos*, meaning "rational." In the mid-1700s, the term "aesthetics"[40] was used to describe the new science by an obscure philosopher whose only claim to fame is the farsighted title of an unfinished work. From here on, the term ceased to designate a human faculty and rose to the dignity of a theory, along the lines of logic and metaphysics. Baumgarten's proposed plurivocal definition ("theory of the liberal arts, doctrine of lower knowledge, art of fine thought, art of the analogy of reason") is nevertheless too convoluted and soaked in archaism to be a legacy for posterity.

The "liberal arts" embrace both the art of persuasion, including the traditional trio (grammar, dialectics, rhetoric), and what in coeval France were rechristened "beaux,"[41] or "fine" arts, which were soon to become the only forms of art deemed worthy of aesthetic contemplation.

The "lower knowledge" intrinsic to Baumgarten's theory pertained to what is intuitive and emotional, thereby producing only *repraesentationes sensivae*, in other words confused and imperfect images, as opposed to the clear, distinct perceptions that belong to the superior stage of knowledge, accessible only through reason and the intellect.

As for "fine thought" (*pulchre cogitandi*), it only partly refers to what was to be called "aesthetic judgment": the fact that the intention was to propose an art, rather than a theory, was because the experience of beauty and of the sublime, as aroused by nature and by art, is simply a special application.

It was rather in the art of common life, particularly the development of a well-rounded graceful individual who could play a spontaneous and articulate role in society, that aesthetics was supposed to have its key influence as a practical discipline (itself an *ars*) concerning—and nurturing— the "lower," sensuous-sensitive faculties.[42]

In conclusion, the "analogy of reason" is precisely where aesthetics hopes to establish a foothold. For this is the "mental universe" parallel to the world of the rational faculties, endowed with workings and an autonomy of its own, whereby the objects of perception and imagination take the place of those of knowledge. Such a world is populated with sub-rational faculties, including the *vis aestimativa* recognized by scholastic culture as something shared by men and animals. The appetites, sexual as well as dietary, should of course also belong here. Largely they do not, however, and for no apparent reason.

In the end it was Kant who took on the role of adjudicator in this matter, despite his own terminological reluctance.[43] In his view, the foundation of aesthetics called for a double delimitation of application. On the one hand, compared with the superior cognitive faculties, *cognitio aesthetica* appeared to be an intrinsically imperfect variation: first because it is inevitably subjective, and thus unsuited to the formulation of any general rule (along the lines of the rhetoric of poetics) that could prescribe or establish which objects are beautiful, and which ugly; and second because it is "lacking in concept," in other words incapable of providing a true cognitive contribution. On the other hand, when compared with ordinary sensibility (in particular with taste in the palatal sense), this special sort of *vis aestimativa* stands out because it is "disinterested," in that it does not concern the object as such, but its form and image. And it is this golden rule of aesthetics that was to shape its historical development and social assimilation.

Granted, this was not Kant's invention. Aesthetic experience, as it is conceived and theorized in modernity, had already been the object of study in antiquity, albeit under a different name. During that period, no less than in the eighteenth century, it was seen to designate the feeling of pleasure aroused at a distance by sight and hearing, in other words the "noble senses" that gave rise to a sort of ecstatic rapture, or suspension of will: the contemplative attitude, shorn of practical considerations or yearning, distinct from greed (or the desire to possess), and also from the other animal instincts aroused by hunger or lust. Enlightenment thinkers strove to isolate and probe into the specific faculty of recognizing beauty. The main aspect that distinguished it from the conceptions of Antiquity and the Middle Ages (and even the Renaissance, permeated with Platonism) was the recognition of its subjectivity, a condition that the taste metaphor suddenly imbued with hedonism.

If taste is a faculty congenitally programmed to achieve pleasure, however, in what way can it be described as "disinterested"? According to Jerome

Stolnitz,[44] what in Kant's aesthetics can appear to be a mere *petitio principii* actually conceals more demanding grounds whose roots can be traced back to morals and theology. For Shaftesbury, an "interested" or narcissistic attitude (*self-interest* or *self-love*) is always to some extent egoistic and often implies a desire to hoard. This thus includes all those actions and motivations in which private good comes before the common weal, personal wellbeing before the interests of the community. The contradictory attitude does not appear in specific reference to aesthetics, but—more coherently—in an ethical, religious context: the virtuous man, Shaftesbury argues, cannot harbor a speculative love for God in the hope of reward in the next life; to be sincere, his love should be totally "disinterested," in other words motivated exclusively by the "perfection of the object." Like other English philosophers (Alison, Hutcheson, Addison), Shaftesbury managed to shift the same moral predisposition to the contemplation of beauty: the term "disinterested" was used to refer to the mental state that set what was useful and pleasurable to one side, in other words that did not take into account the gratification of appetites.

It was Kant, however, who provided the most authoritative and widely read theory of the ideology of disinterestedness as the cornerstone of aesthetic sensibility: by regulating the terms for access to beauty, the *Critique of Judgment* became the breviary of taste that was to shape the Romantic age.

Kant's argument involved four stages, essential to the *ubi consistam* of aesthetic judgment. This was to be:

a. disinterested;
b. universal;
c. pure;
d. necessary.

Each and every moment and attribute simply serves to isolate and differentiate the taste for beauty from the rude and crude original meaning of the term behind the metaphor.

The fundamental moment is the first one, since its goal is to distinguish beauty (or rather the pleasure that derives from it) from what is useful and pleasurable. Kant turned to the famous story of the three iconoclasts:[45] when faced with a splendid palace, it is plausible that an Indian chieftain visiting the Old World might prefer a Parisian hovel offering cheap alcohol and love; that a follower of Rousseau might reflect upon the vanity of the powerful and the poor carpenters whose sweat and suffering went into building it; that a hypothetical Robinson Crusoe would judge it to be unsuitable as a lodging for Man Friday. All three, however, were deemed incompetent in their judgment, since Kant intended something else with his conception of taste. In his view, discussions of beauty had to disregard moral judgments and questions of preference or utility, and instead focus exclusively on the objective description of that state of mind that is aroused by the formal experience itself, shorn of any other consideration. This experience is entirely different from that of the pleasure that the sensation arouses in the senses, because not all pleasures are experienced through sensation. There are also spiritual pleasures, or what Kant refers to as the "pleasures of reflection."

Here Kant makes an essential distinction: what makes sensory pleasure different to the taste for reflection is the fact that the former is aroused by an interest that "excites a desire for objects of the same sort."[46] This aspect of taste as an appetite implies that, unlike the sensation of beauty, the experience of what is pleasurable cannot contemplate its own absence, but instead produces (or reproduces) an inclination that transforms the sentient being into a subject moved by desires. Not that this necessarily implies a process of judgment, however, since the taste for what is pleasurable can be spent through fulfillment, which is the quintessence of pleasure: "those who are always intent only on enjoyment [. . .] gladly put themselves above all judging."[47]

The taste for beauty and the taste for what is *good* are also two quite different things. The former is an absolute term, while the latter suggests the individual perception of what is useful. In both cases, the "pleasure in what is good" always implies the perception of an objective, and therefore a practical or moral interest. Moreover, what is good, conceptually and practically, is different to what is pleasurable, in that what arouses pleasurable sensations (for example, "a dish that stimulates the taste through spices and other flavorings") may still be deemed regrettable from the dietary point of view, which takes its later effects into account.[48]

Aesthetic judgment is a different matter, however: it implies the experience of pleasure, but in a completely different way from the other two, in that it is "disinterested." What is good and what is pleasurable presuppose the existence of an object, which is not the case with beauty. Here the only thing that counts is the representation: taste judgments are formal and entirely contemplative, referring to mere *phantasmata*.

The difference between the three different ways of acquiring access to pleasure is also mirrored in the respective subjects involved in the experience. All creatures, men and animals, can experience pleasure, whereas only rational beings (humankind, but also the incorporeal spirits typical of North European culture, including angels, demons, ghosts, fairies, elves and sprites) can experience what is good. Beauty alone is a specifically human experience, accessible only to rational creatures.

The criterion of disinterestedness is the cornerstone of Kant's aesthetics because, in his view, it gives rise to all the other characteristics of the experience of beauty.

Further into his *Analysis of Beauty* the argument in favor of the universality of aesthetic judgment thus simply relies on an elementary deduction. Given that the pleasure of beauty is not based on any kind of inclination, it cannot depend on "any private conditions, pertaining to his subject alone,"[49] and so it must be universal. Confirmation of this is to be found in everyday linguistic usage: when someone says "I like" something, the subject of the verb is essential to the meaning of the sentence, just as "everyone has his or her own sense of taste." The situation is different when it comes to judgment of beauty, however: "it would be ridiculous if (the precise converse) someone who prided himself on his taste thought to justify himself thus: 'This object (the building we are looking at, the clothing someone is wearing, the poem that is presented for judging) is *beautiful for me*'."[50]

Kant does not appear to be worried by the fact that these very examples are cases of what is "beautiful for us," in that they relate to a particular historic and social context. Indeed, his argument in no way takes into account the succession of styles and fashions, the different degrees of aesthetic judgments, and the process of refining taste (in other words, compliance with cultural constraints). This is no casual omission, but a deliberate, motivated exclusion that is clarified later in the work.

Up to this point, Kant is content with observing that every aesthetic judgment requires the same inspired involvement on the part of the others, who must also either agree, or express disapproval. The very fact that beauty is a question of collective belief, in other words a shared cultural model, implies that there must be a sort of interiorized conformity of sensibility that has acquired mutual recognition. As far as beauty is concerned, this is not simply a matter of personal opinions. What is at stake is the affirmation of shared judgments "supposedly generally valid (public) judgments."[51]

So far this is pretty much what Hume and the other British philosophers believed. However, Kant does differ in the way he aims at something that goes beyond "comparative judgment": for instance the host who refines his judgment so that he can entertain all his guests to perfection. In a case like this, it is simply a question of stipulating a few general empirical rules, based on the casual frequency of similar agreements in the past. In the realm of beauty, on the other hand, the aspiration is to establish universal rules "that govern the judgment underlying the taste for beauty."

In actual fact, for Kant such aims were an illusion, because rules for beauty simply do not and cannot exist. Paradoxically—though not conclusively—aesthetic judgment appears to be hermaphroditic: although it is universal and necessary, it remains essentially subjective, dependent exclusively on the state of mind of the individual and not on the particular features of the object, as the rationalist school claimed to believe. Its universality is thus *sui generis* and refractory to dispute (which means silencing the adversary on the basis of an incontrovertible argument), and yet at the same time questionable in view of the very fact that individual sensations and appraisals can be modified, shared and refined.

This brings us to the third point: to be impartial, in other words universally shared, aesthetic taste must also be "pure." Unlike moral judgment, "it is merely contemplative and does not produce an interest in the object."[52] Unlike what is merely agreeable, the taste for beauty is "independent from charm and emotion."[53] Clearly this line of thought leads to a divorce between taste and sensuality: when taste is referred to figuratively, it implies another type of pleasure, one that is cool, calm and collected—in other words far removed from the heat of the senses: "a judgment of taste is thus pure only insofar as no merely empirical satisfaction is mixed into its determining ground."[54]

Such is the triumph of the rhetoric of refined feelings and noble intentions. To safeguard the fragile paradigm of the universality of taste, to elevate it to the highest pedestal of human illusions, to justify belief in this *auto-da-fe*, all inclinations have to be tamed. The experience of pleasure itself must be reined in and toned down until, completely isolated from the body, it conforms to the rules of public decency. The passions require discipline and control, so that they amount to little more than edifying, innocuous and well behaved pastimes well suited to the hypnotic realms of received ideas.

Everything that does not belong to this reassuring world is impure, and thus worthy of reproach or disgust. Aesthetics as the ideology of beauty aims at teaching and spreading the felicity of faultlessness, thereby also encouraging a degree of recalcitrance. The resulting composure rejects all hedonistic behavior, which is deemed to be so brutish and base that it is far removed from any form of taste, an appellative that pertains exclusively to the superior realms of human sensibility, which is of course pure and disinterested. "Taste is always still barbaric when it needs the addition of charms and emotions for satisfaction, let alone if it makes these into the standard for its approval."[55]

The divergence of tastes calls for and explains the suppression of the body, in that the experience of pleasure effectively produces nothing more than "a pathologically conditioned satisfaction (through stimuli),"[56] which implies a deep-rooted sense of forbidden fruit on account of the obvious affinity with lust and lechery. But even when freed of indecent contaminations of this sort, the pleasure of the senses remains a question of impulse. As Kant points out, since hunger is the greatest cook, the debauchee will binge on any sort of food, with no distinctions: "such a satisfaction demonstrates no choice in accordance with taste."[57] In such a bigoted, provincial world, the figure of the gourmet is absent, or repulsive. Gluttony cannot be considered a possible source of refinement of taste: only when the need has been satisfied, Kant claims, is it possible to distinguish between those who do and do not have taste. But the pleasures of the palate are always interwoven with a physiological or pathological need.

And this leads us to the fourth and last part of the argument. Apart from being disinterested, universal and pure, aesthetic judgment presents an intimate necessity of its own: "whoever declares something to be beautiful wishes that everyone should approve of the object in question."[58] The power of this self-conviction is such that what is really a surrogate for feelings can be passed off as a judgment of reality: "although it has merely subjective validity, it nevertheless makes a claim on all subjects of a kind that could only be made if it were an objective judgment."[59] Thus the paradox of taste again comes to the fore, casting a spell over perceptions and misrepresenting the meaning of reality, so that what really exists within the sentient person is attributed to things. Kant suggests resolving this enigma by resuscitating the quintessential classic idea of "common sense": because we are all programmed in the same way, we feel the same (aesthetic) sensations. His argument sounds very much like a *petitio principii*: to be universally communicable, he declares, aesthetic judgment must presuppose a feeling that is equally shared among all men; by the same token, however, to avoid falling back on psychological justifications, this feeling should be perceived as an *a priori* principle, a necessary condition for the universal communicability of knowledge.

In this way, the problem of the shared subjectivity of taste is dealt with in advance, to avoid getting bogged down in all the historical, social and cultural implications that had hindered the argument during the eighteenth century. While on the one hand Kant's "common sense" supports the idea of the "inner sense" of the Greek philosophers, and the "sixth sense" of the English philosophical tradition,[60] on the other it is invested with a firm new statute that discards all relativism in order to stake its claim among the realm of the transcendental faculties.

It is thus posited as an ideal norm that speaks for the beautiful object of an intimate and uncontestable pleasure: "it is required of every judgment that is supposed to prove the taste of the subject that the subject judge for himself, without having to grope about by means of experience among the judgments of others."[61] Kant seems skeptical about the possibility of educating and refining taste. Regardless of what Hume and the other taste improvers may have had to say, "he should pronounce his judgment not as imitation, [. . .] but *a priori*."[62] In fact, "I cannot be talked into it by means of any proofs. Thus although critics, as Hume says, can reason more plausibly than cooks, they still suffer the same fate as them":[63] that of offering others the fruit of personal introspection regarding states of pleasure or displeasure, thereby soliciting a similar experience, in other words a shared perception.

The established harmony that prevails among human sensibilities is thus the only true, natural foundation underlying the principle of the equality of tastes: "it asserts only that we are justified in presupposing universally in every human being the same subjective conditions of the power of judgment that we find in ourselves; [. . .] since they are subjective conditions of the possibility of a cognition in general."[64]

Granted, even Kant admits that beauty definitely has a social dimension, which progresses in relation to the civilization of peoples and the education of individuals. A solitary castaway on a desert island would not dream of growing flowers to pick for the embellishment of body or hut. Only once human beings come into contact with their peers do they feel the need for sharing the pleasure of beauty with them, for meeting up united by this particular sense of universal brotherhood, "as a property belonging to humanity."[65]

If interest in beauty depends on the nature of the species of sociable animal known as man, and on the degree of civilization he has achieved in the course of time, then the stages of civil progress and the barriers of social discrimination represent no more than an empirical accident that has nothing to do with the argument pertaining to the conditions intrinsic to aesthetic judgment. This explains the Kantian suppression of the historical and social dimension of shared taste: "since the latter indulges inclination, although this may be ever so refined, it also gladly allows itself to blend in with all the inclinations and passions that achieve their greatest variety and highest level in society."[66] So this is precisely the misunderstanding that Kant hopes to avoid by purging the perception of beauty of its frivolous, worldly contaminations.

This in its turn points to the persuasion that contemplation of nature is morally superior to interest for the fine arts and the ornamental use of natural beauty, both of which are potentially insidious sources of vainglory. In keeping with the hoary mimesis paradigm, in Kant's view, the ultimate goal of the fine arts must be subordinated to the supremacy of nature.[67]

The model for aesthetic reception foreseen by Kant is the sort of inspired demeanor of the beautiful soul, the ecstatic rapture of the naturalist "who alone (and without any intention of wanting to communicate his observations to others) considers the beautiful shape of a wildflower, a bird, an insect, etc., in order to marvel at it, to love it, and to be unwilling for it to be entirely absent from nature, even though some harm might come to him from it rather than there being any prospect of advantage to him from it."[68]

All things considered, the emotional contemplation of nature is thus what distinguishes the truly sensitive spirit. Such an attitude is far removed from the aesthetics of those who are fond of beauties that only sustain vanity and at best social joys.[69] And different yet again is the "coarse and despicable" attitude of those who have no awareness of the beauty of nature, and who "confine themselves to the enjoyment of mere sensory enjoyment at table or from the bottle."[70] God forbid that this should be considered refinement!

Value judgments of this sort have an effect on the classification of the arts, in that those that aim exclusively at pleasure are invested with lower status than the arts that elicit the authentic perception of beauty.

The "arts of pleasure" merely procure enjoyment: those pertaining to convivial entertainment, for instance, like the art of hosting a banquet where the only ambition is to ensure that the guests are happy. By contrast, the fine arts are unique in the fact that they embody their own raison d'être, regardless of whether or not they also have secondary effects, including the promotion of sociability among men. For this reason, Kant judges music and embellishment to be two arts that are too "superficial" to arouse truly "pure" pleasure; indeed, they lean dangerously towards enjoyment, which means they are dubious or hybrid in their constitution.

The trademark and common feature of the fine arts is the fact that they arouse a strictly spiritual sort of pleasure: what is essential to them is not attraction or emotion, in other words the pleasure that manifests itself in sensation. If this were the case, the fine arts would be reduced to a mere amusement or pastime.

On account of its connection with the world of frivolity, Kant relegates music to the lowest level of the fine arts, at least as regards its spiritual contribution (it does rather better in terms of hedonistic performance, however, where it gains first place).[71] Music also presents another grave drawback: its irreparable lack of urbanity, given the fact that it invades people's perceptive fields even when they would rather it did not. Contemplation, on the other hand, calls for undivided attention, in other words deliberate and sufficient aptitude of the mind, even when it is just a question of listening. Precisely the opposite happens when someone pulls out a perfumed handkerchief and wafts the scent around so that hapless bystanders feel heady; or during the singing of religious hymns, the expression of noisy and invasive devotion, when "they have forced the neighborhood either to join in their singing or to give up their own train of thought."[72]

So just what kind of pleasure comes with aesthetic taste?

A modest, quiet, solitary and austere pleasure that should never go beyond the uncontaminated intimacy of whoever is wittingly and willingly involved in the act of contemplation. It is thus very much a sublimated, ascetic private pleasure; a sensorial metaphor of the moral idea "which is not gratification but self-esteem (of the humanity within us) that elevates us above the need for gratification."[73]

To support the new ideology of art and the concept of beauty as a form of purity, Kant thus erects his theoretical edifice with its concomitant ethical and moral shield high above need as such, above pleasure, above the differences between humankind, and above their natural or acquired inclinations.

The Pleasures of the Senses Spurned

The aesthetic paradigm establishes a principle, which in its turn acts as a rule of conduct. The apprehension of beauty must be pure, disinterested and edifying; moreover, it must also be impermeable to pleasure and need. To achieve this quintessential state calls for the snuffing of sensuality, a deliberate suspension of desire, abstraction and abstinence from all those states of arousal that underlie the concrete predilections of taste: lust, avarice, exhibition, emulation.

This is the same paradigm that postulates the chosen beneficiary of the work of art as the person who perceives it, thus turning him or her into an institutionalized presence characterized by well-defined behavior and sensibilities. The taste for beauty is the outcome of an educational process that begins at school, continues in the academies and culminates in a collective cult, to be celebrated in museums and galleries and spread by means of manuals and magazine. In time this approach reaches the wider public of amateurs and the curious who, unlike wealthy collectors, can simply enjoy their contemplations without having to think about expanding their possessions.

In view of the fact that the aesthetic paradigm actually invests the cult with formal recognition, it also helps shape and organize the arts. This amounts to a radical change of perspective, by means of which the heritage of the past can be seen in a new light. Human history thus lends itself to interpretation as the attainment of an immanent, free-flowing project that evolves over time and is shaped to a greater or lesser extent by the different periods of history. Thanks to this retrospective invention, art changes its meaning, much as taste and aesthetics have done before. "As for sculpture, we should bear in mind that before the sixteenth century it was never even mentioned as such, in view of the fact that it belonged to a wide range of different trades specialized in particular materials: there were stone carvers (*statuarii*), metal workers (*caelatores*), wood carvers (*sculptores*), people who shaped clay (*fictiores*), others who worked with wax (*encaustic*), and they all used different methods of working (*technai*), and thus all belonged to different trades (*artes*)."[74]

It is therefore hardly surprising that the early classifications of the arts were largely articulated along the lines of the craftsmen's corporations and guilds. These went from the *ars victuaria* (meaning the provision of food) to the *suffragatoria* (means of transport), or the *lanificaria* (clothing) and the *negotiaria* (trade). By the same token, even seafaring, agriculture, hunting, medicine, the theater and war were considered to be arts.[75] Moreover, there were classifications that referred to the different destinations of the arts, although these did not involve any explicit mention of beauty as an end goal for contemplation. Galen and Seneca, for example, spoke of the educational (*pueriles*) and recreational (*ludicae*) arts. Similarly, music and painting were generally considered to be *artes voluptuariae* whose function was to gratify the ear and eye. Indeed, Bacon likened them to cosmetics and medicine, in that he regarded them as serving a practical purpose.

Only poetry was deemed different from the other arts and therefore worthy of greater consideration, because it was held to be inspired (in other words individual) and irrational (or free of established rules and models), the fruit of invention and creativity. Although it was not an art but a form of divination, poetry was paradoxically the activity that was closest to the modern concept of art. In poetry "the Greeks emphasised [. . .] its ability to influence spiritual life,"[76] and believed it to have an edifying, "psychological" effect in guiding the soul: something irrational, that could fascinate, enchant, seduce the mind,[77] fire the imagination.

There was also a close tie between poetry and music: not only because the former was always sung, and the latter voiced,[78] but also because "music and dance, unlike architecture and sculpture, lent themselves to *mania*, to forms of delirium and ecstasy."[79]

While poets were held in the highest consideration (to the extent that it was believed that an arcane, mystical link connected poets and oracles), artists enjoyed very little social prestige. Their works may have elicited admiration, but as people they did not. There was nothing original or exceptional about the artist, who was little more than a skilled laborer, an operative whose job was monotonous and lacking in fantasy. What he lacked was precisely what was to come to the fore in modern times as the distinctive feature of the artist: individual creativity.

Only during the Renaissance were art and poetry to undergo a gradual process of assimilation, when art was freed of its subordination to morals and religion and acquired autonomy and cultural prestige. The discovery or creation of beauty thus became its ultimate and exclusive end. Genius was equated with whoever was able to arouse in others that form of "distance titillation" that coincides with aesthetic enchantment. The manual arts that acquired the epithet "fine" moved camp from the mechanical to the liberal realms. Thus were "art and poetry blended into a single concept on a purely artistic basis, without appeal to mysticism."[80]

The outcome is well known: the *l'art pour l'art* dogma marks the recognition of distance, of pure and abstract reception, of detached formal fulfillment, far removed from any contamination with the kind of pleasure that Kant declared to be unworthy of a place among the dignified occupations of the mind. "The Faustian sense of pleasure, as penned by Goethe, is extremely personal: 'all that is assigned to the whole of humanity, I want to enjoy it from the depth of my inner being.' Today anyone wishing to use this concept in relation to aesthetic experience would be accused of being shortsighted, or overly anxious to satisfy consumer needs in a conspicuous fashion, which would be kitsch. Nowadays to admit to experiencing pleasure through art is only acceptable when it involves tourism."[81]

From here it is but a short step to various forms of ascetic extremism, to the corrective delirium expressed on occasions by Theodor Adorno: "whoever seeks and finds pleasure in works of art is inevitably a philistine: 'expressions such as "a pleasure to hear" are proof of guilt.' The person who is incapable of purifying art of the taste of pleasure is likening art to products of gastronomy or pornography."[82]

What remains to be clarified is exactly why this should be so: what are the causes, the hidden motives, the ultimate aim? Once the taste analogy has been established for the betterment of sensibility and manners, why should the taste for beauty and that of the palate suddenly separate? Did this have to happen?

Clearly the answer to this latter question can be no more than conjecture. At all events, the difference in terms of cultural prestige between the two has unquestionably favored the taste for beauty. As Korsmeyer has pointed out:

> philosophers might have made the opposite move and argued that there are commonalities for shared preferences in food and drink that are as reliable as for objects of beauty. Since literal taste qualities were already accepted as subjective and relative, however, they were left unexamined, assumed to raise no troublesome philosophical issues. But beauty had formerly been conceived as an objective quality, however puzzling. With the advent of empiricism, beauty was newly subjectivized and had to be rescued from the perils of skepticism. Both in formulating the problem of

Taste and in establishing standards for Taste, philosophers saved beauty from relativism by showing how it must differ from literal taste qualities. The all-important problem of Taste was not conceived to pertain to sensory taste.[83]

Although there is clearly some truth in this explanation, it does not appear to go much beyond the surface of things, which means that it fails to address the crux of the matter. Simple though it may sound, perhaps it was not so much the lack of cultural appeal as a shortage of direct experience that hindered the Enlightenment thinkers from perceiving that literal taste, like taste of the mind, can be educated and refined so that it acquires a form of élite inter-subjectivity. Kant's anthropological dissertations would certainly seem to suggest that there is truth in this hypothesis.

For when Kant the moralist declares that he intends to deal with "the knowledge of man as a citizen of the world," in other words as a civilized being, he is immediately establishing a distinction that mirrors his own disdain, mixed with an evident sense of exclusion. The reasons for this lie not only in his difficulty in perceiving the whole question clearly, which would be little more than a methodological alibi, but also and in particular in his total cultural obliviousness to the world of what he perceived as vain and fatuous. "The anthropologist is in a very unfavorable position for judging so-called high-society, the estate of the nobles, because they are too close to one other, but too far from others."[84]

A philosophical inquiry must needs aim higher, seeking what is elevated, ethereal, detached and universal, even when in principle any chance of "participatory observation" is clearly impossible: "the expressions 'to *know* the world' and 'to *have* the world' are rather far from each other in their meaning, since one only *understands* the play that one has watched, while the other has *participated* in it."[85]

This is an event in which Kant has no intention of taking part. His remains the bookish attitude of the provincial, who perceives an obscure harbor city as a narrow, fixed scene that is mistaken for the center of the world: "a large city *such as Königsberg on the river Pregel*, which is the center of a kingdom, in which the provincial councils of the government are located, which has a university (for cultivation of the sciences) and which has also the right location for maritime commerce—a city which, by way of rivers, has the advantages of commerce both with the interior of the country and with neighboring and distant lands of different languages and customs, can well be taken as an appropriate place for broadening one's knowledge of human beings as well as of the world, where this knowledge can be acquired *without even travelling*."[86]

There is no point in hoping for the impossible: every man is brought up within a given environment that shapes his mentality, aspirations, phobias and hypocrisies. So it is unreasonable to expect a person of science, educated in an austere, misogynous, puritan environment, to pontificate about the pleasures of high society when these are well beyond his empirical, moral perspective. Even the most enlightened philosopher must necessarily take inspiration from his own experience and beliefs, as well as conform to the rules of social decency shared by his audience. When aesthetic sensibility is intended as a purely contemplative event, like morals it is considered as a means for elevating the spirits. As such, it belongs to the realms of what is deemed to be civilized by educated gentlemen who go to museums, partake of the grand tour and attend literary salons. However, the category does not include luxury, hedonism, lechery, or the wasteful refinement of the aristocracy. Even Kant admitted that convivial pleasures, unlike erotic delights, could boast an undeniable social dimension. Yet though such experiences are not relegated to the shady sphere of private life, their contribution to human civilization is actually irrelevant, futile and unworthy, given the fact that they are inevitably tied to the dimension of need (hunger) and pleasure (the palate), which constitute the lower states of earthly existence.

Not even this explanation with its empirical, moral connotations is entirely convincing, however. There must be a more persuasive reason behind the imposing theoretical edifice constructed to extirpate relativism as it threatens to spread through the realms of aesthetic predilection. And this leads back to the enigma of the missing metaphor: why should it be possible to establish a universal rule for the taste for beauty, regardless of the evidently transitory, fickle nature of styles and preferences? Why insist on seeking an undeniable, transcendental definition of an ineffable, transient experience: the experience of the perception of beauty? Why should every other form of *delectatio* (not only of the culinary variety) be separated from those forms of "lesser knowledge" (Baumgarten's *gnoseologia inferior*) that are the very salt of life? Why indeed should the address largely focus on distance and disinterestedness?

According to Eagleton, the reply to these questions should be sought in the contribution involuntarily made by aesthetics to the construction and the spread of the very *forma mentis* that was to develop into the bourgeois vision of the world and social relationships. According to Eagleton, aesthetics predisposition suggests "the very secret prototype of human subjectivity in early capitalist society,"[87] nurturing the future liberal democratic ideology. "With the growth of early bourgeois society, the ratio between coercion and consent is undergoing gradual transformation [. . .] Like the work of art as defined by discourse of aesthetics, the bourgeois subject is autonomous and self-determining, acknowledges no merely extrinsic law but instead, in some mysterious fashion, gives the law to itself. In doing so, the law becomes the form which shakes into harmonious unity the turbulent content of the subject's appetite and inclinations. The compulsion of autocratic power is replaced by the more gratifying compulsion of the subject's self-identity."[88]

In the spontaneous and voluntary claim that my own feeling for beauty must necessarily be entirely shared by others, aesthetics comes across as a real paradigmatic model for what is ideological.[89] The ecumenical creation of consensus, the unconstrained acceptance of rules, the harmonization of difference, the toning down of privilege, indeed the consumer view of the world[90] place aesthetic judgment, along with ideological assumptions, within the cozy limbo of worthy feelings, well protected from the asperity and bias of what is true and false:

> the universal quality of taste cannot spring from the object, which is purely contingent, or from any particular desire or interest of the subject, which is similarly parochial; so it must be a matter of the very cognitive structure of the subject itself, which is presumed invariable among all individuals. Part of what we enjoy in the aesthetic, then, is the knowledge that our very structural constitution as human subjects predisposes us to mutual harmony. It is as though, prior to any determinate dialogue or debate, we are always already in agreement, *fashioned* to concur; and the aesthetic is this experience of pure contentless consensus where we find ourselves spontaneously at one without necessarily even knowing what, referentially speaking, we are agreeing over. Once any determinate concept is removed from our grasp, we are left delighting in nothing but a universal solidarity beyond all vulgar utility. Such solidarity is a kind of *sensus communis* [. . .], ideology purified, universalized and rendered reflective, ideology raised to the second power, idealized beyond all mere sectarian prejudice or customary reflex to resemble the very ghostly shape of rationality itself.[91]

Other authors argue that aesthetic predisposition is in fact the symbolic transposition of bourgeois affluence, a social honor that speaks for privilege, emancipation from need. Many people pursue this privilege, but for different reasons:

> the middle class, driven by the necessity to meet standards of "good taste" in order to justify pretensions to join the higher reaches of humanity; the leisure and hypercultivated who have the time (and the money) to devote themselves to the pursuit of "objects of taste and refinement" guaranteed for them by "connoisseurs" of these rare (and rarified) objects, the aesthetes, whose delicate sensibility, aroused only by encounters with "ethereal things," must not be disturbed by passion or impeded by the intervention of moral imperatives. So "taste" and "good taste" have all the earmarks of a bourgeois invention, an arbitrary standard reflecting only a class detachment from life and labor, a conventional badge of status functioning to separate the social herd from the dominant, parasitic social goats in sheep's clothing, a disguised morality pretending to identify approval pursuits and worthy performances by "correctness" of appearance and external form.[92]

According to this interpretation, to be in possession of taste is simply a form of interiorized social acceptance, a theory cogently expressed by Pierre Bourdieu. In an important book devoted to the sociology of taste,[93] Bourdieu demonstrates, with all due empirical evidence, that social stratification is always reflected symbolically by means of interiorized and adopted cultural conventions, most evidently those pertaining to taste preferences. In Bourdieu's view, the symbolic capital of individuals consists in their claim to cultural nobility, which is preserved within the bulwarks of social structure and economic interests.

As a tool of mutual recognition and cohesion (for the members of a certain social circle), taste essentially acts by promoting discrimination towards those who are excluded: among the prosperous classes, possessing taste means, first and foremost, *feeling disgust* for the system of common, vulgar predilections shared by the lower strata; only later does it also come to involve the recognition of what is worthy of appreciation.

Here Bourdieu reconstructs the genesis and outlines the function of *pure taste*, which tends to coincide with "social benefit," in the discriminatory sense described above.

"Pure" taste and the aesthetics which provides its theory are founded on a refusal of "impure" taste, of *aesthesis* (sensation), the simple, primitive form of pleasure reduced to a *pleasure of the senses*, as in what Kant calls "the taste of the tongue, the palate and the throat," a surrender to immediate sensation which in another order looks like imprudence. At the risk of seeming to indulge in the "facile effects" which "pure taste" stigmatizes, it could be shown that the whole language of aesthetics is contained in a fundamental refusal of the facile, in all the meanings which bourgeois ethics and aesthetics give to the word; that "pure taste," purely negative in its essence, is based on the disgust that is often called "visceral" (it "makes one sick" or "makes one vomit") for the everything that is "facile"—facile music, or a facile stylistic effect, but also "easy virtue" or an "easy lay." The refusal of what is easy in the sense of simple, and therefore shallow, and "cheap," because it is easily decoded and culturally "undemanding," naturally leads to the refusal of what is facile in the ethical or aesthetic sense, of everything which offers pleasures that are too immediately accessible and so discredited as "childish" and "primitive" (as opposed to the deferred pleasures of legitimate art).[94]

The class struggle between oppressed and oppressors thus lends itself to cultural translation into the contrast between "instinctive" tastes that are visceral, crude and embarrassing, and "cultivated" tastes, which are of course elevated, edifying and exclusive. To refer this to ideal types, on the one hand there are those who cling to natural needs and do not know how to go beyond basic gratification, and on the other there are those who raise themselves above the *status naturae*, flaunting self-control of their instincts and appetites so that they affirm "their legitimate claim to dominate social nature."[95]

Nevertheless this still fails to explain why the taste of the palate, once it has undergone refinement and become civilized, cannot also take part in the process of social aesthetic elevation. Bourdieu himself, in providing an empirical classification of the tastes of the French, observes close links between cultural and luxury consumption, especially when it comes to food. And yet this is precisely the opposite to what was argued by the philosophers of the second half of the eighteenth century, when "purity of taste" was founded at the expense of sensorial pleasure.

So why should the analogy between gratification of the palate and the sense of beauty underlying the taste metaphor be abandoned? What explains this exclusion?

A glance backwards will reveal that the enigma connected with aesthetic experience consists in the *principle of indetermination* (randomness, fickleness, relativity), which undermines its spiritual and cognitive value. Value lies only in worth, as measured according to a shared criterion.

Although it may be clear why what is fickle (*de gustibus*) should be differentiated from what is mutual, it is not as evident why a pleasure can be shared only at a distance, that is in a disinterested fashion, excluding *a priori* all that arouses the senses or produces some extraneous utility. The underlying tenet is that interest, be it hedonistic or utilitarian, is always something subjective, and thus, by definition, transitory, whereas in fact interests can be shared, ritualized, desired and cultivated within a given social circle. So the problem in this case is not that the pleasure experienced be individual (when in fact it is not); but rather that this sensation should be temporary, debatable, circumscribed to a given moment in time or a particular social environment. At which point it becomes a whim, something akin to fashion, to amusements that are in vogue, where there is no hope of emulating the aristocracy or sharing their privileges.

According to the sociological explanation, distance from the body is a way of sublimating emancipation from need, a symbolic celebration of affluence achieved, a social marker indicating privilege. Yet clearly this is largely apocryphal. Though it may have contained some truth in Bourdieu's France of the 1970s, it certainly did not apply to the Enlightenment period, or to Kant's intentions—even those he was unwilling to confess.

In a similar fashion, Eagleton's approach is reductionist when he claims that "only those with an interest"—in eighteenth-century usage, meaning possession—"can be disinterested."[96] In terms of discrimination, Hume adopts an approach that is more élitist and indeed effective. He sees good taste not as a social privilege masquerading as nobility of the mind, but as an *explicit* expression of advantage. In fact he posits that this requires a process of learning, which includes visiting museums, and sharing certain cultural interests that are "subliminally" instilled by the social environment. Nevertheless, within the great framework of taste as glorified by Hume, the pleasures of luxury goods are fully respected and comprise those of the palate, including the refinement of convivial behavior.

As a result, Bourdieu is unable to account for the fact that Kant's dogmatic, puritanical solution should have prevailed over Hume's hedonistic, conciliatory approach. Nor does he explain why the idea of "pure taste" should ever have risen to acquire cultural hegemony when quite clearly styles have always been transitory. This is particularly curious, because the very dominance of such an idea has circumscribed imagination, fettered the institutions of art, and relegated to the purgatory of frivolity all other tastes, including most refined worldly pleasures. The underlying question is, of course, just why the taste metaphor should have been dismantled.

The idea that taste is simply the symbolic representation of social rank, the emblem of freedom from the constraints of necessity, is thus not a historically acceptable explanation. If anything, precisely the opposite is true, bearing in mind that the Kantian paradigm of pure reception, of emotional candor, of the continence of desire, implies that the aesthetic faculty is accessible to all civilized beings, regardless of class privileges or monopolies of "cultural capital." This explains the emphasis on universality, on the search for what is transcendental, and the mutilation of hedonism. Far from discriminating downwards, Kant actually promotes upwards integration, but only in the spiritual sense. All hedonistic contamination and emulation were carefully avoided, for these were realms he deemed unworthy.

The reason behind the bifurcation of taste is thus basically ideological, even though this may not coincide with Eagleton's inscrutable meaning. For what it all boils down to is essentially "political," which is precisely why it is so persistent.

What the Enlightenment philosophers were looking for was an ethical, epistemological foundation for shared sensibility. Speaking in the name of "mature" civilized humanity, their focus was the attainment of a particular social model, which was claimed to be legitimate in the name of reason. The surrounding context was no longer that of the court, with its ostentation and license. Conventions, decency and measure return to the fore, no longer regulated by appearances, but adopted in order to shape individual morality so that it would work within a society that had little in common with the unrestricted gratifications of the aristocracy. Little of the luxury of the upper echelons of society trickled down to the parsimonious daily habits of the bourgeoisie, where food was nutrition more than refined gastronomy. All things considered, democracy is simply a form of self-control practiced throughout a given society. The utopia of sensibility reflects an evident moral intention: in this sense, elevation towards beauty relates to crude sensuality much as a sense of measure, modesty, temperance and respect relate to promiscuity, abuse, impudence and prevarication. The banquet of the senses is thus inaccessible to the middleclass observer, and all he can hope for is the pleasure of contemplation, which is tame and socially inoffensive on account of the very fact that it can only be activated at a distance, with no need for material appropriation and thus without depriving others of anything.

The Enlightenment social project focused on the dream of universality, and called for an anthropological counterpart in reality. To admit that taste was socially shaped amounted to saying that because aristocratic sensibility was born of greater wealth, better schooling and refinement, it was inevitably

finer, more educated and more receptive than that of the regular bourgeois
citizen. This, however, would have meant invalidating the principle of
universal rights and mutual respect on which the desired model of society
was founded. Aesthetics was born and prospered within a program of
egalitarian social anthropology. It did not accommodate élitist rituals that
were deliberately intended as evidence of social rank, and hence of exclusion.

Having discovered that taste can contain a radically individualist criterion
of appropriation of reality, the thinkers of the late 1700s then came to the
conclusion that the consequences might have been dangerous when such
unprecedented liberty trickled down from the top of the pyramid to the
lesser reaches of democratic brotherhood. At which point a new morality
came to the fore to replace the freethinking, sensual spirit of the aristocracy:
namely, that of middle class romanticism and puritanism. This meant reestablishing a social discipline in the use of pleasure that did not clash with
the ethics of productivity and reciprocity. Clearly all desires had to be
compatible with the new social contract, with coexistence on an equal
footing, with the rules of civil society.

In this the Enlightenment proved to be despotic and totalitarian: "in
Kant's perspective there is still no model for pluralism. He believed in the
primary need for developing principles that could regulate thought and
action, from the point of view of the bourgeoisie, capable of addressing a
religion supported by feudal powers and meeting with the favor of society
as a whole."[97]

This explains why he felt such disdain for "interested pleasures": "Kant
aimed to exclude any connection with the appetites, which do not count as
a basis for determination. His aversion for the concept of interest related not
only to his systematic cogency, but also to the latent political function
implicit in "disinterested pleasure." Indeed, this was directed against the
ideas of luxury and everything else that seduces the perceptions as a desirable
commodity."[98]

At this point it is possible to sum up the tormented evolution of the taste
metaphor. In the bodily sense it refers to the organ entrusted with the task
of recognizing pleasure. It is taste that must decide, instinctively and once
and for all, whether or not something is agreeable. Initially the problem is to
understand why a given item gives pleasure, and to work out to what extent
the phenomenon is cogent or temporary, thereby establishing the conditions
and constraints of the experience, and the rules and exceptions. However,
this "state of innocence" does not last long, because it soon becomes clear
that morals motivated by sensual pleasure would lead to Epicureanism and
dissipation, thereby undermining the foundations of a much more ambitious,
elevated project: within the nascent perspective of Enlightenment political
and social intentions, a hypothetical supremacy of taste evoked the threat of
a licentious and indecent world that would distract humanity from its social
progress, its scientific efforts and its economic productivity.

It was thus clear that a certain prudery of sensibility had to be established:
for the honest man of the eighteenth century, with his strong moral

convictions and a new sense of democratic citizenship, it was edifying to visit museums and go to concerts, to admire cathedrals and paintings, even though this meant shaping the members of society along similar lines. By contrast, it was far less acceptable to take part in refined banquets and thereby to reach the empire of sensuality.

"Good taste," for its part, was supposed to be a rule for behavior that would regulate and promote socially correct demeanor. Yet it was clearly too generic and biased to rival "pure taste" in the hope of gaining the ideological upper hand. Moreover, when developed to excess (for instance, when it became a form of unnatural affectation, a pantomime of mannerisms), it also proved to be politically unacceptable in view of the very fact that it was based on the model of life of the aristocracy, which by definition meant excluding all others.

As for good taste at the table, although Flandrin has expressed doubts concerning the use of the term in gastronomy before it appeared in the sphere of etiquette and aesthetics,[99] *it was not a socially sharable model*: good taste in food was the exclusive privilege of a particular society (those who appreciated cultivated cuisine), and possibly a nation, that of France, where it was born and prospered. It was not until the apotheosis of the *grand restaurant* in nineteenth-century Paris that similar pleasures could become accessible to the middle classes.

4

The Arts of Happiness:
A Journey Through
Impure Tastes

The ideological primacy of the taste metaphor shaped how people felt and thought until well into the eighteenth century, when the social and cultural climate evolved through plenty of lively debate. One outcome was the divorce between what pertained to the mind, and what to the body. For although the term "taste" was still used to refer to both spheres, in actual fact "taste" meaning the sense of beauty increasingly distinguished itself from what had become a sort of bizarre synonym: taste as referred to the palate, which was soon relegated to the irrelevant and intemperate ranks of human sensitivity.

This was a major shift in focus that was to revolutionize perceptions and behavior, forging cultural organization anew and redefining what was deemed to be socially presentable. At the same time, however, the pseudo-science of gastronomy also began to take shape, albeit quietly and without occupying center stage. Initially relegated to the realms of what was considered futile and frivolous, in time gastronomy came to be viewed as a manifestation of *savoir vivre*, which in its turn invested the palate with some degree of respectability. So while Romantic culture preached the sublimation of taste and the ensuing degradation of sensuality, the nascent cult of the gourmet was initially hardly a subject worthy of deep discussion.

Just why was it that an aesthetics of gastronomy built along the lines of eighteenth-century art criticism and philosophy was unable to gain ground and legitimacy within the cultural debate of the time? After all, it did not need to claim an equal footing with subjects requiring intellectual depth and academic dignity. And why should none of the writers who devoted their attention to food have acquired acclaim? Why indeed should writings on gastronomy have been considered a lesser literary genre in Western culture? Apart from the manuals and recipe books aimed at cooks, apprentices and housewives, why is it that publications on the subject enjoyed much the same status as society chatter? Why indeed was it not until the anthropologists and semiologists of the second half of the twentieth century contributed to a change in overall attitude that estimable thinkers such as Lévi-Strauss or Barthes should deign to elevate with their intellectual attention a humble, "minor" subject such as food and cuisine? And even when this did finally come to pass, why were these matters still considered to be less worthy than other disciplines, which admit of their existence merely as a way of providing examples, and possibly a few anecdotes, without ever getting involved in discussions of hedonism and the perception of pleasure? Why indeed should famous writers such as Revel or Aron, who do devote some attention to cooks and recipes, appear to do so as though this were a relaxing pastime, far removed from their more valid intellectual pursuits? These are just some of the questions that this chapter addresses and hopes to resolve.

Gasterea: The Ventriloquist Muse

The history of gastronomy belongs to the entire 1800s, first appearing right at the beginning of the century under the auspices of an obscure bucolic poet by the name of Berchoux.[1] During the course of time, however, its implications and connotations underwent change, ushering in different usage and mentors.

What helped bring about this development was without a doubt the invention of the middleclass restaurant: fare removed from the world of taverns and greasy spoons, which were famously cheap and ill-frequented, the restaurant became the new temple of good taste that housed the daily celebrations of the culinary arts. Thanks to this institution, what was once the conspicuously exclusive privilege of the aristocracy became accessible to a much wider public, thereby allowing a class on the rise to enjoy tangible recognition of the wellbeing it had acquired and to take part in what was shortly to become one of the foremost expressions of French culture, the object of considerable national devotion.

Restaurants started to come into being in Paris a few years before the Revolution, and it was this event that actually spurred their spread. According to an authoritative witness, "in putting the old proprietors on a diet, the Revolution made all their best cooks penniless. At which point these latter chose to exploit their talents differently, by turning themselves into merchants of culinary excellence under the name of restaurateurs."[2]

Zeldin has calculated that less than a quarter of a century after the fateful year of 1789, in Paris alone the number of restaurants had proliferated from fifty to three thousand.[3] Grimod de la Reynière himself also noted that during the same period restaurants outnumbered bookshops in the capital by a ratio of one hundred to one.

There is no doubt that the sudden success of this commercial set-up brought about a revolution in eating habits, promoting the national cult of good food as defined by gastronomy, its high priest, advocate and magistrate. And like all forms of worship, the cult of good food availed itself of evocative terminology, plenty of heart-rending inventive flair and a panoply of initiatory formulae. The use of fantastical terms to shape the sensitivity of the palate and arouse the desire for certain tastes was to become the rich humus that nurtured the seeds of gastronomic discourse.

The idiom itself grew and was enriched within the restaurants by means of the protocol and rituals that preceded and accompanied the serving of food. This meant words designed to conjure up desirable images, shape appetites and ensure that the experience remained printed in the memory. Reading a menu became a sort of sacred genuflection, a manifestation of the desire to partake of an enticing universe, of enthrallment before a lofty style and such inspired poetics. This is precisely what Aron tellingly described as "the rhetoric of the sublime":

> great dishes call for names that measure up to their nobility, such as Chicken Supreme Paris Fashion, or Chicken à la Villeroy, or Tournedos Maréchale. As often as not the origin of these expressions is entirely fortuitous: the name of a famous customer, or of the inventor of the dish, or the fruit of a cook's or a hotel director's imagination. The anecdote is less important than the syntax. To say that a Le Mans capon is stuffed Demidoff fashion with truffles is enough to free the creature from the farmyard and provide it with wings for flight, ennobled with the insignia of the Russian prince who married Matilde Bonaparte. The outcome leads to a revision of zoology as applied to cuisine. The capon is no longer a cock fowl deprived of its male attributes, but a god in the elevated company of pigeons bag-roasted à la D'Uxelles or the fillets of rabbit Conti style. It is a question of dressing up regular products in prodigious disguises.[4]

The construction and the popularization of the imaginary universe of gastronomy underwent further developments outside the restaurant dining-rooms.

This was due to the pens of a new generation of writers, who discovered an irresistible vocation for elevating the inclination for gluttony. From the cultural point of view, the main novelty that came with gastronomy was the invention of a literary genre, or rather the conquest and definition of a *locus cogitationis* that was unprecedented in Western history. "Grimod was the first exponent of the new culinary literature, which differed from the existing handbooks and treatises on account of its 'appetizing eloquence.' Grimod did not so much provide information about cooking as attempt to create a culinary style that associated gastronomy with writing. This toothsome literature was to become a genre that was an artistic event in its own right, moreover one that embodied a degree of perversity because, in Grimod's view, the gourmet was a man of letters, a libertine and an aesthete."[5]

According to Flandrin,[6] the gastronomic "fact" actually existed before the terms coined to describe it. This is certainly true if the gourmet is considered to be a refined connoisseur of the palate, a person endowed with such heightened perceptions that he can distinguish the precise provenance of seafood, the very strip of coastline, rather as certain ancient Romans liked to do; or, as Brillat-Savarin declared, tell from the taste whether a partridge drumstick belonged to a bird that had been shot in flight or when roosting. If this be so, then gastronomy dates back at least as far as the history of luxury foods, whose forerunners would have been the legendary delectations of the Sybarites.

The focus of this study is somewhat different, however: the literature of gastronomy, with its concomitant theories and reflections regarding the pleasures of food. For while there were indeed plenty of writings on food and drink in Antiquity, their focus was diet or education, like recipe books or the manuals on home economics of more recent memory. The desire to write about the pleasures of the palate in a manner that would be perceived as irresistibly enticing only came to the fore in the 1800s, most significantly in France. "Gastronomy becomes the language of the aesthete gourmet. It is he who possesses the word that resolves all issues. This was the era of official counts and artists' readings. Compared with the *Encyclopédie*, there was a decline in interest for art and an increase in the arcane complexity typical of the gourmet. It was no longer a question of practical skill, but of faith in gastronomic essence, in the absolutes of taste. The jury delivered sentences that established culinary culture, which gained further acceptance by means of a specific and highly detailed protocol: the endless formalities were not aimed at indulgence and enjoyment so much as providing the institution with structure."[7]

The choice of a name always implies a degree of destiny. Why did these writers consider themselves gastronomes rather than, say, "culinographs"? The choice is telling, because it reveals how experts and fanatics of all things culinary and food-orientated conceived of their mission. A gastronome was a person who laid down the law, absolved and condemned, rewarded and punished, exercising his competence not in order to improve cuisine, agriculture or animal husbandry, which would have been essentially a service and extraneous to his interests, but in the name of the intimate and inscrutable gratification of the stomach. His intention was never really to spread the word or educate. Instead the goal was to select, classify and appraise. Even the most impartial gastronomic account always conceals a judgment, which ultimately relies on the incontestable verdict of the palate. "Aesthetic judgment and the rules of *savoir-vivre* are both based on the *tyranny of detail*, and both share the same intent to 'teach life' rather as one learns a lesson by rote, especially when the content is not fully understood. In synthesis, it was a question of translating the habits of society's opinion-makers into indisputable axioms. At the outset, this was not really anything new, but the remarkable range of fields of application and the variety of channels by means of which such convictions spread brought about a hitherto unheard of degree of amplification."[8]

There would appear to be two founders of this doctrine: Grimod de la Reynière, who was a militant critic and a gourmet *extra litteram*, rather as Kant had been for aesthetics (which he developed without ever mentioning it in what was to become the accepted meaning of the term);[9] and Brillat-Savarin, the bon vivant theoretician who turned out to be a sterile prophet of a discipline without disciples or imitators.

The backdrop for all of this was the spectacular evolution of the culinary arts, nurtured by the peerless myth of Antonin Carême, the last high priest of the splendors of the *Ancien Régime*. For it was Carême who managed to persuade at least the corporation of artisans that culinary skill was as worthy a form of craftsmanship as the applied arts, thereby providing the purveyors of monumental patisserie with the sculptural illusion that their creations could overturn transience and withstand the tests of human appetites and time.[10]

Of the two devotees of gastronomy, it was Brillat-Savarin who enjoyed the greatest success as a writer. Yet later generations of gastronomes were more inclined to elect Grimod de la Reynière as their point of reference. Grimod was the true forerunner of the food critic, the tireless sampler who took on the role of arbiter of tastes and mentor of the pleasure-loving community. Indeed, he embodied the perfect equivalent of the art critic invoked by Hume: an individual endowed with particular sensibility and encyclopedic tasting experience to whom *gourmands* could look for guidance in the labyrinth of palatal pleasures and the refinement of their perceptual faculties.

The recipe books and culinary manuals of the time were aimed at cooks, whereas the gastronome wrote for an audience desirous of discovering exactly what it should experience, prefer and appreciate. His aim was thus to rule over the appetites of others, to shape them in his own image, to extend his own sphere of influence over other people's inclinations. By so doing, his own particular independence became a widely accepted rule of life, a standard for preference and for a hierarchy of values that no longer depended on bodily needs, social conditioning or the habits inculcated by tradition. Those who were unsure of their own palates could thus rely on a system of regulations established by the gastronome acting as a supreme judge of table manners and good food. All the would-be gourmets had to do was follow suit.

Such ambitions probably owed much to the surrounding political and social context. Grimod was writing during the period that followed the destruction of elegant dining brought about by the French Revolution, and what he essentially suggested in his *Manuel des amphitryons* (1805) was the restoration of a certain *savoir faire*, which he hoped would be adopted by the new middles class. While the restaurant was where the taste for luxury and pleasure could be extended to a wider circle of people, it was in the homes of the new bourgeoisie that hospitality came to imply courtesy and strict etiquette. Granted, the gourmets and their sphere also subscribed to principles of liberty, equality and fraternity when it came to their appetites, but only within the circle of the initiates anxious to save culinary splendor from the Spartan rigors of the Jacobin diet. A new structure of manners thus came into being, whereby a few discerning gourmets endowed with cultural awareness and perceptual refinement ultimately replaced the dynastic aristocracy whose financial means had once assured them the very best. Although it voiced the spirit of the age, gastronomy also had a distinctly nostalgic side to it that mourned the passing of the culinary magnificence of the *Ancien Régime*. Chefs may have freed themselves of servility by bringing about the birth of the bourgeois restaurant and imposing their tastes on others, yet in the eyes of the gastronome they were nevertheless subordinates in the service of pleasure. Thanks to the variety of choice and the independence of taste, the gastronome could hope to regain the privileged position of arbiter of taste by promoting the symbolic restoration of the host over the cook.

This explains the sense of sovereign cultural and social superiority of the gastronome in relation to the sweat and fumes of the kitchen, which remained a sort of workshop devoted to humble, repetitive actions aimed at transforming foodstuffs. By contrast, the gourmet's ability in identifying the ingredients of a given dish, like the sommelier's skill in recognizing a *cépage* or the exact bouquet of a wine, was a way of exercising judgment and showing off unparalleled sensorial discernment. The gastronome's realm did not extend to the capacity for turning raw ingredients into sources of pleasure, which was the cook's sphere of action. Indeed, the former's culinary ineptitude matched the art critic's inability to paint. The gastronome's vocation was not to cook, but to eat. His only interest was to use his personal taste to sample and pronounce pitiless judgments from the height of his self-appointed office. At the very most, like Grimod, on occasions he may have extended the experience to a jury of kindred spirits, thereby transforming the pleasure of eating into a collective experience.

There is something clinically delirious and culturally visionary about claiming to regulate other people's desires. As an overall gastronomic design it involves imposing correctional norms based on purely hedonistic premises and subordinating culinary knowledge to one's personal tastes. This in its turn implies the creation of a sort of cosmology of gluttony that comprises infernal circles, limbos, purgatories and paradises. Perceiving all that is edible as a form of individual privilege is a sort of parody of academia in which "all that pertains to the system of literary awards, rewards and rolls of honor is transposed into the realms of gastronomy."[11]

But was art criticism really the model from which gastronomy took its cue? The metaphor is not entirely convincing. The essential difference between a work of art and a culinary delicacy lies in the fact that only the former is truly a monument, in the sense implicit in the etymology of the word: from the Latin *monere*, meaning to warn, to remind. A work of art is a product consigned to eternity, a one-off item that is born of the artist's inspiration and bears his stylistic stigmata. As such it is likely to appeal to different people in the course of time. Cuisine, on the other hand, deals in ephemeral miracles that are repeated daily, albeit with slight differences; multiples that are produced in order to be demolished. Tasting is a form of gratification that involves seduction, but no form of admonition: a tasty morsel is not a vehicle for memory, but rather a fleeting experience; at the most accompanied by a hint of nostalgia for the sensations experienced during the act of savoring it. The only *unicum* thus lies in the immediate pleasure deriving from individual taste, intensified but not extended by the gastronome's rarely acknowledged discernment.

The whole exercise essentially amounts to a sublimation of oral fixation through a vindication of the palate that eschews universality (gastronomy is founded on the pleasure of diversity), but goes to great lengths in the pursuit of detail. So there is no disputing tastes, not least because the gastronome himself is convinced of the unique value of his own discernment and skill. But there is every reason to criticize and indeed describe the dishes served in a restaurant. Taste thus becomes a sort of ghostly presence lurking beneath the surface of gastronomic literature.

The focus of attention thus became the system of delicacies that could arouse passions and induce ecstasy, which were the two gourmet versions of beauty and the sublime. In this sense, unlike aesthetics, gastronomy was far from providing a phenomenological study, or a comparative, rational account of the individual or shared states of mind aroused by the stimulation of the palate. The desire to impose an "authoritarian vision of things, to make others *learn* rather than make them *understand*,"[12] ensured that gastronomy would always be tied to a "pre-Kantian" stage of development, constrained by the over-classification of foods, recipes and restaurants, without ever managing to explain precisely why any given item should be perceived as good. This was a task left to physiology. Gastronomy did not even contemplate the manuals and recipe books aimed at teaching those in the trade how to transform raw ingredients into tasty dishes. Instead it provided devotional instructions, canons of gastronomic worship, rules for what to expect and how to behave at the table. In other words, it was a "science of nothingness," to use Portinari's caustic but apposite expression.[13]

In its urge to compile, taste and describe in wordy detail, gastronomy confined the appetites within the sphere of sentences, reducing what should have been sensual to a state of imaginary gratification. In this sense it offered something of the consolation of pornography.

Like the pornographer, the gastronome evoked voluptuous experience, titillating the taste buds and promoting lubricious salivation. Gastronomy was not a branch of philosophy, as Brillat-Savarin lamely tried to argue, but of erotic literature, a form of arousal that shared plenty of common ground with the wealth of lasciviously detailed accounts of the many variations on the theme of copulation. "The sexual metaphor is a semantic perspective that prevails in gastronomic literature. When connotations help turn what is essentially culinary into something sexual, the tone becomes libertine. This is no longer the traditional vein of intemperance, but a form of oral transgression that indulges in linguistic perversity. Grimod brought about every possible commutation between the erotic and the gastronomic, combining deliberate crudity with sophisticated literary effects."[14]

Gastronomy acted as the *vade mecum* for gourmands, expressing the morals of dissolution and the art of dissipation. Like sexual obsession, the preoccupation with food achieved visionary seduction and sublimated satisfaction in the literary genre it produced. The idealization of desire and gratuitous gastronomic fulfillment are worlds apart from the aesthetics of disinterestedness. They achieve gratification in the act of consumption, which is unrelated to need. Clearly the analogy with *eros*, with sexual activity freed of the desire to procreate, is more fitting: "the exercise of a desire that is totally pointless."[15]

The pleasures of food, like those of sex, eschew repetition and are constantly changing. Obsessive in their constant search for gratification, both the gourmet and the erotomaniac desperately sought variety, distraction and caprice. Though they may have originated in the same conditions or pertained to the same event, the pleasures of the senses seemed irresistibly different from one occasion to the next, all the more so if they were the fruit of meretricious exchange (the services of a prostitute or a cook, in a brothel or in a restaurant).

Gastronomic experience relied on the literature of enchantment to spread the word. The outcome was thus far removed from the prudish but edifying embrace of aesthetics. The world of the senses offered Dionysiac euphoria, which meant there was no need for philosophical legitimization: "the gastronomic tradition is not founded on knowledge, but on the mythology of pleasure."[16]

Indirectly this accounts for the eccentric orbit of Brillat-Savarin's fleeting appearance in the gourmet firmament. Apart from their common passion for food, his ambitions differed from those of Grimod. In the history of gastronomy, Brillat-Savarin's role was more that of the ideologue than the historian: he saw himself as the pundit of a discipline on an equal footing not with art criticism, but with aesthetics, as a general theory of beauty.

Brillat-Savarin openly declared his intentions in his only publication, the masterly *Physiology of Taste*. His goal was both epistemological and moral: on the one hand he wished to "determine the root principles of gastronomy, so that it may take that rank among the sciences which undeniably belongs to it";[17] and on the other he hoped to celebrate *gourmandise*, the "rational and passionate" cult of good food, as opposed to the inclination for gluttony and intemperance, within the genteel sphere of socially accepted manners.[18]

The epistemological foundation of gastronomy drew inspiration from the circle of philosopher scientists, known as the *Idéologues*, who were the forerunners of modern human sciences. Among these *Idéologues* was Pierre Jean Georges Cabanis, whose treatise *On the Relations between the Physical and Moral Aspects of Man* exercised great influence over Brillat-Savarin. Cabanis's fundamental aim was to overcome the dualism perpetuated by the metaphysical philosophers that divided the intellectual faculties from those of the body. Corporeal reality cannot be separated from the life of the mind because both were functions of the same reality: the human being. Observation of such phenomena led the author to conclude that cerebral activity "secretes ideas," just as the stomach secretes gastric juices. The sphere of the intellect and affections that pertained to "morality" thus arose, he claimed, from the original activity of the sensitive organs, and thus from the "physical" sphere: "the study of vital phenomena and the methodical search for the way in which they are related must ultimately come to physical sensitivity. This is the final or the most general outcome of the analysis of intellectual faculties and the affections of the soul."[19]

In the rehabilitation of the body promoted by the *Idéologues*, Brillat-Savarin found the solution to the problem that had tormented him: attributing cultural dignity to his life's passion. The paradigm established by Cabanis obligingly provided him with the reductionism that allowed him to entrust physiology with the task of "explaining the sensations of taste in rational terms."[20] While the *Idéologues* opposed Descartes' *cogito* with a form of Ur-sensitivity (*sentio, ergo sum*, or "I sense, therefore I am"), Brillat-Savarin overturned the same principle in a mocking "*edo, ergo gaudeo*" or "I eat, therefore I take pleasure," that allowed him to develop the "moral" approach to the phenomenon, along with his leisurely leaning for anecdotes and aphorisms.

As for the "transcendence" invoked in the subtitle to justify the learned gentleman's chosen perspective for gastronomic "science,"[21] it had no claims to mysticism or metaphysics. The term was simply used for "whatever is susceptible to the widest generality"[22] on the basis of a protracted, methodical and dispassionate observation of the facts. Alas, the outcome was pathetic: Brillat-Savarin lacked the authority and the curiosity of the historian (his Meditation XXVII dedicated to the "philosophical history of cuisine" is embarrassingly superficial). Moreover, he did not even have the spirit of observation of the anthropologist, even though Volnay, founder of human geography as a discipline and one of the most eminent *Idéologues*, could have provided him with a convenient model for inspiration: his approach to the relationship between a given geo-climatic condition and the inclinations of the population; in other words, between physical and anthropological reality. In his study of land, climate and demography, he sought connections between the customs, ideas and characters of the inhabitants, and the ways in which they influenced each other.[23] To create a comparative study of eating habits along the same lines should not have been difficult. Yet nothing of the sort is to be found in Brillat-Savarin's "moral" gastronomy, whose epistemological foundations are about as stable as a soufflé. In his chaotic inventory of curiosities, the search for causes and explanations is entirely delegated to physiology. Far from revealing a scientific bent, the author showed no interest in the observation of what was primitive or exotic: he avoided any *instructions de voyage* not because he lacked direct observation (unlike Volnay, Brillat-Savarin was not attracted by travel), but because he eschewed the journey and got straight down to arrival. Hardly surprising, his gastronomic thesis was resolutely teleological and France-centered, with the main focus on a couple of districts in Paris.

Although Brillat-Savarin called himself an "amateur physician," he paid no attention whatsoever to the study of food pathologies and aberrant eating habits, despite the fact that here again he could have looked to several authors for inspiration, not least Philippe Pinel, an eminent specialist in mental illness.[24]

Granted, Brillat-Savarin did devote a couple of chapters to obesity and its remedies, classifying the tendency towards extreme corpulence as one of the rare drawbacks of gastronomic civilization. But this digression, like those devoted to dreams and exhaustion, smacks more of a would-be doctor's desire to sound scholarly[25] than it does of any real desire to understand why people indulge in convivial excess.

The fact is that, despite the smattering of science, the *Physiology of Taste* is not a treatise on food, but simply a manual for gluttony. Brillat-Savarin cared little for the philosophers' pleas for temperance, or the laws aimed at curbing luxury passed by despots, or the church's condemnation of gastronomic indulgence. Instead he argued in favor of the right to binge, not least because he saw that over the centuries the desire to guzzle had survived all social upheavals, to the extent that during his own time "the art of the table grows more florid every day."[26]

The maze of different disciplines that he had announced as being the cornerstone of gastronomic science (a mixture of natural history, physics, chemistry, culinary art, trade and political economy)[27] thus remained an impromptu declaration of intent that others could disentangle, if they felt so inclined. Even the "gastronomic tests" that Brillat-Savarin invented by way of a "dynamometer" adjusted to the different social classes to register the physiognomic reaction of banqueters stimulated by hearing a succulent menu read out loud[28] come across as a farce rather than the basis for an empirical method.

The hoary taste enigma revolving around why people like what they like could not be resolved by gastronomy, whether this was deemed an art or proposed as a science. The one essential difference between these two views mirrored the divergence that separated Grimod and Brillat-Savarin. The former asserts, judges and lays down the law without having to explain anything; while the latter attempts an explanation, but in vain, to the extent that his legacy to posterity amounts to little more than a few somewhat obvious aphorisms: "tell me what you eat and I'll tell you who you are," for example; or "dessert without cheese is like a pretty woman with only one eye"; or "a man becomes a cook: but he is born a roaster of flesh."[29] Would-be gastronomic science, neglected by academic culture, was thus reduced to a series of anecdotes: for the next one and a half centuries, the only people to write about it would be journalists, not scholars.

One point that remains to be addressed is just why the subject should have eluded serious inquiry, understanding and explanation. Why was gastronomy caught within the sphere of the passions, rather than becoming part of a comparative study of people's customs and nutritional predilections? And why did it not aim at transcending mere ingestion, instead of trying to resemble a theory of taste?

In this regard the cultural evolution of taste is instructive: if gastronomy was unable to produce a form of culinary aesthetics along the lines of the philosophy pertaining to art, and if food writing was considered a minor literary genre, this was because the final aim of the discipline, as Brillat-Savarin himself admitted, was the social promotion of its practitioners, "give them the position in society which is their due."[30] Gastronomy simply aimed at being a *vade mecum* for good manners: the best use of the most comfortable of possible worlds. To this end, the parameters for judgment could be somewhat hazy, since simply sharing a hedonistic experience implied no need for speculation or theories. Arguably it was from this point of view alone that gastronomy resembled, or was inspired by, aesthetics: both aimed at celebrating the moral progress of human civilization that had relinquished primordial instincts and achieved an entirely gratifying degree of refinement.

The rest was shrouded in silence. It was as though latent anguish incapacitated the gourmet's conscience, muted by an unexplained state of embarrassment disguised as leisurely wit. If gastronomy concealed pathologies, aversions and cultural relativism, it was to exorcise the sense of emptiness that undermined it from within.

Like an abyss, the stomach threatens the bourgeoisie, which produces comestible edifices to satisfy its demands. I perceive in this silent threat to the deep stomach at the outset of the nineteenth century the first signs of another abyss: the Freudian subconscious. Who, after Freud, would disagree that the cavity of the subconscious is based on that of the sexualized stomach? Everything begins from the lower stomach: the symbols, dreams and neuroses that are food for the soul. The bourgeoisie invents its own absolute, that of gastronomy, perhaps the only answer to the fears expressed by an insatiable stomach, just as psychoanalysis lent itself to addressing the lonely torments of the mind, following the demise of religious certainty and hopes. The gratification of demonstrating self-satisfaction is rooted in the preoccupation with appeasing the stomach.[31]

The two possible approaches to the taste problem are thus either a defense of gluttony, or the study of food predilections. Both embody mutually incompatible opposites: two poles that exclude each other. But then much the same thing happens within the sphere of erotic experience. An *ars amandi* and a *scientia sexualis* will inevitably come to different conclusions, and it is logical that only a clinical perspective could lead to a theory of sexuality. By contrast, far from claiming scientific objectivity, a libertine writing about sexuality would simply be voicing his own freedom of choice to what he defined as pleasure.

Eroticism as a literary genre may give rise to pornography, or even poetry, but it cannot produce a rational explanation of its own essence. In erotomania, as in bulimia, there is no questioning the urge towards the object of desire. It is a raw fact, a compulsive gut sensation, even though it may express itself in the most refined perversions of taste. Describing its progress and listing the sources of satisfaction are both possible, whereas there is no revealing its origins. Taste is inexpressible, the inexplicable drive, the unending urge that belongs to fixation, something that cannot be reduced to a convenient formula to be studied in a laboratory. It is a compulsion that pertains to the individual who experiences it and obsessively tries to share it with his audience, with his imaginary companions in unspeakable antics, whose resulting erection or salivation are secondary effects of the real pleasure to be found in copulation or crapulence.

By contrast, scientific method and clinical inquiry call for detachment, for an impersonal, impartial approach to the given subject. Research into the origins and causes of *gourmandise* would thus have required abstraction from the vortex of the senses, a muting of instincts and reining in of passions: all of which would have been extremely difficult for Brillat-Savarin. Had he but tried to understand the appetites rather than absolve them, had he truly wished to plumb the depths of the stomach instead of disputing in its name, gastronomy would have had to deal with the miseries and anxieties of bulimic civilization. At which point, the learned gentleman would have found himself drawn towards an abyss of obscure and ominous impulses, and this would have undermined his proud belief in a world that needed to establish certainties in order to build up its own identity. The true mission of gastronomy was to advocate the role of fine living and good food in acquiring pleasures and fomenting appetites. For all its edifying aspirations, clearly there was no place or potential audience for a "Critique of Dietary Reason." "In the nineteenth century imagination, the rotund figure of the gentleman engrossed in his own inner world replaces that of the lithe knight gazing heaven-wards in his search for God. Sancho Panza ultimately overthrows Don Quixote and snatches the reins of history from him. The servant becomes the master, turning into the middle-class man who strokes his own fat belly, basks in the arms of his mistress and makes a show of his material success: life is a pleasure, to which gastronomy bears witness."[32]

At which point the only option available to the founder of the discipline is to take refuge in the consolatory canticle of a fictional muse, Gasterea, whom Brillat-Savarin invoked in his last meditation as the patron of the pleasures of taste and the hallucinatory idol of an imaginary science. The backdrop for his delirious descriptions of the goddess's sanctuary was a utopian gourmet Republic conceived as a "vast refectory" resounding with the "general mirth" of jubilant citizens; in other words, a lyrical version of the Land of Plenty, an obsessive dream of a constant, unflagging banquet.

Ephemeral Frenzies: The Feminine Aesthetic

In a footnote[33] that emerges from his misty prose, Brillat-Savarin made at least one observation that calls for comment: "I observe with pride that *coquetterie* and *gourmandise*, these two excellent transformations of our most natural needs brought about by extreme sociability, are both French in origin."

Coquetry and gluttony are thus both interpreted as essential human needs, thanks to the contribution of French genius. Human behavior has thereby benefited from a process of refinement and concentration. Earlier in the book, Brillat-Savarin had established that the concepts themselves owed their existence to the French language, which therefore governed their rightful use. "The *gourmandise*, as the Professor[34] has defined it in this chapter, has no name but in French language; it cannot be rendered by the Latin *gula*, nor the English *gluttony*, nor the German *Lusterheit*; and therefore we counsel those who may be tempted to translate this pithy work[35] to retain the word unchanged; so have all nations done with *la coquetterie* and the words derived from it."[36]

An intriguing parallel that is full of implications, though perhaps not wittingly. Although the term is feminine (a male *coquet* would be as embarrassing for high society as a *gourmande* woman), *coquetterie* no less than *gourmandise* is recognized as being a quintessentially French disposition, a trait that can promote collective passion until it becomes the subject of national pride: just as *gourmandise* nurtures the cult of fine dining, so *coquetterie* furthers the cult of appearances.

Both derive from hedonistic bodily experience: from the perception of the body as a machine for assimilating a pleasure that becomes part of the inner self; or indeed the body as an extension of the inner self, the center from which conspicuous pleasure is projected outwards as a vehicle for social relationships.

The fact that they inhabited the same corner of the world implied their common origins, which in its turn bore witness to the conviction that refinement of appetites and attire arose from a single cultural source and the same social habitat: the splendor of Versailles, that peerless theater of affected taste where elegance, aestheticism and vanity vied with each other in constant competition.

The parallel development also reveals other affinities. *Gourmandise* and *coquetterie* are also both part of the history of costume, in particular of the chapter concerning the discipline of pleasure and the workings of superfluity. In this sense, they represent cultural genres that cannot claim to be on an equal footing with the prestigious model of the fine arts. Instead they rank as paradigmatic expressions of "impure" taste (to use Kant's dichotomy), because they do not represent an end in themselves: by furthering a tendency towards vice, be this gluttony or vanity, they cannot claim to be the object of "disinterested" contemplation, but are rather part of the vortex of luxury, regardless of whether or not they deliberately adopt this heading.

Taste for the superfluous represented the purgatory of brutish sensibility, a realm of indulgence and, at the same time, a sort of correctional center in which the rules of social behavior and distinction were made to apply. Here, the whole point of refinement of attitude and conduct was to act as a parameter for the maximization of earthly happiness. In this regard it clearly differed from the edifying, ecumenical objectives of aesthetics. Nineteenth-century Paris, the mecca of fashion and gastronomy, appeared to the prosperous West as the best of possible worlds: it was here that the last puritanical doubts aimed at opposing the seduction of worldly pleasures crumbled and gave way to collective veneration.

Granted, *gourmandise* amounted to more than the obsessive, ecstatic sampling and ingesting of the finest foods: wines, liquors and tobacco were also part of the enticing picture, and special terms to describe it all were also coming to the fore as part of the initiate's privilege. Along similar lines, *coquetterie* could not be confined within the ample realm of a constantly renewed and expanding wardrobe. It also implied the whole apparatus of bodily ornament, from makeup to perfumes, hairdressing, accessories and jewelry, as well as questions of how to behave in public, including posture, voice, look and general *bon ton*.

That said, however, the two arts of living did effectively establish their respective centers of gravity and main source of pleasure in food and attire. And this does suggest that the spheres of *haute cuisine* and *haute couture* are in some respects related. As an expression of collective aspirations (shared by a community that became less discerning as it grew wider), *gourmandise* and *coquetterie* came to embody increasingly widespread social demands, whose satisfaction called for the invention of two commercial formulas that were destined to play an enormous role in the future developments of "impure" tastes: the luxury restaurant and the fashion house, both of them spheres in which France managed to exercise a world monopoly for the following one and a half centuries.

The institutionalization of these two forms of enterprise represents an essential chapter in the history of taste. By transferring creativity and originality as values from the art market to trade in luxury goods, fine dining and fashion became vehicles of the principle of personal style that two centuries before had freed the artist from the impositions of the patron. This principle also underlay the stipulation of the taste metaphor, conceived as a way of endorsing individual sensibility that was thus ultimately to invest a far wider audience.

As the scions of lesser artisans previously relegated to the outer edge of social prestige, the great chefs and tailors of the nineteenth century transformed their obsequious trade into an inspired art: Antonin Carême and Charles Frédérick Worth were the great forerunners of the celebrity chefs and fashion designers who were to take center stage during the second half of the twentieth century.

The appearance of these new professional figures reduced the potential for individual caprice and eccentricity that had previously been the privilege of any gentleman wishing to show off his refinement of taste. Such personal performance was no longer necessary, since there were professionals to hand who generally did the job better: not critics or tasters, as Hume had predicted, but simply specialist suppliers who were hailed as public celebrities and deified as creators of a new style. This pointed in the direction of predictable forms of taste, predilections that were originally conceived as shared rather than individual, designed to appeal to a range of potential buyers who were free to choose the best offer available. Such tastes were short-lived, however, since they could easily be replaced by other, more seductive commodities, in keeping with the growing plurality of options that had become the rule.

This remarkable change revealed the enormous importance of the supplier's name and fame, which was a byproduct of the increasing democracy of affluent society. However, it also showed that when taste is applied to all forms of luxury consumption as a criterion of preference, in its own right it becomes *the most valuable commodity* the market can offer. "Luxury costs less than elegance," wrote Balzac:[37] by shaping people's fantasies and stirring up their desires, stylistic surplus took over from refinement of materials in the perceived value of a product.

Popes and sovereigns were no longer the only people to vie with each other for the possession of rare resources such as the inspired works of the great Renaissance masters. On a more modest scale, the well-to-do gentleman, his spouse and mistresses, could also indulge in the luxury of a sumptuous banquet or fashionable attire. In both cases, the principle depended on the fact that there was a supplier who towered above the others because he embodied a collectively recognized style, to be sought and rewarded as a model of refinement and object worthy of collection.

Although both derived from and were inspired by court society, *haute cuisine* and *haute couture* were more expansive in their outreach, producing formulas that could be emulated by increasingly wide swathes of the population, and thereby furthering the spread of rules for social conduct. The stylization of behavior as regards food and clothing was thus a facet of social dynamism, initially that of the court, and later of affluent society in general. *Gourmandise* and *coquetterie* became expressions of *savoir vivre*, which in turn implied sensorial etiquette. The ideals of earthly happiness and the ensuing economy of superfluity characteristic of mass society were only a few steps away.

In a civilization that encourages and rewards private gain, promising dreams that come true for all pockets, an increasingly large segment of consumption consists of items that are desirable, but not strictly speaking necessary. Food and clothing are typical of this tendency, in that they are no longer basic requirements, but luxury options. In this way the line that separates the means for subsistence from the ethereal universe of aspirations and gratifications moves forward continuously.

Sets of jewelry and gastronomic delicacies are not the same thing, however: while the consumption of food is generally gratified within the home and the private sphere, anything that pertains to elegance is, by definition, a public event. The very existence of fashion depends on the presence of a social stage suitable for exhibition: the *agora* of antiquity, the Renaissance court, secular festivities and religious ceremonies, fairs and theatrical events, salons and even cities have all hosted, in one period or another, ways of flaunting fine appearance. Such venues were recognized as places in which people could observe others and be observed, introducing new customs and costumes, and encountering new tastes.[38]

It is precisely here that fashion can play its part in shaping and spreading sensibilities. Fashion, like the palate, deals in an ephemeral form of creativity that is far removed from the major arts, be they pure or decorative. Unlike these latter, the products of fashion and gastronomy do not produce "durable" commodities. Yet they play a decisive role that transcends that of other artistic spheres in their ability to construct widespread and highly influential forms of self-image. Described as "the most loquacious of social facts,"[39] fashion has unquestionably proved to be the most conspicuous and captivating manifestation of taste. This was particularly true between the seventeenth and nineteenth centuries, when its visibility and resonance were especially marked.

Within this sphere there are two factors that come significantly to the fore: the first, which also belongs to the world of dining,[40] is the principle of individual choice, which in its turn is related to the dynamism and acumen of suppliers; while the second factor, which pertains only to fashion, is the remarkable appearance and spread of taste among women.

At this point it is worth underlining the fact that the bourgeois fashion orchestrated by the great *maisons*, described by Lipovetsky as "the hundred years of fashion,"[41] was actually born of the "Great Sacrifice."[42]

The stiffness, austerity, and asceticism of his attire would thereafter totally differentiate male from female. The bourgeois drew these elements from an ancient tradition, which can perhaps be traced back to the tightly buttoned, strict dress that appeared at the Spanish court under Charles V and Philip II, then spread to Flanders after the sixteenth century. Adopted by Protestant reformers, by Cromwell's followers, by Puritans and Quakers, it became a point of reference and a symbol for the English bourgeoisie who espoused this elimination of color to repudiate the multicolored splendor of fabrics and finery identified with aristocratic idleness and sumptuousness. Dark greens, blues, grays and especially black denied colors, and with it the distinctions that color emphasized. The extinction of color was a political signal that a new social order had come into being. It also signaled the onset of a new ethic based on will, self-denial, thrift, and merit.[43]

The iconoclastic severity that came in the wake of the great political upheavals did not affect women in the same way, and this was to be of great importance for the future developments of fashion. From this period onwards, fashion became a typically female passion, with Paris as its chosen capital, while London became that of the new, austere version of male elegance. A similar division of spheres came about in the field of furnishings, which is a further manifestation of self-image. From the nineteenth century on, home furnishings became the female domain, well separated from furnishings for the work place, which was a male universe.[44] This division between private and public was not simply a reflection of the social roles of men as opposed to women; it also defined the areas and types of expression that could give rise to opposing aesthetics.

Fashion was nevertheless the most significant phenomenon, not least because it managed to elude the future complaints of the architects and decorators who berated womankind for its love of excessive decoration, ornament, drapes and gaudy colors in the field of furnishings. Although fashion continued to make wide use of the same stylistic elements, it was unassailable, immune to academic debate, a quintessentially female prerogative based on that gender's supposed love of caprice.

Another aspect of the disparity between the underlying ideology of fashion and that of the fine arts lies in the fetishism surrounding commodities that are perceived as beautiful. Because fashion pertains so closely to the individual that it can turn that person into the object of admiration, it tends to lack the "contemplative distance" that Romantic culture considered a requirement for the fruition of works of art. An aesthetic commodity, be it a painting or an ornament, is always an object in itself, with its own inanimate, independent existence. By contrast, clothes cannot elicit "pure" contemplation, and scarcely exist at all when they are not being worn. What is decorative for the home acts differently from what serves as an ornament for the body.

Back in the eighteenth century, the authors of the *Encyclopédie* pointed out that fashion is the fruit of the desire to please, thereby also fulfilling a certain frivolity of spirit. It is thus hardly surprising that the Great Sacrifice should have tightened the close relationship between fashion and coquetry.

The only option that remained open for men was to withdraw from the tournament of appearances, entrusting their wives and mistresses with the task of public representation by means of jewelry and ornament. As for the women themselves, they were not just the opulent vehicles of their menfolk's social status: the very fact that fashion was identified with femininity meant that they had a space of their own in which they could decide, reward, ratify or reject; a free zone for self-expression devoted to "the time-honored portrayals, values and predilections of femininity"[45] and the relative concepts of beauty.

In this regard it is worth pointing out that the birth of fashion, during the early Middle Ages, was explicitly linked to the erotic potential of attire. This regarded both the female sphere, with the introduction of plunging necklines, tight bodices and long skirts, and the clearly distinct male sphere, in which short jackets and clinging hosiery prevailed.[46]

The different conceptions of taste and morals that have come to the fore in the course of time have all had to address the ineluctable question of just how the earliest forms of aesthetic experience embodied the expression of sexual attraction.[47] For though this may have been mutual, the two sides involved were not mirror images of each other. Indeed, they nurtured different visions and ideals in the course of time, in relation to gender, genre and object.

In Ancient Rome, for instance, there were two different types of beauty: the virile and austere beauty described as *dignitas*, and the perturbing feminine beauty that went by the name of *venustas*. The very etymology of the word *beautiful*, along with the Italian and Spanish *bello* and the French *beau*, actually reveals signs of this subtle differentiation. All three words derive from the Latin *bellum*, an abbreviation of *bonellum*, which is a diminutive of *bonum*. The neologism *bellum* only came into fashion during the Renaissance, when it was "initially only used in reference to the beauty of women and children; later the use was extended to the entire sphere of beauty, so that it ended up by replacing the word *pulchrum*,"[48] which had once been used, along with the Greek word *kalòn*, for "invisible" beauty of the intellectual or moral sort. The evolution of these words thus suggests that the history of beauty returned to the origins of sensuality, and it is no coincidence that the taste metaphor came into use during the same period. In his disquisition on the causes that incite love, Hume himself did not hesitate to admit that the first "impression or passion" to arouse him was the pleasurable sensation provoked by bodily beauty.[49]

With the Great Sacrifice, however, female beauty and its various appurtenances ceased to be considered (or indeed stigmatized) as tools of sexual attraction. Instead they acquired a symbolic autonomy of their own, which became the basis of a new conception of taste. It was here that female sensibility was finally able to give free rein to its originality.

This amounted to the institution of a sphere of aesthetics parallel to that of the predominant male universe; a sphere that had its own basic principles, aims, forms of communication, expressive syntax and ephemeral monuments. In an essay written in 1905, Georg Simmel drew attention to the fact that *coquetterie* as an *art* of pleasing (with greater emphasis on the former of these two concepts) was bound to end up as a self-referential, gratuitous, formal performance, even in the most elevated sense of the term: "coquetry stops being a short-lived middle ground and acquires the status of an ultimate value. In so doing, it accomplishes to the full the definition provided by Kant for the essence of art: "finality without an end." The work of art has absolutely no "end," but its parts seem connected in such a meaningful, necessary way that they appear to contribute to a perfectly determined end."[50]

For all that it acts as a means of materialization and gratification, fashion cannot, however, be reduced to *coquetterie*. It expresses more than the simple desire to embellish the body, or the ritualization of sexual enticement, or the exhibition of refinement.

With respect to the earlier tradition that revolved around female vanity, the revolutionary contribution of fashion, perceived as a spectacular manifestation of modernity, lies in the way it impacts on the evolution of individual predilection, in other words on the history of taste. Fashion has always been a forerunner of this history, intersecting with it and injecting it with a degree of irrationality and volubility that accounts for the on-going but uneven appearance in the course of time of new styles and their sudden declines. Fashion has corrupted the morals of this history, undermining its ability to provide a solid foundation for the changeable nature of taste, and thereby disappointing generations of philosophers. Fashion celebrates the triumph of conspicuous display, eccentricity, unpredictability, the rejection of accepted rules and norms, and the ultimate capitulation to the female universe in all that pertains to the handling of this inscrutable hemisphere of sensibility. The outcome is a domain that contends culturally and symbolically with male taste based on a conception of timeless beauty that is everlasting, edifying, monumental and celebratory.

To exorcise the threat to their wavering primacy, men no longer turned to sumptuary laws or ecclesiastical censure, but instead tried to enclose what perturbed them within the confines of a cultural ghetto, so that they could then look down upon it from their lofty moral and intellectual vantage point. This explains why Voltaire denied that fashion could have anything significant to do with taste: "taste is arbitrary in many things: in fabrics, in jewelry, in attire, in all that does not embody the stature of the Fine Arts. In this sense it can aptly be described as fantasy. Indeed, it is fantasy and not taste that produces all these new fashions."[51]

Kant was of the same opinion. In his view, fashion derived from an urge to imitate, which it represented as an evident social phenomenon: "fashion therefore belongs under the title of *vanity*, because there is no inner worth in its intention; and also of *foolishness*, because in fashion there is still a compulsion to let ourselves be led slavishly by the mere example that many in society give us."[52] So, although it is widely believed that "being fashionable is a question of taste," in actual fact this is not the case. As often as not, fashions degenerate into eccentricity in order to be deemed expressions of good taste; moreover, the subjective, instrumental nature of the phenomenon is evident in the way the higher echelons of society drop a given fashion the moment it is adopted by members of the lower ranks, who are thus excommunicated once and for all from the universe of taste. In Kant's view, fashion was not really a question of taste (because it could go entirely contrary to good taste), but of vanity, of the desire to be pointed out and to do better than the next person.[53]

Kant perceived luxury as something different, however, defining it as an excess of social wellbeing *mixed with taste* and spread throughout ordinary life.[54] This involvement is essential: when luxury (*luxus*) is not underpinned by taste, it breaks down into profligacy (*luxuria*). While the former brings elegance and to some degree refines the sensibility of beholders (for instance, at a ball or a show), the latter simply squanders overabundance and variety (as in the case of a Lucullan feast).

As for Schopenhauer, true to his deep-rooted misogyny he expressed even more radical theses regarding the sensibility of women. In his opinion, the fair sex could simply be described as "non aesthetic," in that women were incapable of understanding and appreciating the fine arts, and could at the best ape what others said.[55] Moreover, the innate vanity of women led them to appreciate only material benefits (unlike men, who naturally gave due value to "intelligence, learning, courage"), thus making them squanderers by nature.[56] As for their limited intellectual faculties, in view of their inability to rise above the particular, womankind was deaf to the universe and could hope for no more than the pursuit of interest in novelty and attraction for what is extravagant: what women aspired to was thus curiosity, not real knowledge.[57]

There is no arguing with fashion, wrote a resigned William Sumner at the beginning of the 1900s,[58] redeeming the medieval adage pertaining to the irrational nature of tastes that generations of philosophers had struggled to confute. Since women had been able to say their own and act accordingly, the history of taste had indeed changed. Not only had it suddenly gathered pace, it had also acquired ubiquity. Both were one-way processes that were to be hugely influential.

The role of fashion on the formation of contemporary sensibility was full of fundamental implications. It introduced a period of cyclical infatuation, putting the mechanisms of detached enthusiasm, the cult of the superfluous and the fever for frivolity to the test, thereby preparing the way for what was to become consumer society. In the pantomime of semblance, where the stylized self could wear beauty like a second skin, fashion actually began to shape personal identity. Like a form of collective seduction, it injected social values with a touch of worldliness that colored the present, challenging the ethics of duty with the morals of pleasure. By rallying the aspiration to elegance as a model for aesthetic gratification, fashion directed people's desires towards a certain ideal of beauty, and in so doing paved the way for the aesthetic framework of everyday life that was to become a feature of the following century.

To many observers, the frenzied rhythms typical of the episodic fortunes of fashion seemed like a capricious succession of dictates that called for obligatory compliance. Those who failed to obey were excluded from social and symbolic exchange. But then this is true of all societies and in all ages: regardless of how long they may resist, all past customs were once norms. The oddity of fashion with respect to traditional societies doesn't stem from the fact that its canons of elegance are transitory, that customs change continuously and that the fever for novelty spurs on inventiveness and originality. What really counts is rather the fact that fashion affects the community as a form of irresistible seduction, as the collective enchantment of taste, as the appeal of ostentation and surprise, and as an aesthetic constraint. This is precisely why fashion is bound to be changeable, indeed capricious: it is furthered and spread by a peculiar predisposition of taste. This cult of the ephemeral revolves around the short-lived state of grace to which the individual, under a constant onslaught of heady stimulation, can hope to aspire.

For such is the female universe of taste. Philosophers and sociologists have long done their best to ignore the originality of this sphere of aesthetics, seeking instead to explain the fashion phenomenon as the fruit of conflicts of prestige born of the tendency to emulate the higher ranks of society. Granted, emulation is not necessarily a "vertical" occurrence, in which people lower down the scale try to imitate those above, who in their turn invent new conventions to distinguish themselves from those on their way up (Spencer, Tarde, Veblen, Simmel). It can also be "horizontal," in the sense that it concerns only the ruling classes who vie with each other for symbolic supremacy (Elias, König, Bourdieu). But in either case, the explanations provided all speak through the voice of men: they unfailingly adopt the male perspective, which is blind to the specific dynamics and cultural importance of fashion, with the partial exception of how it effects husbands, lovers and partners. This means paying no attention to the fundamental role that women and female sensibilities have played in furthering the appeal, the satisfaction and the omnipresent taste for the ephemeral.

Gilles Lipovestsky was perhaps the first sociologist who emphasized the crucial and active role of individualism to explain the spread of the fashion phenomenon. For as long as tradition, society, social group and environmental condition decide for us, fashion cannot exist. Rather than social and symbolic rivalry, what really counts in the creation and furtherance of volatility in fashion are "the awareness of being an individual with a specific destiny, the desire to express an original identity and the cultural celebration of personal identity."[59] In his view, increasing social mobility and the ensuing battle for appearances would not have been enough to sow the seeds of such volatility in the Western mentality. "What was required was a revolution in the *representation* of individuals and their view of themselves, such that traditional mentality and values would be overturned. The unique nature of individuals was thus exalted, and as a result social promotion came to be identified with the ostentation of difference."[60] Interestingly, it was arguments of this sort that brought about the taste metaphor as a way of explaining the individual nature of the expression of sensibility.

This is more than mere similarity of intent. For it is fashion that catapults taste onto the social stage, establishing it in the middleclass mind as the crossroads between reality and fiction, perception and imagination, enchantment and habit. Essential to the creation of such acquiescence and the ensuing devotion to stylish products has long been the predominance of the female sensibility. This had led to the adoption of an aesthetic radar system that controls all aspects of surrounding reality. The outcome has been the pursuit of happiness and the underlying sensuous morality of a society fired by material desires.

5

The Economy of Taste in Consumer Society

Paris in the nineteenth century was not just the capital of luxury in the fields of cuisine and fashion. It was also the high temple of taste regarding everything that had to do with renewal in trade, the invention of sales techniques that are still in use today, the unrestrained profusion of goods, and the rampant yearning for what was superfluous among increasingly widespread strata of the population. Paris was the city that first introduced department stores, thereby bringing about a revolution in the landscape and symbolic meaning of consumption.

Bewitching Commodities

In 1883, Émile Zola provided a lucid account of the heady increase in temptations that dazzled the Parisian middle classes, undermining what had become time-honored habits. In this he was a forerunner of the moral judgments that were later to accompany the chronicles of the inexorable rise of consumer society.

> As though he were divulging a secret of the sort men sometimes like to share with others of their kind, he finished his explanation of the mechanisms behind modern department store trade. What appeared to be at the very top of the whole edifice was the exploitation of women. Everything came down to this: the constant renewal of capital, the system of piling up commodities, the "good market" that works well, the price displayed that reassures the purchaser. It was women that the stores strove to attract by means of competition, women who could never resist those special offers, especially once dazzled by the shop windows. In the female bosom they had awoken new desires, flaunting tremendous temptations to which women were bound to succumb, first giving in to necessary purchases, and later to mere whims, to consuming obsessions. As they increased sales tenfold, bringing luxury within the reach of wider circles, the department stores exercised an irresistible urge to spend,

thereby ruining the family economy and fomenting the increasingly costly madness of fashion.[1]

The person expounding such wisdom is Octave Mouret, a ruthless self-made man who owns the department store that provides the novel with its title. One after another, Mouret's store puts the dusty, family-run shops in the district out of business. Towards the end of the story, he falls in love with a recalcitrant, virginal shop assistant from the provinces, the granddaughter of a traditional mercer whose business folded on account of her suitor's merciless commercial acumen. A melodrama for modern times, with a happy ending that only slightly sweetens the bitter pill of the effects of trade on human relationships. Though Mouret himself may be a figment of the author's imagination, he stands for a category on the rise, his store clearly alluding to Bon Marché, a highly popular institution in late nineteenth-century Paris. Zola had studied the evolution of the phenomenon carefully, illustrating its development with tabloid-style sensationalism rather than the detachment of the novelist.

The remarkable success of the new model of distribution did not come about overnight. There were forerunners in the shape of the *passages* and the *magazins de nouveautés*.

The former began to spread through Paris between the second and the third decade of the 1800s. An illustrated guidebook of the time described them as follows: "These arcades [*passages*], a recent invention of industrial luxury, are glass-roofed, marble-paneled corridors extending through whole blocks of buildings, whose owners have joined together for such enterprises. Lining both sides of these corridors, which get their light from above, are the most elegant shops, so that the arcade is a city, a world in miniature."[2]

The new commercial spaces called for attractive display to emphasize the seductive power of commodities, and this in its turn boosted a form of voyeurism that revolved around the urge to acquire. To be seen and thus become desirable, an object required window-dressing. The outcome was shopping as a socially shared pastime.

The arcades of Paris aimed at seducing the beholder and thereby gaining custom. Gas lighting, which was first used in these *passages*, provided increased and extended visibility, as well as a gratifying sense of progress. The urban landscape was thus enhanced.

In a famous pamphlet on the subject, Walter Benjamin drew attention to another innovative aspect of the development: the use of iron in construction, initially in the arcades themselves, and later in other "transit buildings" such as railway stations or exhibition halls. An intrinsic part of modernity, this new technique also embodied the experience of mobility that was a feature of the age.

The itineraries provided by the arcades were psychological as well as topographical, underlining a principle that was to become an essential tenet of consumer society: the fact that the desirability of commodities could become an event in its own right, a show capable of arousing individual fantasies within an irresistible collective experience that involved the entire civilized population (in other words, the nascent middle class).

The theatricality that ran in the veins of modern trade gave the new stores hypnotic powers that furthered the mirage created by commodities. Things were brilliant and full of wonder, as though the waving of a magic wand had brought about a new mixture of ideology and make-believe, cultural display and sensorial stimuli, prestige and representation. Such was the contribution of the *passages*, and their apparent showiness. "The arcade is a street of lascivious commerce only; it is wholly adapted to arousing desires. Because in this street the juices slow to a standstill, the commodity proliferates along the margins and enters into fantastic combinations, like the tissue in tumors."[3]

By erecting their own aesthetics and promoting their own mythology, commodities took on a dream-like aura that projected them, once and for all, onto center stage. And the department stores represented the apotheosis of this development.

The *magasins de nouveautés* that took root in Paris between the 1820s and the 1830s further paved the way for the triumph of the department stores. While the novelty of the *passages* lay in display, the outstanding feature of the *magasins de nouveauté* was the range of products they stocked.

Trade had traditionally taken place in specialized shops that focused on the sale of one type of merchandise. To go into such a store meant buying something that satisfied a specific need. Moreover, the choice of both the shop and the item to be purchased took place without the customer having any preliminary idea of the prices, which ultimately were the result of a certain amount of bartering between shopkeeper and customer.

With the advent of the *magasins de nouveautés* all this changed radically: a wide range of goods were suddenly available under one roof, and each bore its own price tag. To add to which, commodities could be returned and exchanged, and potential customers were welcome to have a look around, without necessarily having to buy anything. In this way real need was no longer the reason for entering the store. Instead, those who ventured in were likely to feel drawn, first and foremost, by the delectable contemplation of what was displayed.

When need was no longer the reason for shopping, to wander in and out of stores became a form of self-indulgence, a quiet luxury, especially when the store in question promised a proliferation of "novelties." For varied supply was able to arouse impelling needs and insuppressible sensations that tended to lead to demand. The desire for fashion, born of visual stimulation and the ensuing powers of suggestion, was the fairy godmother of commodities in all their ostentatious splendor.

The glorification of whatever was new grew apace, changing and transfiguring what people thought about things, and thereby shocking generations of philosophers and polemicists, who saw in all this the signs of wasteful obsession: "Newness is a quality independent of the use value of the commodity. It is the origin of the illusory appearance that belongs inalienably to images produced by the collective unconscious. It is the quintessence of that false consciousness whose indefatigable agent is fashion."[4]

With the birth of the department stores, this trend came into its own: the theatrical nature of the arcades married with the vast range of products typical of the *magasins de nouveauté*, thereby creating a phenomenon of enormous impact. In next to no time, the Bon Marché stores, the first of their sort, became the diorama of desires spread before the rising middle classes, who were thus happily able to invest in their appearance.

In people's minds, the overt splendor of the goods displayed in the shop windows replaced the aristocratic ostentation of wealth that enhanced the splendor of the court. The department store thus promoted and extoled what Zola defined as the "democratization of luxury." Anyone was free to enter, indeed was explicitly invited to do so: there was no need for coats of arms, for social pedestals or the exercise of carefully refined sensibilities. Inside the emporium all the goods had already been selected to appeal to everyone, as though displayed in a museum of ephemera. Once an inaccessible sphere that required initiation, luxury had become available to everyone, an ecumenical phenomenon based on the heady rhythms of fashion. Supply preceded demand, which it fashioned in its own image: thus consumer society came into being.

Bon Marché was not just the *arbiter elegantiarum* for the masses on their pilgrimage towards material grace. Apart from selling commodities, the store helped shape a view of the world, which it delivered along with the instructions for use. It thus became a secular cathedral whose consecration lay in the catechesis of consumption.

> The Bon Marché came to serve essentially the same role as the Republican school system, at least for those of middle-class means or middle-class aspirations. It became a bourgeois instrument of social homogenization, a means for disseminating the values and life style of the Parisian upper middle-class to French middle-class society as a whole. It did this by so lowering prices that the former's possessions became mass-consumer items. But it also did so by becoming a kind of cultural primer. The Bon Marché showed people how they should dress, how they should furnish their homes, and how they should spend their leisure time. It defined the ideals and goals for French society. It illustrated how successful people or people who wished to be successful or people on their way to becoming successful lived their lives. In its pictures and in its displays the Bon Marché became a medium for the creation of a national middle-class culture. Thus, through the Bon Marché, Paris and the countryside became more alike. The millions of catalogues mailed from the center to the provinces carried the message of a set way of life, much as the textbooks the Ministry of Public Instruction sent to the communes carried a set vision of society.[5]

Advertising, which began to be used widely in order to promote the department stores, also made an essential contribution to developments, acting as a dress rehearsal for the fundamental role it was shortly to play in the construction of the consumer mindset and imaginary sphere. In this sense, it was also, and from the outset, distinctly innovative. Thanks to advertising, even when people were actually unable to see the goods in question, they could at least imagine them thanks to the contribution of newspapers, magazines, postcards, flyers, almanacs and calendars. Moreover, alongside the engraving that portrayed the desired item, and the trademark that identified it, there was also a symbolic corollary interwoven with images and slogans aimed at lubricating the memory and stimulating desirability. By means of such "appeal at a distance," the magnetism of goods became insistent and pervasive, like a recurrent chimera.

The universal exhibitions completed the process of transformation. Reassuringly reminiscent of popular fairs, they promoted the collective celebration of what Benjamin criticized as being "the enthronement of commodities with the surrounding halo of distraction," in an age when the entertainment industry was still in a seminal state. "World exhibitions glorify the exchange value of the commodity. They create a framework in which its value recedes into the background. They open a phantasmagoria which a person enters in order to be distracted. The entertainment industry makes this easier by elevating the person to the level of the commodity. He surrenders to its manipulation while enjoying his alienation from himself and others."[6]

The trade in inexpensive items promoted by the department stores clearly furthered the voyeuristic tendency implicit in consumerism, it was the universal exhibitions that took this trait to hitherto unimaginable heights. Window-shopping became a leisure activity in its own right, a popular cult that revealed the veneration of commodities implicit in consumer aspirations.

The overall show was designed to dazzle observers. Human eyes had never previously beheld such an impressive aggregation of goods in one place. This was the deliberately designed high temple of trade. Even the containers, fittings and furnishings devised for the purpose helped reshape the urban landscape by creating futuristic settings: in 1851, the vast Crystal Palace built in iron and glass in London; in 1889 the soaring Eiffel Tower in Paris; again in Paris, the triumph of electrical lighting that gave new brilliance to the French capital in 1900, suggesting the proud epithet of *Ville Lumière*. Moreover, starting with the 1867 Universal Exhibition in Paris, the goods displayed spoke eloquently for the triumph of industry and technology, an accomplishment that was to shape the coming years, forging people's perceptions and imaginations. As consumption and progress began to mean much the same thing, these spectacular events gave resonance to the ideology of prosperity that was to culminate in mass society.

The outcome of all these astounding novelties heralded the arrival of a new age. Thanks to the arcades, the department stores and the universal exhibitions, pleasure and consumption, dreams and commodities, trade and leisure pastimes interweave and affect each other. Unleashing the imagination no longer means succumbing to the enchanted worlds conjured up by the arts of suggestion: literature, music, the theater. Taste as a system of shared preferences becomes the perfect tool for self-identification.

The idealization of commodities was the key event of the late nineteenth century, because it nurtured people's tastes by providing them with concrete stimuli and fulfillment. To possess something, to be able to buy it rather than simply gaze at it from a distance, was decidedly more gratifying and reassuring than the "disinterested" participation promulgated by the aesthetics of Romanticism. The attractions of symbolic compliance with established privileges faded as people began to realize that accessibility to the world of ownership was gradually expanding, and would soon become inclusive.

As desires became commodities, the relationship between available funds and shared aesthetics underwent a process of symbiosis that redefined and established in measurable terms the value of things. Under the bewildered gaze of the Marxists, commodities underwent a metaphysical transformation, accompanied by the liturgy of frivolity.

> Once escaped from the hand of the producer and divested of its real particularity, it ceases to be a product and to be ruled over by human beings. It has acquired a "ghostly objectivity" and leads a life of its own. "A commodity appears, at first sight, to be a trivial and easily understood thing. Our analysis shows that, in reality, it is a vexed and complicated thing, abounding in metaphysical subtleties and theological niceties." Cut off from the will of man, it aligns itself in a mysterious hierarchy, develops or declines exchangeability, and, in accordance with its own peculiar laws, performs as an actor on phantom [. . .] The commodity has been transformed into an idol that, although the product of human hands, disposes over the human.[7]

When commodities began to cast their spell over people and consumer society first established itself as a way of life, the "democratization of luxury" also came to mean the *democratization of tastes*, which was a much deeper, more radical phenomenon. The consumer myths were naïve and sickly-sweet in their rhetoric, with terrible stylistic blunders and plenty of disarming vulgarity. Yet their development also ushered in an unprecedented novelty: for the first time in the history of Europe everyone suddenly had the right to desire.

By rapidly increasing the range of individual aspirations, mass society shaped itself around desire: the desire to consume, and the freedom to desire. Desiring something that had hitherto been out of reach meant not being resigned to acceptance of the status quo: aspiring to improving one's lot, regardless of one's origins; pursuing greater expectations. This was the age of opportunity, which egged on social mobility. Both were the fruit of the widespread, compelling urge that derives from the taste for what is superfluous. The taste for wellbeing was something everyone could enjoy.

Luxury certainly fueled taste, but taste did more than simply drive capitalism, which it had done since the twilight of the Renaissance. At the dawn of the twentieth century, it also became the focus for the urge to consume, and in so doing gave modern democracies their cohesion and consistency. As far as the aims of this book are concerned, it is sufficient to observe that the conquest of desire automatically gave rise to a system of preferences that redefined in aesthetic terms the relationships between people and things.

When taste expresses itself in consumption, it conjures up fantasies, adopts a stylistic universe of its own, and is sensitive to the power of suggestion. Harris has identified the main categories of the consumer aesthetics shared by the American middle class at the end of the twentieth century. Cute, quaint, cool, romantic, zany, futuristic, delicious, natural, glamorous and clean describe the stylistic repertoire of everyday normality, "a kind of collective aesthetic unconsciousness, a psychic realm that serves as a storehouse for faint memories of the extraneous designs on trash cans, jelly jars, and milk cartons."[8]

A century earlier, in the department stores of London and Paris, it was the idea of "the exotic" that held stylistic way. Of this obsession Williams writes in *Dream Worlds*:

> To criticize the chaotic-exotic style as "bad taste," a frequent condemnation even around the turn of the century, misses the point. As a quality of aesthetic judgment, taste does not apply to transient décor whose purpose is "to attract and to hold" the spectator's attention. Why the reliance on fake mahogany, fake bronze, fake marble? Because the purpose of the materials is not to express their own character but to convey a sense of the lavish and foreign. Why the hodgepodge of visual themes? Because the purpose is not to express internal consistency but to bring together anything that expresses distance from the ordinary. Exotic décor is therefore impervious to objections of taste. It is not ladylike but highly seductive. In this aesthetic demi-monde, exotic décor exists as an intermediate form between art and commerce. It resembles art, it has recognizable themes and stylistic traits, its commercial purpose is wrapped in elaborate visual trappings; yet it does not participate in traditional artistic goals of creating beauty, harmony, and spiritual significance. This hybrid form is an illusion of art, a so-called artistic element posing as the genuine article.[9]

With its mechanisms of solicitation and enticement, its overt avowal of intent and its immediate accessibility in monetary terms, the stimulation of taste in the service of commerce came across as radically different to the aesthetics of solemnity pertaining to the fine arts. For in this latter sphere it was the ascetic paradigm of contemplation at a distance that held sway.

Far from standing aloof, taste was involved in the new arts of entertainment that helped shape popular culture in the twentieth century: movies and photography (especially snap shots and postcards featuring photos), light music and video clips, light reading and comics, television and advertising, holiday villages and theme parks: in all these cases, immediacy of enjoyment was more important than any claim to artistic content. It was inevitable that the Kantian dichotomy between pure taste and taste as a pleasure should return to the fore. These two different aesthetic inclinations naturally gave rise to contrasting artistic products: Le Corbusier, Picasso and Schönberg, as opposed to Disneyland, Hollywood and Madison Avenue.

On the one hand, there was the taste of the élite, refined by expertise and inclined towards a coldly formal approach to the perception of aesthetic stimuli. Such a stance viewed any involvement relating to immediate, sensorial pleasure with disfavor, condemning it as "impure" and to be contrasted. Entirely serious and intellectual, the pleasures of contemplation required detachment, and devotion to patient cultural apprenticeship.

On the other hand, plebeian taste was spontaneous, coarse, heady, full of cheap emotions and inclined to dwell on the sensorial roots of a metaphor that had begun its life as a corporeal preference, before being elevated to the lofty realms of the spirit. Little wonder that any show of uneducated taste was likened to gluttony or lechery, as though spontaneous preferences of this sort were unable to rise above the *status naturae*:

> "vulgar" works, as the words used to describe them indicate—"facile" or "light," of course, but also "frivolous," "futile," "shallow," "superficial," "showy," "flashy," "meretricious," or, in the register of oral satisfactions, "syrupy," "sugary," "rose-water," "schmaltzy," "cloying"—are not only a sort of insult to refinement, a slap in the face to a "demanding" audience which will not stand for "facile" offerings [. . .]: they arouse distaste and disgust by the methods of seduction, usually denounced as "low," "degrading," "demeaning," which they try to use, giving the spectator the sense of being treated like any Tom, Dick or Harry who can be seduced by tawdry charms which invite him to regress to the most primitive and elementary forms of pleasure, whether they be the passive satisfactions of the infantile taste for sweet liquids ('syrupy') or the quasi-animal gratifications of sexual desire.[10]

The contrast did not only consist in the division of the spheres of sensibility, according to social circumstance and condition. Cultivated taste did not oppose the predilection for what was trivial, commercial, obvious and common with an exhortation to undergo the aesthetic initiation of formal contemplation, which would have been unpalatable and anyway practically impossible for simple souls. Instead it pinpointed the objects of popular taste and inveighed against them. While unrefined taste delighted in sugary, melodramatic effects and excess, cultivated taste expressed its distance by means of disgust and contempt, deeming such vulgar realms to be nauseating and intolerable. Where cultivated taste became most belligerent was not within the esoteric labyrinth of modern art, however, but in the crusade against bad taste. Inevitably *kitsch*, the overwhelming rise of mass taste was deeply offensive and called for outright rejection.

The appearance of a new taste with widespread appeal, commercial intrusiveness, semantic cacophony and obtuse enjoyment was bound to meet with opposition. Cultivated taste organized some energetic resistance: the rights and privileges of the intellectual caste had to be defended, and this meant stemming the rising, malodorous river of consumer aesthetics. Such was the battle that was to underlie the phenomenology of taste in the twentieth century.

Ease and Progress

As taste came into contact with the artificial paradise of consumerism, the elective supremacy of personal preferences expanded beyond measure as regards both the universe of the goods themselves, and the realm of those who possessed them. From this point on, taste became the yardstick for individual sensibility, thereby directing the redistribution of social roles. Increasingly a person's position in society could be defined in terms of his or her system of predilections: people were what they consumed, and they consumed what they desired, and desired whatever fascinated and bewitched them. Taste thus became the cornerstone of the process of aestheticization of social identities.

Central to this development in post-war years was the concept of "lifestyle," which spread throughout Western society and behavior. Coined by sociology and spread by marketing, "lifestyle" soon found its way into everyday language, thereby explaining the system of ramifications underlying what Kant had described as the "taste for what is delightful." In actual fact, taste was not a singular phenomenon, because *tastes* proliferated with the spread of their possible applications, as did the preferences of single individuals. The outcome was more like a patchwork of arbitrary choices than the cogent emanation of an inner faculty.

Understanding a person's tastes thus came to mean keeping tabs on his or her spheres of interest: favorite shows (cinema, concerts, plays, television), musical preferences, what he or she liked to read, his or her dream car—or more realistically the car that would ultimately be bought, choices of food, holiday destinations, favorite sports, most visited websites, hobbies and leisure activities. Taste had become as extensive as leisure, mixing with it as the passing generations expressed their rites and fashion imposed its whims.

As Pierre Bourdieu pointed out in his famous study of 1979,[11] the regularity and correlation of tastes to be found within the same social group increasingly had less to do with a common social background and more to do with membership of the same aesthetic tribe. In this sense it had become a criterion of social aggregation; one that was to disintegrate towards the turn of the millennium as myriad sentient but disconnected individuals anxiously tried to pinpoint their own faltering preferences, overpowered by the growing obsolescence of objects and desires. At this point the consumer schedule could no longer reflect a cultural background, be this inherited or acquired through education, shared values, existential aspirations, ideological orientation or religious beliefs. Instead it had become the fluctuating consequence of the constant and ever increasing onslaught of commodities.

To put it briefly, taste became a prosperity detector and a compass of leisure, marking out the time devoted to personal wellbeing rather than to work. The society of desires thus revealed its hedonistic soul, and its individualistic, utilitarian bent. The commercial success of commodities and services increases in ratio to the intensity of the promised happiness: such is the laconic moral of consumer civilization. For this is a civilization in which taste is no more than the sensation that urges us towards something that is supposed to give us intrinsic pleasure, a form of enjoyment that does not depend on anything beyond immediate gratification. And this, in its turn, is the paradoxical reversal of the enlightened aesthetics of "disinterestedness" that many people find to be deeply disturbing.

Granted, this equivalence did not come about overnight. Instead it developed gradually, once it had saturated the desire to hoard and the urge to acquire the goods that stand for social preferment and membership of the society of wellbeing, well removed from any earlier state of need. In this context, the democratization of luxury foretold by the critics of consumerism proves to be no more than an oxymoron. Luxury is, by definition, something rare, available only to the élite. Its status has little to do with the materials or workmanship involved, because it ultimately depends on the distribution of wealth, in other words on limited availability in relation to a virtually unlimited demand.

Although luxury as such cannot be available to everyone, faking it is within most people's means: "this is alchemy reversed, whereby gold is turned into iron pyrite, silver into nickel, leather into pleather, tapestry into upholstery, painting into lithography, lace into tulle, substance into ornament, solid into veneer. This is the rising tide of what is similar, pseudo, bogus antique; of boundless imitation that fears no excess, since it is making up for earlier deprivation that focused on junk, or faux items, or even unique objects that mass production has abolished, or the original model that is out of reach anyway."[12]

All of this has devastating effects on the rules of elegance, upsetting its significance, ruining its ceremony, and provoking horrified reactions on the part of those who reject imitation because they have the discernment to recognize the value of the original. Rather than making privilege available to a wider segment of society, the "democratization of luxury" thus represents the spread of that sense of satisfaction (it matters little whether this is illusory or fake) that comes with the availability of commodities. The idea of comfort, which began as a yardstick or excuse for such goods, soon proves to be closely related to the figurative meaning of taste.

At the same time, however, comfort also ratifies the legitimacy of desire: the desire for what is superfluous, for what is pleasurable, and surplus to real requirement. In this sense, it actually has something in common with the aristocracy's love of luxury. Moreover, comfort also lends itself to sensual gratification. It arises less from pride of possession than from a particular and distinctly more intimate gratification that derives from the mixture of wellbeing, reassurance and familiarity that we obtain from the objects that surround us, from the environment in which we live, and from the clothes we wear.

The current meaning of the word "comfort" dates back to seventeenth-century England. In earlier times, the term was used to signify something closer to its Latin origins: to "give comfort," meaning to "restore strength" to a body or spirit tried by fatigue. Apart from giving rise to the concept of the "*restaurant*" with its focus on *gourmandise*, this restoration not only offered "comfort," but also adapted its meaning to embrace the growing civilization of society, acquiring independence from the sphere of material needs and increasingly tending towards that of luxury.

In Italian there is an expression that translates this modern sense of the term effectively: "*sentirsi a proprio agio*" means to feel at ease, whereby the faculty of feeling (*sentirsi*) blends with the assurance of comfort that derives from financial wellbeing (*agio*), and with the sense of intimacy that brings these two connotations together into a single concept (*proprio*—self). Comfort is thus poles apart from the impersonal exteriority of decoration, which inevitably smacks of decorum and respectability; in other words, of duty as opposed to pleasure, and of outer as opposed to inner wellbeing.

There is even an aesthetics of comfort manifest in the furnishings and appurtenances of the home. Far from being pure, cold and disinterested, this form of aesthetics pertains to a realm of gratification that transcends the functional purpose of things. Function was only to recover some of its earlier importance during the 1900s, with the mechanization of daily life. By contrast, during the nineteenth century, it largely regarded the aesthetic and the symbolic sphere, commemorating the past rather than heralding the future. "The psychological comfort provided by familiar, reassuring motifs in the home was fundamental to the image of domesticity which, in turn, was linked to the idea of virtue and respectability. These meanings were also communicated through the level of comfort provided to ease the body as well as the mind. The "Victorian" interior was characterized by a preponderance of upholstered furniture, and by a liberal use of draped textiles to increase a sense of privacy and to soften the environment, both visually and to the touch."[13]

The fragmentation of tastes unleashed a surge of unregulated eclecticism that succumbed to the wildest desires, stimulating and gratifying regressive instincts by proposing vulgar imitations of models from the past as though they were the ultimate cornucopia. As a result, the high priests of cultivated taste reacted across the board, promoting rectification for the deplorable degeneration of "bourgeois taste."

What was denounced was not so much the advent of a new style, or indeed its regrettable decline, but rather the lack of coherent taste, the chaotic dispersion of the applied arts in a thousand pointless rivulets, and the want of an authoritative model that could act as a mentor for a new age and turn the tide of the spreading commercialization of beauty.

The nineteenth century was the century of ugliness: our parents, our grandparents, and we ourselves have lived and still live in surroundings more ugly than any before. I repeat: look at everything with unemotional eyes, and when you have compared what we have today with what was there in earlier times, you will become convinced that not one of the objects used by our parents and ourselves today can be called beautiful, whereas those that still look attractive tend to come from an earlier century [. . .] A certain consecration of life is lacking, ultimately a lack not of education—for we are more educated than our predecessors and no longer have funeral pyres, inquisitions, or slaves—but of culture, which is something quite different. For is not culture the accord between a spiritual core, the result of communal aspiration, and its reflection in material form, that is to say, art? Humanity, seen as the community, no longer has an ideal. Personal interests have replaced mutual, spiritual interests and have assumed a purely materialist form—money.[14]

The real threat was not the prospect of seeing unruly hordes undermine the privileges of the well-to-do. During the 1900s, there was no automatic relationship between refined taste and social prestige, since the two were often in open conflict. The spread of mass taste and the so-called artistic production that was supposed to gratify this taste was not experienced as a symbolic attack on the upper echelons of society: indeed, in the eyes of the lower classes the ostentation of luxury on the part of the wealthy continued to be worthy of admiration and emulation. What was more significant was the loss of authority experienced by those who felt their education and learning should have made them absolute arbiters of taste. It was the architects, designers and academics, in other words all those who considered themselves the rightful creators and custodians of true beauty, who felt their role begin to vacillate and their declarations go unattended. Disconcerted and discomfited by the relentless proliferation of decorative excess, they had visions of having to bow their heads once more. Following the momentous emancipation of art that characterized the Renaissance, they now found themselves having to pay lip service to the foibles of clients, most of whom were philistines whose lack of taste went hand in hand with their extravagance.

All of this was not far removed from the bitter polemics and total contempt expressed regarding ordinary people's tawdry desires, the dogmatic attitude towards those who refused to toe the line, the iconoclastic fury with which the privileged few tried to reshape the present, and their visionary despotism applied to the future. The outcome was the excommunication of what was seen as the vilest abomination of taste: ornament.

It was the Viennese architect Adolf Loos who unleashed this particular crusade. Having adopted the principle that "form follows function" from his American colleague Louis Sullivan, he was unable to contemplate the idea that form might actually have something to do with the simple gratification of the senses, and instead set out to indoctrinate the Old World with a formula that soon became an evident and powerful dogma for the Modernist Movement. Granted, the basis of this theory was distinctly ideological, since its very cornerstone was a concept that required further definition: the exact meaning of "function," and of the underlying idea of comfort. The cult of modernity and the ideology of progress rooted in rationality gave rise to an ethics based on efficiency and profit, and this inevitably breathed new life into the concept of the "use value" of objects as a criterion for mass produced desires: in the efficiency-oriented world of industrial productivity, there was no longer room for whim and fantasy, which were deemed the despicable waste products of a world in dissolution.

The gradual emancipation from the "slavery of ornament" soon turned into a Darwinian criterion of cultural selection among the various stages of humanity, regulated according to its degree of civilization—a concept that embraced the moral as well as the aesthetic sphere:

> in the womb the human embryo passes through all the development stages of the animal kingdom. At the moment of birth, human sensations are equal to those of a newborn dog. His childhood passes through all the transformations which correspond to the history of mankind. At the age of two, he sees like a Papuan, at four like a Teuton, at six like Socrates, at eight like Voltaire. [. . .] The child is amoral. To us the Papuan is also amoral. The Papuan slaughters his enemies and devours them. He is no criminal. If, however, the modern man slaughters and devours somebody, he is a criminal or a degenerate. The Papuan tattoos his skin, his boat, his oar, in short, everything that is within his reach. He is no criminal. The modern man who tattoos himself is a criminal or a degenerate. There are prisons where eighty percent of the inmates bear tattoos. Those who are tattooed but are not imprisoned are latent criminals or degenerate aristocrats.[15]

In this context, Loos theorized, the tattoo was considered emblematic of a need felt by primitive peoples to camouflage their bodies and products because they were not content with showing them and using them for what they really were. Ornament was thus simply the transferal of this impulse to architecture and furnishings. Modern times had emancipated humanity from this naïve desire, however, making such activities seem like a symptom of cultural or indeed mental backwardness. Loos was finally able to show the world that "the evolution of culture is synonymous with the removal of ornamentation from objects of everyday use."[16] The ineluctable march of progress thus heralded the advent of a new era characterized by the elimination of superfluity, whereby "the furnishing of a prison cell by the royal upholsterer Schulze or by Professor Van de Velde[17] will be considered an aggravation of the sentence."[18]

The predilection for shapes with sharp corners, for smooth, polished, monochrome surfaces, for unaffected clarity, for the aesthetics of sobriety and containment implicit in the tenet *less is more*, could not be entirely reduced to the battle for progress. It was also a battle between the sexes charged with misogyny: the taste to be established in the name of modernity derived from the measured and austere demeanor of the industrial bourgeoisie that stigmatized (or at the best excused) women's enjoyment of the frivolity of fashion as an expression of incurable fatuity. Clearly such short-lived, wasteful tendencies were blameworthy in their effects no less than in their intentions: "if I falsify an object by decorating it, I limit its duration because, through being subject to fashion, it is condemned to die earlier. This waste of good material can be justified only by womanly caprice and ambition, for ornament in the service of woman will live forever. Objects of limited durability such as fabrics and wallpaper remain subject to fashion, and therefore to ornamentation. [. . .] Ornament in women substantially corresponds to that of the savage, and is erotic in essence."[19]

To counteract all this was the aesthetics of "modern man," who relinquished all desires for ornament on reaching the age of reason: "a man of modern sensibility has no need for ornament, indeed is disgusted by it. All those objects that we call modern are free of ornament. *From the French Revolution on*, our clothes, our machines, our leather items and all objects of everyday use have been unadorned. Except the objects that pertain exclusively to the realm of women."[20]

From the cultural and anthropological point of view, the advent of the Modernist Movement and its enormous influence on the world of design amounted to a celebration of the "Great Revenge" of male taste, following the previous century's "Great Sacrifice" to the fair sex in the sphere of attire. A new division of competence and sensibility thus informed the design of the home and shared perceptions: the world of technics, efficiency and productivity in contrast to the world of feelings, protection and care.

The rivalry between the architectural and decorative styles of the early years of the century can largely be attributed to a dispute between the two sexes. It was not simply a question of traditionalists opposed to innovators. The competition between the schools that voiced the pressing need for radical stylistic renewal also expressed the dichotomy between taste conceived as contemplation and taste conceived as enjoyment. This naturally widened the cultural divide between the two archetypes of aesthetic sensibility: on the one hand what was formal, Apollonian and masculine; and on the other, the sphere of all that was sensual, Dionysiac and feminine.

The contrast between Art Nouveau and the initiators of what was to become the Modernist Movement made this contraposition quite clear:

> not convinced by the notion that hard edges and plane geometry were the components of an elemental and "honest" vision, the various contributors to the Art Nouveau delved, instead, into the polymorphous sensuality of some imagined, primordial life [. . .] Rational modernism was an appeal to the cold and distant eye. It was the product of a deliberate calculation. Art Nouveau, on the other hand, evoked the more intimate and provocative senses of taste, touch, and smell. Rational modernism pointed

toward a mathematically synchronized social order; Art Nouveau spoke to the impetuous hungers of an inner, private realm. Rational modernism drew its inspirations from the metallic and uniform properties of the machine; Art Nouveau drew the visual metaphors from a pre-civilized conception of nature [. . .] Against the predictable symmetry of rational modernism, the netherworld of Art Nouveau was irregular, tantalizing, protoplasmic. If rational modernism represented the arenas of work and production, Art Nouveau was languid, sensual, organically reproductive. Its sense of motion did not mimic the forward-driving pistons of the locomotive, but of the uncanny, damp of post-orgasmic repose.[21]

The cultural message that underlay these two aesthetic factions also spoke for their different spheres of influence. The sensuality of Art Nouveau permeated a number of different countries, acquiring different names as it spread: *Art Nouveau* in France, *Jugendstil* in Germany, *Sezessionstil* in Austria, *Liberty* in England, *Floreale* in Italy, *Modernismo* in Catalonia, *Tiffany* in the United States. In becoming a worldwide fashion, it was applied to a wide range of products (buildings, furniture, lamps, jewelry, everyday objects), enjoying great success among the public in a relative short timespan. Indeed, it provided the first heady celebration of the wedding of art with trade.[22]

The genesis and fortunes of the Modernist Movement could not have been more different. Right from its polemical outset, the movement was a distinctly academic phenomenon involving the sphere of intellectuals. It advocated a "superior" sort of taste that neither met with nor catered to public acclaim. Instead it preferred to acquire critical endorsement.

The adepts of the Modernist Movement expressed disdain for what was "fashionable" in the architecture and design of other schools, and this went hand in hand with their aim at spreading their own unshakable aesthetics, even among the vulgar ranks of the uncivilized. What they were promoting was not an airy-fairy imaginary future, but the ideology of modernity in the making, of a present that could be shaped in relation to designs for the future. Le Corbusier's concept of the *Ville Radieuse* was not supposed to be a futuristic utopia, but an ideal model to be adopted in order to solve the problems of urban development.

The Modernist wished to overcome the chaotic, anti-economic world of crafts production, and instead to design what was "rational," along the lines of mass production. The idea was to stop mass society from allowing all sorts of styles to proliferate and compete among themselves, as they had towards the end of the 1800s. In an age dominated by progress and technology, a "Taylorization" of desires was required in order to rein in and align tastes. To achieve this, according to Le Corbusier, the retrograde figure of the architect, with all his romantic myths, could not become the champion of the Great Revenge. This was the task of the engineer, who was free from stylistic fetters and fatuous ornament. He alone could "make human products resonate with the order of the universe,"[23] overcoming the individual foibles and the conditioning of history. Glorifying in the a-temporal pleasure of geometrical figures, the engineer could at last bring about the complete suppression of style, negating the very existence of comfort and the value of individual tastes.

This was tantamount to a radical turning point in the history of twentieth century taste. The apostle of the Modernist Movement had absolutely no interest in trying to arouse or convert the general public in their leanings. It was of little importance that the pavilion designed by Le Corbusier for the 1925 Paris Exhibition of Decorative Arts attracted very few visitors. There were loftier things at stake, because the role of the new aesthetics was to attend to the birth of a new era, an age marked by progress, by technics and reason. This redeeming mission underlay its claims to being infallible, its intolerance and the attitude of visionary paternalism that the acolytes of functionalism adopted when dealing with the philistine inclinations of simple souls.

The devotees of Modernism fought the good fight to "integrate the industrial proletariat into the urban community"[24] (such was the underlying ideology of the Bauhaus) in the name of "economic efficiency and instrumental rationality,"[25] in keeping with the dictates of the International Style that had found great favor in the United States. The basic idea was always the same: complete rejection of the regressive desires of ordinary people, and instead the enforcement of their own view of beauty, and the world in general.

The enlightened taste of the few was expressed in vitriolic terms against the wretched taste of the masses. There was no point in trying to attract or convert the vulgar; and no need for diplomacy in what amounted to a war of religion. The aesthetics of the Modernist Movement were thoroughly authoritarian, unheeding of ordinary people's ideas because their very desires and gratifications were considered deplorable.

It was a dialogue of the deaf. In the *querelle* between enlightened and vulgar taste the question was not the right to possess certain commodities, but their aesthetic accessibility. Desire and imagination could easily overcome any material barriers, so these were not central to the debate. In their place, however, there were well-traced cultural boundaries dividing unrefined tastes from those upheld by the Modernists, which would have appeared totally incomprehensible and unacceptable to those not "in the know." The supporters of refined or educated taste made no effort to win over the "unenlightened," and instead focused their attention on achieving spiritual supremacy. The important thing was to exercise control over the education of taste and the production of style: in other words, the universities and academies, where the Modernist Movement was to exercise a crushing ideological supremacy.

As Hume had predicted, in mass society the arbiters of taste were to be few in number: architects, designers, gallery owners, art critics, fashion designers. To exercise and perpetuate this oligopoly, they had to impose their role as the high priests of beauty and make others feel like lesser beings.

Wherever people were free to choose for themselves according to their own predilections and foibles there could only be bad taste, in other words items so far removed from the lofty echelons of the enlightened that they necessarily belonged to the wretched sphere of shameful hideosity.

Such was the aesthetic paradox of the 1900s. By challenging common opinion and trampling on most people's sensibilities, educated aesthetics rejected shared tastes and established a distance between itself and the naïve but reassuring world of what people actually claimed to like, transforming its symbols and undermining its intrinsic scale of values. This radical divide became a feature of the entire century, with highbrow culture taking a stand as far removed as possible from the noisy vulgarity of the hoi polloi.

For a long time, the middle classes as well as the petite bourgeoisie looked upon the bare, spare taste of modernity with the utmost suspicion, preferring traditional styles for their own dwellings. Indeed, the new aesthetics only began to gain in impact when architects started persuading builders to adopt Modernism as the most "rational" way to shape metropolitan development. The tyranny of Modernism was thus responsible for the concrete and glass tower blocks that housed not only factories and offices, but also people's homes, thereby disfiguring cities and creating horrible outskirts without ever managing to tame and manipulate people's tastes.

The aesthetics of Modernism were dull, desolate and repetitive in their linear purity, better suited to hospitals and prisons than to real people's homes. Yet they held sway in a remarkable fashion, purporting to embody an abstract Platonic ideal that everyone was supposed to embrace. It is hard to explain just how a series of hideous buildings, uninhabitable houses, unlivable districts and furniture better suited to mutants can possible have influenced generations of architects and designers so deeply. Interior design had come to mean products for "men redesigned as cubes, and women redesigned as spheres."[26] Or equipment for masochists such as the chairs that "hold the human frame as if in permanent traction; they bruise human skin each time one skirts too closely to them," [27] rip the clothes of whoever uses them, and require the help of a physiotherapist when the unfortunate sitter finally decides it is time to get up. To say nothing of the back-breaking beds that challenge human physiology and patience, the "modern clocks and watches that captivate the eye, but don't tell the time; the educational toys that our children hate; water pitchers that titillate your visual perception while wetting your pants."[28] How on earth was it possible that a taste utopia of this sort managed to take root in society, redesigning our everyday reality?

The Modernist Movement gained ground thanks to the shock that came in the wake of the democratization of luxury, the desire to defend artistic independence and the prerogatives of the intellectual caste, the determination never to give in to the meretricious matrimony between art and mass society. Yet this is still not sufficient to explain the degree and extension of the success of Modernism.

Architects could easily have adopted a different approach to further their taste supremacy. Without putting themselves to too much trouble, if they had simply manipulated traditional elements of style in order to create impressive make-believe environments, even on an industrial scale, they would have elicited enormous admiration on the part of potential clients and those who looked on from afar. Indeed, this was precisely what a few of their fellows did, drawing critical sneers from those in the know, and enthusiastic acclaim on the part of the public: forty years after its construction, the picturesque lakeside village of Port Grimaud, designed by the prophet of "vernacular architecture" François Spoerry, is still one of the most visited "monuments" in France.

So why did the Modernist Movement choose a more difficult path, challenging the dominant taste of the time and eliciting general incomprehension? The obvious answer would seem to be that Modernism by definition could hardly have chosen a different route.

The essential ingredient of the Movement was the myth of progress, which fueled the underlying ideology and pumped up its visionary impact. The idealization of technology and the absolute faith professed in reason both seemed to point towards a glorious future, one in which town planners would provide the key to untold possibilities and important change. All this was very much part of the cultural design of Functionalism, to the extent that "it would have been inconceivable without modern technology just as Christianity would have been without the symbol of the cross."[29]

Le Corbusier himself invited the unseeing architects of his day to admire the imposing mechanical totems of the modern age: airplanes, steamships, automobiles. Even people's homes were considered *machines à habiter*, thereby underlining the irrelevance of any criterion that was not strictly related to the efficiency required by the pressing needs of progress.

Yet among the aesthetics that heralded the future, the aerodynamic style of streamlining that met with widespread acclaim in the United States between the 1930s and the 1950s not only competed with Modernism on its own ground, but also proved to be infinitely more eloquent and incisive in the way it contributed to the idea that objects fashioned in a particular style could actually embody and promote the popular cult of progress.

Unlike Modernism, streamlining was fortunate in appealing to everyone right from the outset. But then it was designed to gratify and be successful, by stimulating consumption following the Great Depression of 1929. Those who promoted streamlining were very different to the Modernists in background: as a designer, Norman Bel Geddes was an eclectic visionary who came from the world of advertising, which offered rules and guile that could be adopted and adapted to understand and cater to people's tastes. Far from being an academic indoctrination conceived along the lines of the Bauhaus, streamlined design was the art of salesmanship mixed with the aesthetics of profit, "an alliance between popular mechanics and the psychology of advertising,"[30] in which form no longer derived from function, but was used to transform the product by means of attractive packaging. The aerodynamic lines of the product were simply a stylistic expedient, often completely lacking in any functional justification, which invested industrial products, from steamships to pencil sharpeners, with the seal of progress. And this was enough to spread the myth further and wider.

The American dream to which everyone paid happy tribute was projected in the tailfin of the Chevrolet, in the rounded fronts of locomotives and toasters, in the streamlined outline of motorboats and irons, and in the convex casing of the jukebox and the Vespa. According to the collective illusion, the there was nothing to stop people shaping the future, furthering progress and improving their own social condition. Why be happy with what you are, with what you have and what you know? Mass individualism, that strange oxymoron, was there to forge the destinies and desires of the industrialized Western world of the twentieth century.

Both Modernism and streamlining affected a very wide range of everyday objects, some of which acquired their intrinsic identity by means of such stylistic elements. The Modernist Movement drew special inspiration from the chair, that simplest and most Spartan of everyday objects. By contrast, streamlining achieved its apotheosis in relation to the product that best embodied dreams of future happiness, or indeed social envy: the automobile. The chair did at least respond to a physiological need, and was in one way or another already part of ordinary households, without necessarily suggesting idleness, luxury or waste. But the automobile was something very different, a "compensatory fetish" that fueled exhibitionism and competitive emulation, symbolizing opulence, aggressiveness, narcissism and sexual prowess.

For the Puritan spirits of functionalism, the gleaming, streamlined automobile bodywork fashionable in America in the 1940s and 1950s represented the most despicable depths of consumer hell, a metal leviathan that the advocates of good design chose to condemn outright: "In its monumental size and showy shape, the customized car, a monster of luxury and speed, was the very symbol of kitsch."[31] Streamlining paid exclusive homage to the seduction of what things looked like, to increasing a product's exchange value. By suggesting what was futuristic rather than harking back to the past, it thus ratified the restoration of ornament in everyday objects. Discerning taste could never accept the fatuous nature of streamlining, denying that such objects could belong to the selective sphere of design. Streamlining was no real industrial art, but simply a form of styling that had nothing to do with functional requirements.

Yet styling ultimately proved to be the meeting point between modern design and popular taste, a repository full of desires that was poles apart from the rigors of Functionalism. In the history of design, it represented the payback of the market, promoting an aesthetics of the present with which the consumer could identify. The concept of comfort was thus recovered, modernized and invested with symbolic and psychological values so that it could act as a gauge for desired and acquired wellbeing.

To Modernist Movement diehards, all this sounded like utter blasphemy. In their view, functionalist design was to streamlining what ethics was to cosmetics. The cult of "beautiful form," the seduction of appearances, and gratification of the eye all took design back to the dark age of Mannerism and ostentation, sinking what had been a noble project in the slough of the "commercial arts," like futile fashion shows. Indeed, styling was but a capricious imitation of fashion characterized by similarly facile, short-lived appearances.

This explains why it was rejected by critics and never really managed to compete with Modernism in terms of cultural stature. Streamlining was too emphatic, too commercial and too easy, just as certain music—especially jazz—was judged to be too catchy. Indeed, streamlining was a parody in bad faith of the austere aesthetics of true design, the very apocalypse of good taste:

> for quite a while, the principle of streamlining was extended, as though it were a principle of modernity, to shape totally immobile objects such as radios, irons or hairdryers. Over and above any considerations regarding mass communication, much of the styling that changed the shape of objects went only skin deep, and aimed solely at promoting consumption. In so far as manufacturers and designers continued to consider product design as a form of publicity rather than an intrinsic design process, ornament and bodywork maintained the upper hand, often giving rise to a triumph of chrome parts and blinking lights that projected the image of a status symbol that built-in obsolescence was soon to banish to the realms of kitsch.[32]

Thus the myth of progress is not enough to explain the Modernist Movement's aesthetic fundamentalism and icy composure. Nor can it account for the pulpit from which the Modernists expounded their cultural hegemony, unheeding of the congregation's evident disinterest. Only the Modernist Movement was invested with aesthetic authority, an acknowledgment that was denied to the promoters of streamlining, or indeed to the supporters of Art Nouveau and Art Deco, despite their efforts to make products more appealing to consumers.

The criticism leveled at "consumer aesthetics" revolved around the fact that they were contaminated by desires, by values that had nothing to do with appropriate form. In this sense they were impure, justifying the application of the *conventio ad excludendum* that already held sway in the fine arts: to appraise an industrial product, instead of turning to stylistic analysis or critical judgment, the point of reference became the phenomenology of taste. This alone could decide whether the object in question belonged to the realms of good design, or should instead be relegated to the realms of inferior sensibility, with no claim to artistic merit. This in its turn depended on how the object elicited pleasure: as the result of an aesthetic judgment, which implied the presence of "true," and thereby pure, contemplative beauty; or as the fruit of the taste for pleasure, which was no better as an appetite than the desire for bingeing or fashion.

The ideological supremacy of the Modernist Movement was able to hold undisputed sway through to the last quarter of the century[33] on account of the fact that it paid due homage to this principle, the only one still fashionable in the applied arts.

Despite the declarations of intent pronounced by its gurus, Modernism was far from saving money or the environment. Indeed, it was responsible for economic waste and ecological failure, founding not a science, but an ideology. As a result, it promoted an aesthetic, but not a technique.

Far from banishing beauty, the preconceived rejection of ornament was supposed to provide access to it, to a world that was diaphanous and purified, in keeping with the precepts of Romantic culture. This was deemed to be the only way to rescue industrial objects from their everyday ordinariness, and to imbue them with an aura of art.

In a famously critical essay, Peter Blake takes a close look at the premises and illusions underlying the ideology of Modernism.[34] The myth of purity, which Blake considers the third axiom of the Movement, could never have acted as the inspiration for an applied art if it had not been able to rely on the solemn paradigm relating to the sublimation of taste and the eradication of pleasure. By availing itself of its well-established prestige, the dreary aesthetics of the Modernist Movement were able to attract proselytes and claim cultural superiority over all competitors. At the same time, however, the myth of purity was to compromise its own future by imposing a number of strict restraints: to rise above the vulgarity of trade, to escape the stylistic obviousness of consumer culture, to repress the desire to succumb to the market, all products had to be carefully "decontaminated" and cleansed of the desire for hoarding. Cool, detached contemplation was the only answer: a curious approach to objects made to be sold.

If any of the prophets of Modernism had happened to read Kant's *Critique of Judgment*, they would no doubt have agreed with the philosopher's adage according to which the ultimate end of beauty is to arouse "the self-esteem . . . that raises us above pleasure." Suffice it to replace the term "pleasure" with "comfort," in the sense of private ease and public vanity, to find the perfect moral and theoretical justification for puritanical paternalism applied to industrial design.

Modernism thus brought about the most rigorously Kantian aesthetics ever applied to everyday objects, pursuing an ideal of beauty that was spectral, lofty, unattractive and lacking in any purpose other than the abstract beatification of function. Any aesthetic gratification deriving from this state of affairs could only be formal and detached.

Clearly the influence of Le Corbusier contributed to this state of affairs, especially in the thoroughly Kantian distinction between the pleasures of the senses and the feelings of the intellect. To add to which there was also the banishment of color. "Every human manifestation requires a certain *quantum* of interest, especially in the aesthetic field; this interest is sensorial and intellectual in nature. Decoration is a primary sensorial experience, like color, and as such is well suited to simple peoples, to peasants and savages. Harmony and proportion arouse the intellect, drawing the attention of the educated man. Peasants like ornament and paint frescoes. Civilized gentlemen wear English suits and possess easel paintings and books."[35]

This explains why two centuries after the invention of aesthetics, the division of tastes continued to exercise its draconian influence over discrimination between predilections, where beauty is contrasted with desire, pure with commercial, plain with comfortable.

According to the egalitarian ideals of the Enlightenment, "contemplation at a distance" was supposed to guarantee the universal separation of aesthetic pleasure from the actual possession of the commodities, in other words from social rank. But this tenet was then turned upside down when distance became the means by which the social and cultural élite could separate themselves from the vulgarity of common taste.

The aversion towards the deplorable leveling of tastes was to be even more dramatic in the sphere of the "fine arts." Indeed, in the twentieth century the term itself came to be considered archaic.

The Gallery of Iconoclasms

In the history of taste, no battlefield has been more ferocious, cruel and devastating than that of modern art. No other expression of culture has exceeded the avant-garde art movements of the twentieth century in disconcerting the common conception of beauty by inflicting outrage, derision and invective. It was a battle of tastes that proved to be uniquely traumatic, dismissive and venomous.

The production of art in the twentieth century brought about a drastic caesura with respect to all earlier ages. The sacrificial victim and target of polemics was the Enlightenment idea of socially shared beauty, such that taste, that particular sensation able to activate and appraise aesthetic perception, was belittled, derided and excluded.

In mass society, taste migrated from the fine arts, where it was born and nurtured, to the arts of what was pleasant, shaped by commerce, show, emotions and amusement. As for *good* taste, that self-satisfied privilege of being able to refine one's capacity to recognize valuable commodities, it was turned upside down: the stolid, dreary pleasure of agreeing with the general perception of what was deemed "beautiful" was transformed into acclaimed disgust. Art refused to have anything to do with the commercialization and mechanization of beauty, rightly perceiving that it was no longer able to operate according to its own traditional precepts.

The extraordinary but inevitable consequence was that art divorced from aesthetics, which was relegated to the attic: only one and a half centuries after its invention, it had become obsolete and useless. When art was no longer able to arouse the sense of beauty, or rather deliberately refused to do so, aesthetics became pointless, unable to understand the inner workings and cultural impact of a new, alienating form of artistic production. In what was later to be described as the "civilization of the image," the cult of beauty was to be celebrated elsewhere, largely through photography and television. What came to be worshipped was a certain ingeniously projected image of the human body, as personified by movie stars, top models, bunny girls and Miss Whatevers. In consumer society, beauty began to show itself in puerile forms, at least according to the defenders of highbrow culture, even in the pre-packaged emotions of the entertainment industry. Art would have nothing to do with all of this: it was not concerned with the fate of beauty, but had other things to keep it busy. As for aesthetics, it was to become a branch of archeology, an approach to studying the vestiges of earlier ages and civilizations, or a way of thinking about individual choices.

Once alienated from aesthetics, the art of the twentieth century was no longer the object of collective devotion, and instead became an initiation rite that was to discriminate against the tastes of the masses, to challenge people's ability to comprehend, and to mock their primitive sensibilities. In an age dominated by communication, modern art expressed itself through events rather than works. Scandal, paradox, profanation and enigma became central to its being. No longer a moment of celebration for society, it turned everything upside down by means of criticism: the critique of the values, aesthetic conventions and ideological premises that had hitherto glorified the great artifice of beauty.

Unique in its historical development and aims, modern art was born with the explicit intention of *not pleasing*, of being a sight for sore eyes, of offending the sensibilities of the average beholder, denying the common sense of what art was all about. Since the invention of the figurative meaning of taste, people had believed that aesthetic experience was the ultimate goal and purpose of works of art. Secularity had triumphed as art gained independence, so that sacred subject matter had begun to waver. As a result, the social function and ideological justification for art revolved around spiritual elevation achieved by means of the gratification of the senses. This was the edifying paradigm rejected by the modern school, which opted to spread its own word by means of a utopia based on desecration.

Therein lies the "scandal" of modern art: in the rejection of outer beauty as ideal inspiration and in the denial of its value as a shared criterion for the transfer and validation of works of art.

Ordinary people from ordinary backgrounds with ordinary tastes began to feel they could not understand art already in the 1800s. The term "avant-garde" was borrowed from military usage to refer to the most recent trends in art, the works that went well beyond what was obvious, reassuring, tried and tested. It was nurtured by the myth of the bohemian artist whose life was governed by his creative demon, a figure unheeding of the opinion of his contemporaries because his gift to posterity was visionary genius. Thus Van Gogh came to symbolize the painter-hero, scorned in his own lifetime and hugely admired following his death. At more or less the same time, the phenomenon of *Kitsch* first came to the fore, a source of naïve pleasure for common people and an abomination of taste for more refined palates. What was *Kitsch* was cheap and obvious, something that catered to those whose

sense of the aesthetic was non-existent or underdeveloped. Art thus ceased
to be a single, coherent, consolidated and shared heritage. Even among the
prosperous classes, it came to signify something that was complicated and
difficult, the object of violent passions and bitter polemics.

The criteria for appreciating works of art inevitably began to vacillate.
One of the most emblematic chapters in this development regarded the
querelle concerning what was "finished." During the nineteenth century, the
art market spread to embrace "a large and undiscriminating public, interested
only in small pictures, either of genre or depicting an affecting story, and,
above all, highly 'finished'."[36] Meticulous definition of detail thus became
the guarantee of "painterly work," a sort of instructions sheet attached to
the artistic product: "the *fini*, or 'finish,' provided evidence of work, and
work was what appealed to the newly enriched middle classes as opposed to
the spendthrift aristocracy; moreover, 'finish,' by reducing the role of the
imagination and the part required of the spectator, was a safe, easily
verifiable means of judging the value of a work of art (aesthetically as well
as financially) for those without educated taste."[37]

At this point clearly there were two conceptions of art, according to
whether an individual claimed to be *tekhne* or *poēsis*. The former implied
naivety and backwardness, meaning that the painter was still considered
simply an artisan endowed with a manual technique that called for practice
and effort. Thus a portrait or a landscape could be no more than ornamental
objects, the product of well-established rules and parameters. The latter, on
the other hand, involved élitist sophistication, and a perception of the artist,
like the poet of antiquity, as a person imbued with supernatural inspiration
who could transfer their creativity to his canvases. Collectors thus acquired
items that embodied true originality, products whose value was proportionate
to the stylistic distance separating them from earlier works. In essence, the
work of art was merely an imperfect projection of the artist's genius, which
made it secondary in relation to the personality of the artist himself.

During the 1800s, however, this contraposition still responded to the
traditional dynamics of "emulation/differentiation" that turned up in many
other spheres as well, especially that of fashion. A taste for what was strange
and original was deemed to be the proper inclination of the connoisseur, the
educated mind able to appreciate an elevated aesthetic order, in other words
true beauty, in advance of ordinary people. Granted, the masses were likely
to catch up later, as the enormous success of Impressionism, despite its
distinctly innovatory character, went to show.

Only during the 1900s did avant-garde art take on the role of preconceived
rejection of aesthetics as an obligatory approach to the reception of art.
Repellent in form, disconcerting in content and irreverent in style, the
modern genre came up with the same line time and again in its efforts to
provoke scandal, appear inaccessible and undermine the aura traditionally
recognized as belonging to works of art: "the decadence of the bourgeoisie
was accompanied by rapture, which became an asocial school of behavior
in contrast with amusement. In effect, the Dadaist manifestations allowed

for distinctly violent amusement, turning the work of art into a scandal. The work of art was supposed to satisfy a need: that of arousing public indignation."[38]

The manifesto of this spirit of desecration was a carefully organized event that was designed to shock: Marcel Duchamp's urinal, exhibited under the title *Fountain* in 1917. The then 30-year-old Duchamp was considered by his older brothers, who were well-known artists, to be so little gifted as a painter that they tried to discourage him in his efforts to make a career for himself in this field. What he lacked in talent, however, he made up for in temperament, and an indomitable spirit of revenge that led him to send a urinal purchased from a plumber's hardware store as his entry for the Salon of Independent Artists in New York under the pseudonym Richard Mutt. At the time Duchamp was also part of the organizing committee, and when his fellow committee members rejected the work, judging it to be a practical joke,[39] Duchamp actually resigned. Moreover, he later published an enthusiastic critique of the work in the review *The Blind Man*, of which he happened to be the director.

Without this providential media redemption, the "scandal" would probably have passed unobserved, as indeed did the original work, which ended up in a public waste dump. In this Duchamp proved his worth, at least as a forerunner of future trends. Having moved in artistic circles, and being a natural showman, he managed to turn what was basically a flop into a "case," recovering the item from the cemetery of cultural trash and turning it into a totem of contemporary art. From this moment on, the resonance of a work of art became part and parcel of its value. Henceforth, for a contemporary artist "the worst setback was not to be insulted, rejected or mocked, but to be ignored. True discredit was no longer measured in terms of scorn, but in terms of silence and disregard."[40]

With Duchamp the legend of the rebel artist gained momentum, the image of the visionary hero who took the mickey out of the establishment, thereby initiating a completely new way of conceiving art. This was a matter of breaking "the rules in order to introduce derision as an artistic value, and iconoclasm as a creative tool."[41]

Duchamp's *Fountain* was an artistic event in the mocking shape of a paradox that was both aesthetic and intellectual. It amounted to a hugely important statement that was to have enormous repercussions in the art world, contributing more than any other single work of the early twentieth century to undermining the conviction that the only validation principle of art should be aesthetics. If it was sufficient to take the lowliest of everyday objects, turn it end upwards, sign it, date it and give it a title in order to place it as a sculpture in an exhibition, then the value of art was irreparably illusory, conventional and fictitious. Clearly what turned an object into a work of art was not the skill of the artist, but the eye of the duly indoctrinated beholder. In a word, as Duchamp himself was to declare, "it is the beholder who makes a picture," and taste is no more than "a habit, the repetition of something already accepted."

This "demonstration" nevertheless contains a shaky premise: the urinal can pretend to be a sculpture, but is obviously not one in point of fact. "It was apparently shown that aesthetic contemplation and gratification implied nothing other than an act of faith. Once this demonstration was over, the conviction itself inevitably proved to be self-destructive. To know that a snow shovel is a work of art simply means being informed of the fact. But to believe it is absurd, because it means acknowledging the magic of the artist and succumbing to the enchantment of the fetish."[42]

And yet, like a self-fulfilling prophecy, right from the outset Duchamp acted as though he were a sort of Midas capable of turning pottery into gold, an anonymous, mass-produced object into a masterpiece. It was not so much that anyone really had to believe in it, but that everyone should behave as though it were true. As in many other episodes of modern art, what really mattered was the echo of the scandal, which had got off to a slow start and only later proved its worth.

Part intellectual game and part aesthetic provocation, the diabolical, defiant seduction of Duchamp owed much to the way he rallied unceasingly with new expedients and contrivances. He set himself up as the doyen of profanation and rebellious ecstasy, a man capable of turning the concept of painting upside down, of professing aesthetic nihilism with a touch of excremental, necrophilic hyperbole,[43] of making outré statements as an act of liberation and an expression of the myth of the *maudit* artist. Duchamp's scorn for manual talent with brushes and color (which he described as "olfactory masturbation"), his mocking pity for works that tried to elicit sensorial pleasure (*ars retinica*), his gratuitous delight in puns and wordplay, his view of creative sterility as voluntary exile from the world of art, his pseudo-scientific charlatanism regarding the pictorial portrayal of the "fourth dimension" and the esoteric wit of his main works all contributed to the fact that his ineffable monuments to nothingness actually lasted for the whole of the twentieth century, like impregnable fortresses that resisted the assault of interpretation. Such was the legacy of the man some considered a genius,[44] and others deemed an impostor[45]—a paradox common to much of the art of the twentieth century.

The unpopularity of avant-garde art was part and parcel of its iconoclastic nature. It deliberately created an abyss between the wide world of the uninitiated and the select circles of those in the know, a divide that was to grow deeper and wider in the course of time.

Before Dada it was the experts—art critics, painting juries, academic big-wigs—who decried the anathema of the whatever in modern art and judged in outrage that it didn't deserve to be called art. The public at large—the crowd of laymen—for the most part abstained from such legislating judgment (for which it didn't have the political means anyway), but it showed through its interest that it perceived some of the social issues at stake in modern art, and thus, that it by no means held modern art as just anything whatever. After Dada (or after its reception, its "recuperation"), things were reversed. Since the experts—at least those who legislate over current artistic practice—proselytize ceaselessly their interest in contemporary art, whose name "art," they seek to justify on the basis of all the qualities that make it anything but whatever. And the public at large has lost all interest in art. Deaf to the explanations of the experts, it persists in seeing in contemporary art a huge whatever to which it remains indifferent.[46]

Duchamp called his works "*ready-mades*" because they did not require any manual input on the part of the artist, apart from the mocking "corrections." Like the famous urinal, they consisted of objects selected from the prosaic world of functional products removed from their original context, so that their intrinsic function became entirely useless. The idea was to disorientate viewers, undermine their aesthetic "superstitions" and accentuate the degree to which convention guided all judgments of taste: "*Ready-mades* are of greater critical and philosophical interest than they are of sculptural importance. It would be useless to discuss their beauty or ugliness: they are beyond beauty or ugliness. They are not works of art, but question marks or denials placed before these works."[47]

Official hagiography has underlined the demystification implicit in the *ready-made*, claiming that Duchamp used three-dimensional paradoxes to make fun of aesthetic conventions, thereby denying the role of contemplation and taste in the enjoyment of art.[48] In rejecting the reification of art,[49] Duchamp refused to gratify the sense of beauty,[50] and instead transformed art into intellectual anagrams.[51] Certainly no artist of the 1900s had greater impact on the anti-aesthetic tendency of modern art.

Granted, once the outré art of Duchamp had pulled the chain[52] on the age-old ideal of Beauty, what remained was disconcertingly sterile. Following extended exile from the art scene, his work became electively hermetic, solipsistic, deliberately incomprehensible and intent only on provoking objections on the part of those very viewers who were supposed to "make the picture."

And yet, as the inventor of the *ready-made*, Duchamp earned himself a place in history as the high priest of the iconoclasts. It was they who allowed him to overcome the barrier of anonymity and acquire miraculous powers that were far beyond what he could have hoped for as a lesser exponent of the widely scorned "retinal" art. In his conceptual ascent, Duchamp inaugurated a new genre founded on collective autosuggestion, on witting mystification and paradoxical tautology. "According to Duchamp, the artist was no longer defined by the nature of his works, but because he was recognized as an artist, a being able to make an object artistic thanks to the power of his signature, invested with belief in his artistic nature, just as— according to Mauss—the witch-doctor was not defined by the nature of his deeds, but thanks to the fact that he was recognized as a sorcerer, a being able to make a given deed efficacious solely in virtue of the power of a ritual, invested with credence in its magical nature."[53]

With its witchcraft, its "black masses" that defy naïve feelings regarding beauty, modern art thus ended up by resembling a modern theology,[54] which developed and spread thanks to sectarian logic. Like religious creeds, aesthetic conviction depended on oracles and prophecies, relics and exegesis, dogma and inquisition: "it is not only a question of accustoming the eye, but also of converting it."[55]

The repulsive heresies of the avant-garde (Duchamp's urinal, but also Malevitch's *Black Square* or Picasso's *Les Demoiselles d'Avignon*) set fire to the myth of Beauty: the Platonic, edifying, "disinterested," timeless beauty that Western culture had pursued for the previous twenty-five centuries. Yet modern art did not arise from the ashes of this particular bonfire.

Aesthetic vandalism merely paved the way for the founding epic, adding to the impact of the legend among acolytes and imitators. Modern art could only really get off the ground once the canonization procedures were under way. Before the rules of art, its communication, its shared terms and values could undergo any radical change, iconoclasm required museum status, with all due beatification of the heretics.

The cultural paradox of modern art consisted in the very transformation of iconoclasm into objects of iconolatry. How on earth was it possible that a product deliberately chosen to repel aesthetic perception should become an object of veneration? What explains the spread of an ideology that managed to introject iconoclasm as the only presentable new orthodoxy short of the absurdity of *Kitsch*?

In actual fact the few heartfelt critics of modern art who did raise their voices tended to be self-professed reactionaries (for instance, Ortega y Gasset, Coomaraswamy and Sedlmayr),[56] which meant that they were soon censured by modernist conformism. As for "politically correct" literature, it was only prepared to admit that in recent decades contemporary art had been excessively exhibitionist and academic, thereby losing edge and inventiveness.[57] To question the legends of Dadaism, Cubism, Abstract Art or Surrealism would have been a taboo. No one is apparently prepared to admit that the dissolution of modern art actually began one hundred years ago, when iconoclasm first burst onto the art scene. It is still there to this day, which explains the thread that ties Duchamp to Warhol, Klein, Arman, Christo, Burri, Fontana and Manzoni.

It is not the object of this book to provide a succinct account of these events. As far as the history of taste is concerned, however, what is interesting is the way the triumphal march of modern art gathered widespread acceptance. Just how did it come about that Western culture began to adulate something that set itself up as a severance, a breach, transforming what was supposed to be the negation of aesthetic indulgence into an object of cultural veneration?

The justification of iconoclasm involved an initial legitimation that was entirely ideological. Over and above any sporadic alliances with political movements (Suprematism and Bolshevism, Futurism and Fascism), in cultural terms the artistic avant-gardes of the early twentieth century shared the revolutionary ferment typical of that period. This explains the irreverent tone, the anti-bourgeois thrust and the anti-conformist impetus. It was but a short step to the aura of heroism and martyrdom attributed to those who fell in the name of a noble cause.

In the end, it was not so much the scandalous exhibitions that provided the avant-garde with its place in history as a derogatory show organized to denounce such art by the Nazi regime: "ironically, the century's most highly attended exhibition of advanced art was mounted as an attack on the new painting and sculpture. Over two million people visited the Exhibition of Degenerate Art (*Entartete Kunst*) in Munich, with crowds averaging more than 20,000 a day during the exhibition, which lasted from July 19 to November 30, 1937, extended from September due to the popular demand. Some came to see old friends, works confiscated from museums and marked for elimination. But most came to view the mental and moral degeneracy that National Socialism sought to eradicate, art so shocking that no children were allowed into the show."[58]

To compensate for this cultural holocaust, the guilty conscience of the West beatified modern art to a far greater degree than the artists themselves could ever have dared to hope. The success of the movement, both ideologically and commercially, owed a great deal to this moral stance. Once it had divested itself of its earlier revolutionary intent, the avant-garde kept up its aura of rebellion, but with little underlying substance. The outcome was a sort of self-referential *hortus clausus* that was politically innocuous, though not neutral: during the Cold War, in fact, it stood for the Western world.

Serge Guilbaut provides us with a meticulous reconstruction of the ideological and political background that allowed New York to oust Paris as the international art capital. "The unprecedented success on the national and international scene of the American avant-garde was not only based on aesthetic and stylistic phenomena, but also (and perhaps largely) on reasons that could be described as ideological resonance. I do not wish to claim, as certain authors have insinuated, that the post-war American avant-garde was incongruous or totally manipulated. Rather, that in the wake of the general enthusiasm, critics often neglected the aesthetic and political matters at stake in the definition of this style of painting."[59]

For the construction of the new American cultural identity, the imported myth of a rebellious, proud avant-garde that had become a victim of totalitarianism came in very handy. It was well suited to the image of a young, energetic, victorious nation that had finally freed itself of its earlier inferiority complex regarding the Old World because it now had a role in History as the champion of planetary freedom. The creative paroxysm of avant-garde art gained kudos by being indigenous, so that it was able to symbolize the values of individualism and liberalism essential to Western democracies, thereby investing the United States with an emblematic role as the bulwark of freedom.

During the immediate post-war years, various fashion magazines devoted their covers to the artistic avant-garde, a subject that also became the focus

of articles in periodicals devoted to the cultivation of the middle classes. The
famous feature on Pollock published in *Life* with the aim of making
American art sound like the best possible output in circulation[60] earned
itself a permanent place in the collective conscience of the United States,
creating a wave of unexpected national pride concerning that country's
artistic endeavor.

Clement Greenberg, the art critic who started out as an angry Trotskyist
and ended up as the most authoritative ideologist of the canonization of the
avant-garde in the United States, was also a talent scout for Abstract
Expressionism. His intellectual evolution was emblematic of the process of
"normalization" that modern art was in the process of undergoing. The
Greenberg cultural project was clearly expressed in a seminal article
published in an influential radical review in 1939.[61] His argument was based
on a triple equation. Good taste is opposed to bad taste just as avant-garde
art is opposed to commercial art (identified as kitsch), and freedom of
aesthetic judgment to ideological propaganda:

$$\frac{Cultivated\ taste}{Bad\ taste} = \frac{Avant\text{-}garde}{Kitsch} = \frac{Freedom}{Totalitarianism}$$

The cornerstone of Greenberg's stand lies in the zealous dualism with
which he opposes avant-garde and kitsch. This line of reasoning inevitably
has moral and political implications.

In Greenberg's view, the advent of the avant-garde should be viewed
within the cultural climate of the early 1900s, whose salient feature was
the demise of the principle of authority. The avant-garde took part in the
cultural ferment that encouraged the West to take a close critical look at
the certainties inherited from the past. The aesthetic equivalent of the
epistemological revolutions that led to the redefinition of the exact sciences,
the movement was like a form of deep introspection, an invitation to think
seriously about expressive abilities and conditions; a self-analysis that was
pictorial in idiom, rather than critical and philosophical.

For Greenberg, the paradox of modernity lays in the fact that the birth of
the avant-garde went hand in hand with the development of kitsch, a sort
of reverse mirror image. How could it be that the same civilization produced
both Eliot's poetry and audiocassette music, paintings by Braque and covers
by Norman Rockwell?

Greenberg traced the social origins of kitsch back to the changes brought
about by the process of industrialization and urbanization: the new cultural
habitat that tore the masses away from their traditional folklore brought
about a state of symbolic disorientation and loss, which in its turn led to a
demand for new cultural parameters in line with the commercialization of
culture itself. The naivety of taste of the masses greatly widened the customer
base for what was kitsch, since such people were attracted by forms of "art"
that were in actual fact bogus and simplified. The new symbolic ABC
supplied by the arts of entertainment also proved to be a remarkable aid to

persuasion and political compliance, which explains why the rhetoric of kitsch was adopted by both Hitler's Germany and Stalin's Soviet Union.

In view of its polar opposition to kitsch, in Greenberg's view the avant-garde acted as an antidote to the commercial prostitution and ideological exploitation of art. The mixing of morals with aesthetics led the author to declare that "the alternative to Picasso is not Michelangelo, but kitsch."[62] In this rose-tinted account, the avant-garde was like the teleological fulfillment of the Renaissance tradition, intent on furthering the independence and secularization of art, on freeing it of the rhetorical and celebrative functions with which it had been invested in the past. The myth that taste should be disinterested and "purely" receptive, intended during the Enlightenment as a defense of this historic process, thus came to be ascribed to the avant-garde as one of its merits. Indeed, Greenberg deemed abstract art to be practically uncontaminated by content as a function, which meant that it could not be accused of being ideologically manipulated.[63]

For Greenberg, taste was the receptor of avant-garde art. The difference with respect to the past lay in the fact that taste groped its way forward in exemplary solitude. Because it could no longer rely on the "instructions for use" that earlier canons of beauty had once provided,[64] it could solely depend on its own ineffable perspicacity.

Rather more Kantian than he was wont to admit, Greenberg was getting close to Hume when he upheld the indisputable nature of the critic's judgment (in other words, that the opinion of the recognized expert shaped the consensus of tastes). And when he argued that the advent of Abstractionism had made art self-aware, bent exclusively on the exploration of its own expressive potential and subject only to the constraints of canvas and color,[65] he was not far removed from Hegel.

Regardless of who his philosophical ancestors may effectively have been, Greenberg is the last important thinker to have tried to place modern art within an aesthetic paradigm of Enlightenment derivation. Unfortunately for him, only Cubism and Abstractionism came within his interpretative framework. The rest of the avant-garde eluded his inquiry, especially the thoroughly American trend that was soon to explode in the wake of the irreverent heritage of Dadaism: Pop Art.[66] In the face of all empirical evidence (public and critical acclaim, commercial success), in his work as a critic Greenberg did all he could to minimize its importance.

Harold Rosenberg, who was a contemporary of Greenberg's, clearly had a better grasp of modern art: the cults of the new and aesthetic heterodoxy[67] were what he judged to be the fundamental ingredients of the avant-garde cacophony. In his view, the task of modernity was to promote works of art that did not try to gratify taste (not even that of an enlightened critic like Greenberg), but to establish a break, to violate the aesthetic, conceptual and material barriers contained in earlier art. It was not only a question of abandoning the superstitions of the past. Following half a century of ups and downs, even the avant-garde had gathered a history of its own and established a tradition. The constant tension that urged it beyond the transitory arrival point was indeed the very engine of modernity: the cult of the new, which was the artistic equivalent of the myth of progress and the future that was replacing the broken idols of the old world.

Rosenberg was perhaps the first specialist—certainly the most influential— to come up with an explicit theory of the uselessness of aesthetics as a way of enjoying and validating modern art. The advent of the avant-garde had, in his view, revolutionized the way works of art were received. It was no longer possible to establish the value of a work by looking at it: to the uninitiated, modern art was intrinsically unattractive, irritating and enigmatic. There are plenty of works that cannot even be collected or shown: earthworks, for example. All that remained of art's onetime splendor was its self-satisfied gratuitousness, which was simply the symbolic opposite of an age dominated by efficiency and profit. Contemporary works were like a new sort of show, a happening that the artist, or *showman* (to use Rosenberg's term) used to attract proselytes, or viewers.

Modern art was thus poles apart from the Enlightenment aesthetic. It was the deliberate fruit of iconoclasm, in that it aimed at discrediting, profaning and sabotaging the edifying complaisance of aesthetic pleasure. In its efforts to make fun of naïve, shared tastes, it upset tame contemplation. In other words, it developed within the aesthetic paradigm in order to contest it in a crescendo of perceptual provocation:

> the transgression of the academic rules of representation on the part of Impressionism; the transgression of the codes of figuration by means of color on the part of Fauvism; then the creation of shapes on the part of Cubism; the transgression of the norms pertaining to figurative objectivity on the part of Expressionism; the transgression of humanist values on the part of Futurism, of the criteria of seriousness on the part of Dadaism, and of real possibility on the part of Surrealism; the transgression of the very need for figuration on the part of different forms of Abstractionism, starting with Suprematism and Constructivism, through to Abstract Expressionism: generation after generation, modern art upsets and betrays the established norms of art. And in so doing creates scandal.[68]

Regardless of Greenberg's declarations, the viewer could not be left to face the work of art alone because the viewer was simply not in a position to understand it. To appreciate a work of art called for instructions, and this meant expertise: an explanation of the artist's recondite intentions, and a certificate of originality. This cultural mediation redefined behavior regarding the perception of works of art: it was an exercise in intent, a painful initiation, an "aesthetic leap" into a parallel dimension, a quest into the ultimate essence and murky confines of art that was a goal in its own right.

In modernity, aesthetic agreement (the instant recognition of what is beautiful) was turned into an ontological challenge, which involved vacillating arguments about the nature of art, especially where no one ever previously presumed it to exist. The outcome was that the naïve taste for beauty was condemned as despicable, and the conventions of the past were upturned and mocked.

Modern art thus dictated the epilogue of aesthetics. It celebrated nothingness, rejecting the social consumption of beauty for which the Enlightenment had identified a faculty. Modern art required initiation, and was deliberately incomprehensible to the masses, who found in it nothing of aesthetic value. Though it may have created a scandal at the outset, in the course of time it lost its edge and became almost predictable in its ritual self-desecration.

One provocation after another, in time the principle of affront became a self-deceptive, self-referential convention. But then if the ultimate goal of the avant-garde is to make viewers think about the real essence of art, it is hard to imagine how the constantly repeated question can represent a shared criterion of appreciation: "the quality of a work cannot be measured in terms of the meaningfulness of the ontological questions it raises, since even an ugly picture can raise a debate of this sort. Moreover, the intrinsically fascinating question regarding the definition of art will only interest the philosopher of aesthetics, not the art lover or the critic. Lastly, the question itself is no more essential to the contemplation of a work of art than any other insoluble matter (for example, the meaning of time, of love, of truth, etc.)."[69]

Since the 1980s, a spirit of resignation has made itself felt among enthusiasts, such that contemporary art somewhat resembles the proverbial moonless night when everything looks much the same shade of black. Thinkers such as Belting, Danto and Morgan[70] have argued that the avant-garde has lost its purpose in the "delta of modernism," where everything is allowed and, with varying degrees of amusement, accepted.

Regardless of whether it is considered ritual suicide, cultural treachery or ideological fraud in grand style,[71] modern art eludes all classification (in Duve's view turning from concept into proper noun)[72] because it no longer has anything to communicate, other than its desperate need to survive and nurture its own myth.

Three centuries after the original, modern art seems to be reinventing the Don Quixote myth: just as this latter played on the discrepancy between events (the deeds of the hero) and meanings (a context in which those same deeds became grotesque) to present the collapse of the courtly epic, so modern art portrays the collapse of aesthetic experience, the disintegration of the underlying values and the failure of ideals that have no reason to exist in modernity. In its battle against the windmills, the avant-garde uses distortion, ugliness and derision of artistic beauty to mock aesthetic perception as a dated form of sensibility that relates to a defunct system of aspirations and representations.

The gallery of iconoclasms thus represents a way of processing loss. The conception of beauty as an allegory of beauty, a way of evoking ideals beyond sensorial perception (the sacred, power, human brotherhood, the bourgeois possession of the world) that has been definitively deposed, reviled and abolished. Rather than encouraging the spectator to look beyond what is obvious, conventional and reassuring, modern art tells a far more upsetting and painful tale: the disenchantment of looking, the loss of the shared sense of beauty, the fact that it is no longer possible to enjoy anything according to the rules that worked in the past. For thousands of years art did its best to "show off (present, exhibit, materialize) by means of a sensorial support (color, sound, stone) what was considered a superior truth,"[73] but this aim is now lost for ever. The burden of the sacred is undone, and in its place evanescent secularity weighs down on the shoulders of post-Enlightenment humanity in all his solitude. As for the artist, the latter bears emblematic witness to this change, but with detachment.[74]

A world that no longer has dreams to share unless they are part of a nightmare (the domination of technology, totalitarianism, world wars, genocides, arms of mass destruction) cannot express accepted forms of aesthetic devotion. Adorno predicted that after Auschwitz it was no longer possible to write poetry: in other words, just like in Don Quixote, there is no way to propose anew any edifying aesthetic without appearing ridiculous. There is nothing to celebrate other than the ephemeral myths of consumer society; nothing that can move us to the devoted detachment and sense of sacredness that Beauty (as an absolute idea) can induce; nothing indeed that can warrant the arcane and paralyzing experience of the Sublime.

In an era dominated by technology and information, reality seems to have nothing to hide, nothing that cannot be understood, calculated and programmed. It is as though Hegel's prophecy had come true: once humanity reaches the height of its spiritual progress, it loses the state of innocence that allowed it to contemplate the world aesthetically, such that the need for art is no more.

Looking backwards, the appearance of aesthetics in Western culture comes across as a casual, short-lived event: before the eighteenth century, art had goals other than simply gratifying the eye of the viewer. One and a half centuries later, the dissolution of art seems to mark the end of an age and a utopia.

In Kant, the inheritance of Enlightenment ideals in the definition of the aesthetic event is as clear as can be, not least in view of the way he attributes universality to a faculty of judgment that was really the outcome of social privilege. Aesthetics sanctioned the democratization of tastes, which had hitherto been the prerogative of the court, and the spirit of the French Revolution brought about the ensuing symbolic expansion. What did extending the flag of 1789 and the cry of "Liberté, Égalité, Fraternité" to the sphere of taste really mean? Desiring the superfluous was evidently a form of Liberté, and the contemplation of beauty a sublimated version of this. Égalité meant giving everyone the right to enjoy the pleasures of this same beauty. And Fraternité stood for the sharing of taste, which accounted for the edifying, collective nature of the phenomenon.

In mass society, these achievements come across as obvious, to the extent that they are relegated to the constantly expanding realm of what is pleasurable. If cultural entertainment has become accessible to everyone, then there is no longer any need for beauty, at least for the sort of beauty that transcends individual sensibility and affects the shared human spirit.

In processing this loss, the edifying contemplation of beauty can only survive in the form of nostalgia: this explains the tendency to admire the relics of the past, still subject to the dictates of Romanticism and the Enlightenment. For example, in 2001, the West was shocked by the destruction of the gigantic statues of Buddha in a desert torn by religious enmity, perceiving this as a crime against the (aesthetic) dignity of human kind. The entire planet thus becomes a sort of living nativity scene, a heritage to protect, a show to eternalize, where natural beauty and works of art coexist, just as Kant would have wanted.

As a museum, however, it is sterile: there can be no introduction of new products, conceived, constructed and enjoyed according to universally accepted rules. A permanent schism has come about between the meaning of the art of the past and that of the present, which looms over us, insensitive and ineluctable. Modernity has disowned Beauty like a deposed deity; in its stead there is a constellation of minute events, a kaleidoscope of transient aesthetic models whose only possible archetype and parameter is fashion, the ephemeral art of vanity. The aesthetics of modernity is subject to the same frenzied rhythms, the same capricious temporality: everything is subjective, short-lived and unconvincing. Instead of the icy discipline of awe, we have the heady tyranny of seduction.

Beauty has been deposed in favor of a new catalyst of sensibility: Style. The real outcome of the autonomy achieved by art is the transformation of aesthetics into the frenzied production of signs that flutter into our consciences and make their presence felt without requiring any center of gravity or direction. Taste is no longer the faculty for recognizing an abstract ideal, a shared goal towards which all ages in history were supposed to draw closer. It is Style that commands, the prototype of all individual predilections: gratuitous, revocable, and yet at the same time irresistible and inexplicably contagious.

Why Style? Because taste looks to Style for individuality, for the relic that seems authentic in a world of shiny, prefabricated fakes. The idealization of style amounts to a symbolic tribute to the individual, a protected species in mass society, a talisman against mechanization, mass production and the alienation of the modern world.

A bottle-carrier, a torn canvas, what seems to be a can of soup, a wrapped building or a mound of trash obviously have no claim to arouse a sense of beauty. A caustic celebration of the discomfort of civilization, they stand for the refusal to submit to conformism, and as such are bearers of style, without which they would never have been noticed, let alone considered works of art. They have to be the original article, however, rather as other memorabilia are sought at auctions simply because they once belonged to celebrities. In other words, their value resides in the fact that they came from an artist, and has nothing to do with how they are made.

The "transitive principle" of the artistic aura gained strength from the object's power to shock and surprise. Duchamp was well aware of this when he first proposed his *ready-made*: the magic wand for turning a banal functional item into a work of art was style, which allowed him to exploit one original idea, thereby justifying a form of plagiarism that inevitably led to creative sterility.

The contemporary artist was no longer expected to be able to draw or paint, but to be original. As with Don Quixote, the traditional canons of artistic beauty became farcical when applied to the present. The outlawing of kitsch ratified the displacement between a declining cultural mythology and a new world that embraced the ban while knowing it to be insufficient. Thus Dorfles could preach the divorce between artistic "talent" and "taste": the latter alone could inspire a style, while in its pursuit of a conventional ideal of beauty the former inevitably ended up in mannerism. The technically perfect but soulless work of Pietro Annigoni, official portraitist to Queen Elizabeth ("an academic work whose 'pleasantness' and skill are not sufficient to make up for the lack of a contemporary 'taste' or style"),[75] is thus stigmatized in favor of the crude primitivism of Jean Dubuffet, "a deformation of what is figurative in which the 'unpleasantness' of the image is justified by the topicality of the 'taste' and the technique involved."[76]

By the same token, no painting by Picasso can reasonably be considered "beautiful," although his output—at least from the Cubist period on—undoubtedly reveals distinct personality. The works of Warhol or Lichtenstein cannot claim to be "beautiful" either, but they are certainly not short of originality: a mere glance is sufficient to recognize them. The criteria for judging art thus undergo radical transformation. The true object of veneration is no longer the work, but the celebrity artist. And if style is the indelible mark of his individuality, his work will become "a highly refined visiting card":[77] "for modern viewers, the work acquires meaning only when it refers to subjectivity, becoming a pure and simple expression of individuality: a unique style that does not try to mirror the world, but to create an imaginary world within which the artist acts. Though we may be allowed to enter this world, it in no way pretends to be a universe that is shared *a priori*."[78]

The ousting of beauty and the enthronement of style are symptomatic of a wide phenomenon that has shaped Western sensibilities in the age of massification: the idolatry of individuality, and its transformation into an object of collective worship.

Well before Coco Chanel, Greta Garbo or Elvis Presley, modern art gave rise to the modern myth of individuality. Before the phenomena of emulation promoted by fashion labels and the collective hysteria unleashed by the stars of show business, avant-garde art had already started to glorify individuality, thereby preparing the way for much of the behavior typical of the society of frivolity: the bawdy-house of celebrities, and the surrogate for holiness in a secular mass society. Art was to lend this cult of the profane its workshop and testing ground. By establishing a new form of aesthetic production and reception, art thus prepared the way for the history of modern taste because it wielded the power to create artifacts for exhibition. No other activity was better suited to shaping the social consumption of images.

The 1900s were not only the century of the avant-garde movements, that is, of the loss of the edifying sense of beauty. They were also the century that witnessed the triumph of Style: that aura of singularity that raises us above everyday ordinariness, the symbolic antidote to the mechanization of the world, the new hypnotic source of the seduction of tastes. This phenomenon found its most evident expression in fashion, which it easily transcended to establish a *forma mentis* that redefined the Babel of human preferences.

Tattooed Man

Fashion designers bear witness to the fact that the twentieth century elected style as a dominant ideal of taste. Moreover, the twenty-first century appears to further the veneration for ideological and commercial stardom of this sort.

This is particularly visible in the media, where fashion designers enjoy a prestige hitherto unequaled in the history of consumer society: "there is no writer, painter or film director with such a visible claim to fame. Only the fashion designer can aspire to see his or her name identified with a label and exposed to such public appraisal and awareness, from city shop signs to logos on every item of clothing sold. A successful businessman may become a household name, but never with the visibility of a fashion designer. The difference lies in the fact that the fashion designer is still considered akin to an artist."[79]

Such social and symbolic acclaim turns the cultural coordinates of aesthetic appeal upside down. Artists, architects and product designers may be the darlings of critics and journalists, but they are usually unknown to the public at large. Fashion designers, on the other hand, tend to be foreign to the realms of academia and intellectual pursuit, yet are venerated as idols by wide swathes of the younger generation whose tastes they help to forge. The protagonists of the star system may not be the subject of many learned treatises, but they are certainly the focus of endless magazine cover shots and feature stories, of advertising and megastore distribution.

Yet what fashion designers produce cannot be relegated to the realms of kitsch, the repository of so much that triumphs on the mass market. On the contrary. The fashion designer is by definition an arbiter of elegance, someone who lays down the laws of vanity and defines the sphere of luxury, inventing and imposing new laws of apparel. Indeed, fashion designers are perceived as clairvoyants invested with the gift of foreseeing women's whims in clothing. They are the modern Prometheus, stealing the fire of fashion and giving it to mortals in a constant cycle of renewal.

All this is but a short step from the Renaissance, when the high priests of taste were artists. Through their art they reshaped collective awareness and renewed aesthetic parameters, leaving their own seal on works of great inspiration.

The etymology of the word "style" makes this clear. The term derives from the Latin "*stilus*," which refers to the pointed tool used by the ancients to engrave wax tablets. In designating the quality of expression, style acts like a trademark that reveals the personality of the designer.[80] Clearly the next step is the concept of style as a characteristic of a given period or aesthetic trend. In both instances, today no less than in the past, the essential characteristic is individuality.

It is interesting to note that the word "*griffe*" also derives from the sphere of writing ("*gràphein*") and designates individual creativity, like a sort of overall fingerprint, except that fingerprints are hereditary and therefore involuntary, whereas the written expression requires the power of will and reveals indelible personal traits.

In the fanciful world of fashion, the various *griffes* provide canons of taste that effectively aid people in their choices of what to wear. Granted, this suggests a large number of competing systems, which are all based on the charismatic figure of particular designers. What is important, of course, is the fact that consumers recognize their chosen style guru and blindly trust in his/her every expression. The outcome is a convenient solution to the enigma of taste that has fascinated generations of philosophers engaged in defining beauty in art. Just why we should accept and embrace the dictates of taste regardless of our own deeper feelings and perceptions is a question that remains unanswered.

Consider further the mechanisms of contemporary fashion. "Taste always refers to the preferences and the choices of an individual and is totally private by its very nature. Everyone is supposed to choose what feels good. At the same time, the ideal of good taste is meant to be beyond the individual, and to be socially binding. It offers a universal standard, potentially applicable to all members of a society. It is an ideal which everyone is supposed to follow. Furthermore, it is a standard which is socially communicable even though it can never be conceptually determined."[81]

By contrast, the classic aesthetic norms in art largely pertain to the desire for timeless beauty. Fashion, on the other hand, focuses on the ephemeral criterion of elegance, which can be turned into a socially recognizable cult. This is a major difference. If beauty is linked to the present, and elegance prefers action to contemplation, then the public stage of social competition becomes its sole focus. The system spawns must-have objects to be grabbed and shown off as symbols of privilege and distinction. The key concepts are thus self-image, exhibition and seduction. Little wonder that the thinkers of the Enlightenment saw fashion as an illusory expression of human vanity lacking in any real aesthetic stature: fashion could never be widely accepted, because if it were it would no longer be fashion.

With respect to this framework, however, contemporary fashion has introduced something entirely new. With the spread of wellbeing, fashion has become less exclusive and showy, and instead has developed symbolic and psychological values that have little to do with economic factors. Consumer society relies on the principle of access, such that social distinction is no longer the main function of fashion, which in its turn grows more universal, available and repetitive.

It is the fashion designers who are responsible for this. Thanks to the proliferation of collections (from ready-to-wear to casual and sportswear) and in particular to the way licenses have expanded to embrace all manner of objects, the style trade has grown at an astounding rate. What it has lost in impact it has gained in accessibility, drawing into the realm of fashion a vast range of previously unrelated commodities. In so doing, it has also reshaped terms of reference and consumption.

A great deal has happened since 1921, when Chanel No. 5 was launched and soon became the most famous scent in the world. Increasing numbers of fashion designers have invested products once extraneous to fashion with their personal charisma to further their commercial success. In 1948, Christian Dior lent his name to a collection of hosiery in the United States. Forty years later, Pierre Cardin had accumulated 800 licenses ranging from garments to cosmetics, chocolate, furniture and appliances that bore his name throughout the world. Among the 200 licenses collected by Yves Saint Laurent, the *enfant prodige* of Parisian fashions, there was even the *YSL* brand of cigarettes. To this day, the main source of income for fashion houses derives from brand licensing. The seasonal collections that receive so much press coverage are what establish, develop and maintain the designer's image. Because they are costly to produce, they do not always yield income.[82] Little matter, however, for this is the job of the vast array of brand accessories.

Fashion today is a heady, often showy enactment of style. It embraces not only choices to do with clothing, or indeed consumer behavior, but also the attitudes, interests, desires and preferences of individuals. It is thus evident that while designer labels represent only a fraction of the variegated universe of fashion, they encapsulate most aspects of the phenomenon, especially its causes and symptoms.

Moralists[83] complain that fashion has made label slaves of helpless, innocent souls duped into thinking that they too can enjoy the thrill of luxury. Yet a more detached view of the whole world of logos simply reveals to what extent the demand for fashion has spread throughout contemporary society. After all, it was the power of the label that turned tailors and dressmakers into the high priests of taste, their *griffe* into a magic wand.[84] Logos have dematerialized style and turned it into a fetish, capable of investing mass produced objects with an aura of exclusivity. "It's the rarity of the producer that makes the product rare. The magic of the logo is what explains the conceptual difference between the true item signed by the master and a mere copy, though the two essentially differ only in price."[85]

Of course it's true that there may be practically no difference between a genuine designer garment and a fake version of the same thing, at least as far as look, finish and materials used are concerned. Yet the symbolic divide between the two is unbridgeable. Acquiring a designer garment is like an entry ticket to dream world, a sort of aesthetic affiliation, a declaration of faith, a form of devotion. Buying a fake designer garment is the equivalent of prizing a postcard from an exotic destination one has never had the privilege of visiting.

The miraculous power of designer logos resides in the ability to turn personal charisma into a magic talisman that can elevate banal commodities into precious and desirable items. Iron becomes gold in an act of "symbolic transubstantiation that eludes any real transformation."[86]

Fashion achieves ubiquity thanks to designer logos. It transcends social barriers and commodity categories, is universally accessible and infinitely repeatable. For this is the magic charm that eliminates the contrast between sacred and profane, precious and banal, authentic and fake, exceptional and ordinary. The oxymoron triumphs within the realms of taste, as the principle of authority and free will coexist in a constant, euphoric flurry.

The great Post-Modern saga is the product not so much of architects as of fashion designers. When product designers rebeled against the grey predictability of the Modernist Movement, their provocative counter-proposals went largely unnoticed by the public at large. When fashion expanded to embrace all manner of products, on the other hand, the phenomenon swept the whole world along with it, shaping and spreading "the postmodern condition."

The foremost exegete and hagiographer of postmodernism was Lyotard,[87] who described it as the eclipse of the accepted canons of artistic and scientific discourse: where there are no established rules, the "truth" of a work or a theory becomes intrinsically volatile. When applied to the profane world of trade, this implies the loss of convertibility between symbolic value and economic privilege: the value of fashion becomes a form of autosuggestion.

Other authors have argued in favor of an intimate connection between consumer society and postmodern sensibility. Lyons[88] talks about the closing of the divide between cultured and mass taste brought about by the spread of consumer logic throughout all aspects of cultural production. Jameson[89] describes how aesthetics and culture have become revocable, superficially chosen commodities. This followed Baudrillard's original perception[90] of a collective indoctrination to the religion of consumption and the aesthetic hallucination of reality. As for Featherstone,[91] he identifies ubiquitous fashion as the most evident symptom of the postmodern revolution that has brought about the implosion of symbolic hierarchies and the aesthetics of daily life.

Logos are so seductive and contagious that they have spread beyond the confines of gadgets embellished by the golden designer touch. A growing number of industrial brands from both the luxury and the mass-market sectors now claim to be designer labels. This is visible not only in the multiplication of commodity genres (design labels now ennoble anything from cigarettes to clothing, cigars to scents, fountain pens to wrist watches, travel gear, shoes and even car tires). What is particularly noteworthy is the metamorphosis of brands into the symbols and mirages of lifestyles.

According to Naomi Klein, whose pamphlet criticizing the globalization of logos met with widespread acclaim,[92] the phenomenon is actually the fruit of a deliberate strategy on the part of the huge multinationals to counteract the increasing banality of commodities, their interchangeability when it comes to performance, the growing indifference of consumers to advertising. When manufacturers started outsourcing production to low wage countries, it became evident that what they were selling "were not things, but *images* of their brands. Their real work lay not in manufacturing but in marketing."[93] As for advertising, Klein regrets that its appeal has "gradually taken the agencies away from individual products and their attributes and toward a psychological/anthropological examination of what brands mean to the culture and to people's lives."[94] Unsurprisingly, when you consider that the goal of advertising has always been to endow goods with a special "aura" that differentiates them from competitors and makes them more in the eyes of the public. What is more, just as all consumer goods embody a great deal of symbolic content, so the exchange value of logos implies a premium with regard to their use value. The "scandal" deplored by Klein consists in the global manipulation of minds whereby consumers attribute such symbolic value to a logo.

Whatever the social and moral implications of the phenomenon may be,[95] it is clear that the process of spinning dreams around logos has borrowed a page from the "ubiquitous fashion" book in its efforts to imbue goods with symbolic and emotional content. In its own way, a logo is a magic talisman that repeats the formula of designer labels: there is no substantial difference between the person who purchases an Armani scent or pair of Dior specs and the consumer who opts for a Marlboro Classics bomber jacket or a Nike cap. Both are lifestyle brands, which allow their owners to partake of a special world of their choice.

The very fact that the charisma system created by fashion designers can actually be applied to a wide range of different products reveals to what extent the social and cultural meaning of fashion has changed. In becoming more "democratic," it loses its aura of luxury and becomes a trait common to consumer goods in general, or at least their outer appearance. The traditional parameters of what is and is not considered a luxury thus fade into non-existence.

The vertical structure of preference and the way taste percolates down from the top of the pyramid to its lower echelons defined in the past the exclusive nature of luxury. Fashion was explained in terms of the two polar extremes: imitation of the leisured classes on the one hand; and differentiation from the newly moneyed on the other.

Gone are the times when style rivalry could be explained in terms of competition between social classes. Today fashions often begin at the grass roots level, spontaneously and unexpectedly, transforming city streets into catwalks that often act as inspiration for fashion designers themselves.[96] Social fragmentation has given rise to the proliferation of intermittent, interchangeable fashions which spread in mysterious ways: "contemporary dress fashions are neither as universal nor as symbolically focal as they once were [. . .] Nor do fashions today seem capable of enforcing uniform like compliance throughout society and across all class and status groupings."[97]

This brings to the fore the paradox of fashion in the contemporary age. Pluralistic and polycentric, intrusive and blasphemous, fashion is like a kaleidoscope that encapsulates and abandons short-lived styles and products. No longer is it a vehicle for social mobility or privilege. Fast food fashion,[98] as it has been called, is available to everyone everywhere, which entirely undermines the real desire for fashion. What do we really want? This is the question that only a history of contemporary taste can hope to answer.

The Far East is in the social and cultural vanguard when it comes to "ubiquitous fashion." For an overview of the relative model of development and consumption suffice it to turn to Japan, and other prosperous Asian countries following its lead. Not only do they represent highly profitable markets for Western luxury products, they also provide a precious observatory for the anthropology of contemporary fashion.

The essential feature is the sense of loss brought about by the adoption en masse of Western clothing. Traditional costumes have all but disappeared, replaced by "modern" garb that does not embody similarly meaningful norms, values and prohibitions.

According to Donald Richie, in *The Image Factory*, "The Japanese, having scrapped their own native costumes and having proved understandably maladroit in handling the various nuances of Western dress, are now presented with a new problem—or rather, the same old problem under a new guise: how to present the social self, given only the highly individualized clothing styles from which they must choose."[99] The outcome is that fashion is suddenly called upon to provide "instructions for use" for an alien sort of elegance. For an Asian consumer, bowing to fashion (including the worship of logos) has become a rule of life that supplies a ready and reassuring solution to the latent need for self-expression.

This explains the obsession with a given look, not only in clothing but throughout the whole range of consumer products. Teen magazines are full of features that nicely illustrate the situation. "The *taipu betsu*, or classification of types, in relation to the clothes, products and accessories that each individual prefers. Not even the most ordinary products can elude this analysis. From the brand of a packet of cigarettes, for example, you can identify the "type," specifying in detail the global characteristics of his or her personality: style, tastes, weaknesses, education. There are all sorts of *taipu betsu*: in relation to haircut, clothing, music, sport, leisure pursuits, food, cosmetics, preferred reading."[100] Little wonder, then, that the streets of Tokyo far outdo those of Paris, Milan or New York when it comes to parading comatose, passive fashion victims. In Omote-sandō, the fashion avenue is flanked by megastores and the logo sanctuaries erected by famous architects to attract swarms of devout pilgrims, dazzled by the spectacle of consumer paradise and the beatification of fashion designers whose products are purchased and treasured like sacred relics.

The place of initiation into the cult of adult fashion is Harajaku, a fairground of trends much beloved by adolescents. Here "you can discover exactly what is cool and *naui* (from 'now'), which pop stars are in or out, which clothes, accessories, hairstyles are on the crest of the wave, which cocktails prove one is not *dasai* (out), which crepes or pizzas will still be in fashion by the end of the month."[101]

Shibuya is a picturesque district that provides further insights into fashion in Japan. Its inhabitants tend to be young: nymphets duly attired and made up; young mothers wheeling colorful pushchairs bearing infants with trendily bleached hair. Amid this daily fashion, carnival girl groups form to establish their look and exhibit their identity as brazenly as possible. To shock is to succeed because it means being noticed, which is much, much better than the gray anonymity that would otherwise engulf them.

The *ganguro-gyaru* (literally "dark-faced bad girls") are a case in point. They meet up and give free rein to self-expression, safe in the fold of the group. Only thus can they claim visibility: "it is evident that the *ganguro* reject the very concept of Japaneseness, which they do their best to alter by modifying their look. It's as if these girls were hell-bent on achieving a transformation involving hair, skin and features that allows them to elude the perceived constraints of their real lives. The *ganguro* style is closer to disguise than it is to fashion."[102]

These extreme manifestations of fashion actually contain an element of explanation. As a crossroads between culture and commerce, aesthetics and custom, elegance and disguise, they are essentially theatrical events, at the same time both élitist and popular, in which the actors draw in the audience to take part in a play whose theme is how to be different.

Style worship in Japan achieves such paroxysms of exhibitionism that the country has become the apotheosis of Western fashion, a land in which fashion fever and the cult of the look define the existential game of reshaping one's inner and exterior being. That said, something remarkably similar is also going on in the outskirts of the West. In the globalized world, fashion has become the buzz, the upper, the trip that gets people through the day: aesthetic Prozac plus social aphrodisiac.

So, far from being the manifestation of ease and refinement it once was, fashion is now equated with labels and logos following hot on each other's heels in a frantic race without a finishing post: run, run, as fast as you can . . . it will leave you too breathless for Angst.

Of course, since time immemorial, human beings have devoted thought to appearance. "Before embellishing fabrics, man decorated his body with scars and tattoos. The origins of the symbolic aspect of ornament lie in man's innate need to dress up in order to show who he is."[103] From this point of view, though contemporary fashion may be widespread, pluralistic and accessible, it still manages to express the ritual function of ornament typical of archaic societies: that of defining the signs of social identity.

Yet there is one basic difference: in modern democracies, social identity has become a stage for acting out competing aspirations, and as a result it is also a source of frustration, insecurity and neurosis. For fashion today is fluid, risky and unstable. The construction of identity is not something that can be passed down from one generation to the next. Rather, it is an individual conquest in which fashions and logos inevitably reflect the temporary, volatile character of an indeterminate reality. "Today there is no fashion: there are only *fashions*. [. . .] *No rules, only choices* is the current claim. [. . .] Everyone can be everyone. In fashion, as in much of the imagery of a mass culture, we confront the echoes of our own desires."[104]

The mirage of fashion often embraces what can appear to be some worrying distortion. For instance, the youths whose fashion fetish leads them to have the Nike logo tattooed onto their skin. But then, all the other kids are wearing the same logo anyway, so what real difference does it make?

Even the loudest and showiest icons of fashion do much the same thing, except that they're applied to our second skin: clothes and accessories. Hence the double G buckle denoting Gucci, the Bulgari logo that dominates a wristwatch, the Louis Vuitton monogram disseminated over a vast range of products as an ornamental motif. Such are the tattoos of modernity. Those who show them off are asserting their identity as part of the flow of fashion. They are armed with the right passport for entering the hallowed realms of here-and-now society.

An intriguing study by Alain Ehrenberg describes the clinical and social development of depression during the twentieth century.[105] According to Ehrenberg, depression can be seen as a symptom of the "pathology of change." The trigger is the rise of mass individualism as society demands and imposes a process of autonomy on each and every citizen. "The 1960s saw the collapse of the prejudices, traditions, constraints and limits that had hitherto given structure to people's lives. We grew emancipated, in the true sense of the term: the modern political ideal, which frees men and women from being docile subjects and turns them into self-proprietors, is extended to all aspects of existence. The sovereign individual, as predicted by Nietzsche, has now become a common condition of existence."[106]

The society of autonomy does not countenance superior nature (we fight age, our hereditary traits, our physical imperfections), and has banished any trace of an interior moral law (gone are the sense of guilt, the taboos of desire, the constraints of pleasure). What we become and how we behave depend exclusively on our own will and abilities. "Our reality has become a world in which the individual is freed of morality and shapes his or her own being, thereby becoming a superperson in his or her tendency to transcend individual nature through action. This individual, however, is often fragile and rarely has the courage of his or her convictions. Weighed down by autonomy, he or she feels aggrieved and dissatisfied. Depression is melancholy amalgamated with equality, the quintessential sickness of democratic man. Such is the ineluctable endowment of the individual who has become his or her own sovereign."[107]

Since the spread and degree of depression is directly proportionate to the process of social autonomization, the ailment can be seen as the toll of modernity, along with substance and alcohol addiction: two forms of self-defense against depression, both of them pathological in their own right.

Contemporary society expects us to construct an identity, to maintain it and defend it from ourselves and those who surround us. All this clearly comes with a psychological and social price tag. The miraculous mission of fashion is to reduce this price tag, which it does with the help of logos and labels. Society is thus supplied with a simplified recipe for elegance based on fragments of identity ready for use.

The central question of this chapter centers on the conviction that what people seek in fashion today is a transfiguration of self that can help alleviate fatigue of self. In the melting pot of an ambivalent, contradictory society in which individuals have to choose their own fate, fashion acts as a social panacea that mitigates the discomfort of autonomized identity.

The condition of autonomy, long desired but frustratingly difficult to handle, looks to fashion for a paradigmatic model of the contagious state of permanent over-excitement that underlies the collective yearning for individual happiness. It sustains the self by encouraging desires for every sort of consumer commodity that can provide momentary gratification. In this sense it is the ideological imperative "that characterizes the second half of the twentieth century, attributing value to everything in terms of pleasure or disappointment. Those who do not take part in the euphoric ritual are condemned to shame or relegated to a life of discomfort. The imperative is based on a double postulate: either get the most possible out of life, or suffer and feel wretched because you haven't."[108]

The irresistibility of fashion lies in its ability to foment desires and encourage the compulsion for luxury, or at least what is superfluous, in the name of self-realization. This is inextricable from modernity, in which the multiplication of individual aspirations goes hand in hand with an economic system that promotes and gains from the mirage of universal happiness: "what underlies capitalism is no longer the concept of production based on labor and saving, but rather that of consumption, which brings with it expenditure and waste. In this new strategy, pleasure has taken the place of exclusion, thereby blurring the divide between the economic machine and our whims, which become the true engine of development. The Western individual is thus freed of public shaming, which was a feature of the early, authoritarian stage of democracies, and is encouraged to acquire full autonomy. In his freedom, however, he no longer has any choice: with no obstacles between him and paradise, he is "condemned" to be happy. If he's not, he only has himself to blame."[109]

In reality, of course, the individual is beset with a feeling of inadequacy, the fear of being excluded, the unmentionable anxiety of not quite managing to enjoy life quite as one should. This is simply the hidden face of fashion, not the panacea of self-realization, but the empty chimera of unfulfilled promise. What underlies both aspects of the phenomenon is narcissism, which can be joyous gratification or a tantalizing and ultimately frustrating projection of the self. In this latter case, the individual becomes the "prisoner of an image that has been so idealized as to be paralyzing. The outcome is a constant need for reassurance resulting in dependence on those who supply it":[110] a condition that is intimately linked to the frenetic volatility of fashion. To be fashionable means constantly trying to improve one's look, and being frustrated in so doing. The concomitant anxiety is simply due to the impossibility of the task: an ever-receding goal.

The mirage of self-image also suffers in relation to the direction that society is taking. In the days when fashion represented the choreography of progress, the stage costume for a play about us in which we all took part, it seemed to be positive and desirable. Nowadays, however, "the fear of going backwards and being excluded far outweigh the hopes for social preferment. We all change, inevitably, but without the sense of making progress."[111]

Having reached this peak, the focus on self no longer seems like the existential project it once did. Instead it looks worryingly like a form of autosuggestion, an ugly mirror image of a society that has lost its vision. Fashion no longer appears to embody excitingly contagious novelty. On the contrary, it smacks of an endless, errant pursuit of the present. The fruit of this is self-disappointment, leading in its turn to further striving towards surrogate identity. In this vicious circle of aspiration, effort and dissatisfaction, the ultimate goal grows increasingly evanescent. Little wonder, then, that fashion should reflect that sad state of affairs.

The Odyssey of Appetites

We live in an age of overabundance. By affecting our eating habits, the age of overabundance has greatly expanded our range of choices and revolutionized the way in which we exercise them: "yesterday choices were limited and imposed by resources, membership, tradition, rituals and representation. Today the atomized individual of modern civilization is like a particle of mass society, totally disconnected from family, social and cultural ties, and lacking in reliable points of reference for making such choices."[112]

In premodernity, people ate according to availability without thinking too much about their stomachs. What and how they ate depended on their roots, family and social milieu. Nowadays, unlimited freedom of choice means that we are constantly forced to make decisions of our own. Feeding becomes a question of individual responsibility, and the constant search for guidance and confirmation, criteria for appraisal and reassurance regarding our eating habits. This explains people's extraordinary readiness to let their minds and palates be swayed by myriad different stimuli, fashions and precepts. It also accounts for the random role of taste in shaping our preferences and dislikes.

In all ages and civilizations, the taste for food has meant more than simply gratifying the palate. Above all it has stood for adaptation to a given system of practices and images regarding the way nature (the foodstuffs available and the requirements of the metabolism) is subjected to culture (the techniques involved in processing and preserving these foods, combining their tastes and controlling the manner in which they are consumed). When a particular culture gives way to the overwhelming impact of what is new (new products, new lifestyles, new orientations), taste inevitably grows irresolute in the face of so much that is seductive and dissonant. The inner compass that governs our feeding habits thus gets stuck, and we lose our inner feeling for what is "ecological" in terms of food. The traditional relationship between individual, landscape, social context and material history begins to collapse, and in its stead we experience a nostalgic longing for what is perceived, often erroneously, as being typical and traditional.

To account for the food taboos characteristic of tribal societies, Lévi-Strauss came up with a famous declaration according to which animals and vegetables do not become food because they are "good to eat," but because they are "good to think"[113]—in other words part of the classification system that defines the sphere of what is edible. In today's food system, however, the saying is no longer applicable: between the response of the palate and the image the food conjures up in the mind's eye, where once there was harmony, correspondence and mutual support there is now suspicion, aversion and reciprocal deception.

Modernity has revolutionized the world of food, redefining its tutelary gods and rewriting its myths. The cacophony of dietetics and gastronomy has spawned contradictory stimuli that torment our desires, and weigh down on our preferences. We are no longer what we eat; we eat (or at least try to eat) what we would like to be. And when, as often happens, we fail to achieve this goal, we are unable to be self-accepting and instead give in to feelings of guilt and inner conflict. We desire foods that are less suited to satisfying bodily needs or whims of the palate than they are to nurturing the imagination and appeasing the conscience: foods that contribute to our narcissistic self-image.

The aspirations and goals that shape food preferences change in the course of time. Taking part in modernity calls for detachment regarding the heritage of the past. The tyranny of mass communications and individualism imposes forms of self-idealization aimed at exorcising the specter of physical decline and concomitant social marginalization. In so doing it distances us from ancestral traditions, which are perceived as being aesthetically and substantially inadequate, symbols of poverty and protracted privation, of early ageing, of the fatigue and hardship that mark the body, of an archaic condition of existence and its underlying aspirations.

To return to such a state would mean giving in to the ineluctable nature of the past, enduring its disgrace and relinquishing the challenge to sway the future. And this in its turn would imply giving up all hope of prosperity, renunciation of the collective dream of inexorable, unlimited progress, and rejection of the mirage of omnipotence in shaping one's own fate as expressed by a slim, attractive and eternally young body.

There is indeed little that is comforting or gratifying about becoming part of modernity. The globalized standardization of supply is shaped by market interests and objectives that reflect changes in the way society and the family are organized. The quiet murmur of the well-oiled wheels of consumer behavior cannot entirely block out a sinister background noise.

Modernity multiplies the deceits, anxieties, doubts and frustrations regarding the identity and effects of the foods we ingest, underlining the rift between what we think we ought to eat and what we actually consume, between looking after ourselves and giving in to temptation, between control and indulgence, longevity and satiety, duty and pleasure. Apollo and Dionysus are the two gods that upset the new food theogony. The object of clandestine liturgies and sacrilegious cults, they can stand for orgies or penitence. Stigmatized as heretical with respect to the salvific religion of nutritional balance, bulimia and anorexia reveal the uneasy conscience of contemporary appetites.

Certain critics have tried to explain alimentary modernity in terms of a contrast between junk and light foods, perceived as polar opposites in the problematic handling of the hunger instinct. This apocalyptic view is reductive, however, because it fails to account for the complexity of the phenomenon. Outside of North America, the threatened "Macdonaldization" of eating habits is a sociological caricature,[114] and the so-called "lipophobic society" of people so terrorized by fat that they subject themselves to hideous dietary torture belongs more to the world of dreams (or nightmares) than to that of real consumer behavior.

The revolutions and rediscoveries in what people think about food have not only reshaped the appetites of the Old World. They have also helped mitigate the divide between the demands of the palate and duties involved in healthy living, between the myth of lost genuineness and the reality of the industrial food chain. To put it briefly, "good to eat" and "good to think" are now slightly less out of tune with each other.

Etymologically speaking, gastronomy is the discipline of the appetites (from the roots *gastros* meaning stomach or greediness, and *nomos* meaning precept or custom). By instigating the seduction of the palate, gastronomy has effectively returned to a meaning that resembles its Renaissance usage, when it pertained to the doctrine of honest pleasure (*honesta voluptas*), to the art of remedy, to the methodical reduction of damage: in other words, when it was the catechism for moral consolation.

The most significant events to have influenced the way we think and act concerning food can all be traced back to the conflicting elements in this concept. With the breakdown of rules, the disintegration of reference points and the clash of contradictory convictions, consumers have begun to feel torn and unhappy about their choices. Yet the goal of modern food science has also been to define *new gastronomies,* thereby reestablishing rules, reintroducing regulatory principles and returning to certain paradigms of taste.

In this sense, the Mediterranean diet, the French paradox, our gastronomic treasures and creative cuisine all help shape how we think about food, introducing new mythologies destined to influence what and how we consume. Each of these will be treated in turn.

The first and most influential of the modern gastronomies, at least in Italy, is the Mediterranean diet. Right from the outset it has always come across as an ideological rather than a dietary solution to the discomforts of modernity. For generations of people brought up to believe in the religion of wellbeing, the advent of nutritional prosperity has failed to fulfill its promise of happiness. The variety and profusion of foods available to everyone, the abolition of the principle of fatigue, restriction and renunciation, and the daily accessibility of foodstuffs that earlier generations could not have hoped to enjoy, except perhaps on special occasions ("Sunday lunch is no longer anything special in relation to the festivity: from this point of view every day is a Sunday"),[115] transform the achievement of prosperity into a self-destructive threat.

The damage that derives from overabundance of food has been a matter for debate for some time now, thereby spoiling the voracious appetites of opulent society. Modern dietetics no longer addresses the ills of malnutrition, but focuses its energies on trying to cure the effects of overeating, a practice that has reached epidemic proportions. The new mortal sins of overfed society are the plague of obesity and the spread of cardiovascular illness (according to statistics, one of the main causes of death). From this point onward, freedom of choice must go hand in hand with a sense of individual responsibility, the delights of pleasure with self-control, gluttony with the ability to look after oneself, conviviality with temperance, bingeing with life expectation. "The contemporary condition is intimately related to education: knowing what one is eating and what one should eat. No longer imposed by cultural background or family habit, such rules for behavior are shaped by dietary information and aesthetic aspirations, common opinions and personal idiosyncrasies."[116]

Historically and ideologically, it is within this context that the "Mediterranean diet" has enjoyed such widespread success. As a scientific theory, it was promoted by the American nutritionist Ancel Keys in a series of pioneering studies undertaken in the 1950s. A further three decades were to pass, however, before it acquired widespread acceptance, establishing itself as the new bible for healthy eating.

The success of the Mediterranean diet is largely due to the fact that it reconciles our eating habits with our dreams about food. In other words, it lessens the inner divide between our taste for luxury and our witting choices shaped by nutritional considerations. "People tend to see the Mediterranean diet as a sort of *nutritional counter reform*, the very answer to the constraints of modernization. The food image of the 'North' is technological and full of proteins: the steak myth, for instance, or the astronaut's pills, or slimming diets, or precooked convenience foods. By contrast, by offering a dietary model based on its own history, Italy comes across as a model of nutritional wisdom, scientifically ratified by the United States, that most advanced of countries, and widely admired and copied."[117]

The discomfiture of modernity is thus resolved by repudiation. In advocating a return to earlier times, the Mediterranean diet actually makes a myth of what people really used to eat, inventing a state of something akin to nutritional innocence, authenticity and purity, surrounded by an aura of cleansing frugality that opens up a path to nutritional redemption for the benefit of an overfed civilization. Rescued from the folly of modernity, longevity is the golden fleece that we should all try to attain by means of the rediscovery of simple, healthy, natural food. The echo of the phenomenon goes well beyond the spheres of diet and gastronomy: underlying the myth of the Mediterranean diet are implicit judgments concerning duties and pleasures, temptations and renunciations; in other words, suggestions for how to behave regarding the insidious threats of food and the onslaught of models of consumption that are not only heinous, but also contagious. In people's minds, the world of food thus takes on edifying precepts of an essentially moral, ideological nature, thereby shaping what is perceived as being "good to think."

Granted, the condition of those brought up on hamburgers, fries and Coca-Cola is different. Here change involves behavioral adjustments that resemble conversion to a foreign religious sect. The first requirement is to bury the deeply interiorized practices of the recent past, which is altogether a different approach to that of those accustomed to eating bread, pasta, vegetables and olive oil, and who have only recently achieved sufficient prosperity for a daily slice of meat. In this latter case, the Mediterranean diet comes across as a delectable form of symbolic and cultural revenge that erases all feelings of guilt, inadequacy or inferiority. The Mediterranean cult provides new generations of Italians who have been temporarily "corrupted" in their eating habits with a way of plotting a safe course in the labyrinth of food. "In actual fact the Mediterranean diet resolves the 'omnivore's paradox' described by Claude Fischler because it helps reconcile the tendency to innovate with resistance to change, such that earlier behavior can go hand in hand with the urge to evolve. In the Mediterranean diet, the *greatest alimentary modernity* coincides precisely with the *least innovation*, or, to put it differently, with the *greatest gastronomic regression*. To feel that one is keeping up with the times it is no longer necessary to revolutionize one's habits, but simply to carry on eating as one always has done, with the glorification of pasta."[118]

The Mediterranean diet has managed to assure pasta and olive oil a place in the High Temple of Comestibles, rather as the "French paradox" has resulted in a similar revalorization of red wine. In 1990, the American review *Health* published a report written by correspondent Edward Dolnick on the state of health of the French.[119] As in the case of the Mediterranean diet, the whole argument depended on epidemiology. Why is it, the author wondered, that death rates due to cardiovascular disease in France are two thirds lower than they are in the United States, despite the fact that the French consume such abnormal quantities of animal fats? To answer his own question, Dolnick quoted the unorthodox theories of nutritionist Jacques Richard concerning the unexpected virtues of his fellow countrymen's eating habits: it was the daily doses of red wine that kept the Gallic arteries in order.

The French paradox had to wait another year before it could reach a wider audience. This happened thanks to an episode of the popular *60 Minutes* show specifically devoted to the subject. Glued to the screen in the comfort of their own homes were twenty million viewers,[120] which meant that the miraculous fame of red wine spread fast, thereby provoking a major rise in consumption.[121]

> For the first time in the United States restaurants began to sell the same quantities of red and white wine. In early years, white wine had dominated by 80 percent. What was it that managed to overturn American preferences to such an extent? A television broadcast: in France, it was declared, the death rate for heart disease was three times lower than what it was in America, despite the fact that fine eating was still the favorite pastime of the French. One hypothetical explanation for this scandal was that red wine was responsible for protecting them. For Americans, health is a difficult goal to achieve, one that calls for effort in adopting an "appropriate" diet. For the French, on the other hand, it is a blessing that permits the elect to enjoy life: for them, wine is not a magic potion, but a pleasure. In France people drink to other people's health, in America to ensure their own.[122]

The analogy with the phenomenon of the Mediterranean diet is evident: yet between the two cases there is one substantial difference. While Mediterranean eating habits can be described as a "diet," albeit a highly enjoyable one, providing followers with a yardstick for alimentary temperance and nutritional balance, the French model has no such claims, which is precisely why it comes across as a paradox. That said, however, what is most disconcerting is not the disputable nature of its scientific premises or its empirical validation, but the fact that it violates an ideological prejudice, the very one that underlies the Mediterranean paradigm: the idea that frugality is healthy, morally edifying and ecologically sound. In the view of nutritional puritanism, "the French paradox represents an ethical scandal in which perceived sin is rewarded."[123]

A value judgment of this sort naturally calls for contextualization. For centuries, wine had led two parallel lives, especially in France: aristocratic and plebeian, sophisticated and humble, refined and vulgar, according to the circumstances in which it was consumed. It thus projected two separate images, of which one (that of quaffing wine) began to fade as consumption diminished, while the other rose to wider acclaim as it gained recognition and kudos as a blazoned drink to be enjoyed in the right company.[124]

Flasks, demijohns and large bottles with crown caps gradually began to disappear, leaving more room for 75 cl bottles embellished with labels and closed with cork stoppers. Clearly this was not simply a question of appearances. The symbology of wine and the anthropology of wine-drinking had grown more refined, thereby distancing themselves from the archaic experience of peasant culture: once a proudly home-produced source of energy that could contribute to the household economy and was never missing at mealtimes, wine was gradually turning into a quality product for hedonistic consumption, a drink for convivial occasions that was invested with the gastronomic and emotional significance that had once been the prerogative of a narrow circle of privileged people.

In the epochal transition from "wine as nutriment" to "wine as pleasure," the inclinations of taste and the variables of appraisal underwent substantial change: the senses grew more discerning, the range of choices became wider, and the drinker was increasingly expected to be well-informed. Once wine had become a symbol for prestige, subject to ceremony and viewed as a sign of *savoir vivre*, its consumption moved away from need towards choice, and from ordinariness towards refinement. By the time the expression "the French paradox" gained acceptance, the transformation of anonymous plonk into a desirable, select wine had already come about. Once it had established itself as a luxury product, wine could hope to emulate the prestige of the great labels, which had always been considered symbols of pleasure-loving dissipation, gastronomic squandering and ostentation (nothing at the table can be as expensive as a rare cru). All this was clearly poles apart from the ideals of frugality suggested by the Mediterranean diet.

The image of wine thus underwent a new metamorphosis, becoming an elixir that remained a source of pleasure and a sign of refinement. Accompanied by polished wine-talk, its consumption was beatified, freed of feelings of guilt and invested with salvific virtues, such that it ousted alcoholic chastity and abstinence in representing nutritional probity.

The perception of wine as a herald of health coincided with the gradual collapse of the moral juxtaposition between sensuality and sensibility, pleasure and temperance, squandering and need, alcoholic inebriation and dietary redemption. This in its turn meant redefining the system of values and images that considered the drink an object of desire.

Like the Mediterranean diet, the French paradox rewrote the instructions pertaining to earlier consumption, which thus acquired a new light that allowed them to become, all of a sudden, "good to think." The "new gastronomy" thus gained ground, upheld by consolatory morals. The French paradox taught how to sin and save the soul at the same time, dispensing nutritional absolution to the epicureans, and paving the way for luxury consumption and gourmet inclinations. It thus reconciled desires with reassurance, melding self-image with self-respect, translating self-indulgence into self-esteem, and assimilating vice and virtue within the mirage of joyous longevity.

The myth of origins and authenticity, with its surrounding aura of ethical correctness, is even more evident in another recent phenomenon: that of the gastronomic glorification of small local producers whose very existence is at risk, of purveyors of specialties known only to initiates. Italy abounds in such products: cave-ripened cheeses that have aged in straw-lined subterranean shafts, Colonnata pork fat that is brine-seasoned in marble vats, Zibello *culatello* pork rump matured in underground caves, to mention but a few of the area-specific products that have been invested with almost magical qualities. It is interesting to note that these three at least owe their cultural tradition, gastronomic identity and special flavor to the fact that they are in some respects "sepulchral foods," products that have been "buried" in their place of origin.

As often as not, products such as these also embody something of the epic and legendary in the way they tell the tale of whoever founded or discovered them. For instance, the practice of burying foods in caves or shafts was originally adopted to protect them from the bandits who raided the Romagnolo countryside; and the custom of salting pork fat in marble vats was simply a way of using locally available products for the seasoning of foodstuffs that could be taken up to the quarries by Tuscan quarrymen.

Food writer Davide Paolini, a pioneer in seeking out realities of this sort in Italy, describes the ideological delights of discovering "gastronomic treasures" in the following terms:

> anyone who observes, smells, touches and tastes these items is well aware that they are far removed from the "standardized" foodstuffs that are produced industrially and in great quantities. These realities are like mines from which rare tastes can be extracted, veins of precious gastronomic substances that are the fruit of knowledge and skill handed down through the generations, of manual expertise that cannot be replaced by machinery or technology. The production of these foods is made up of various stages, such as cutting, seasoning, salting and breaking that are akin to the manual gestures of the artist, something individual that becomes part of the country's heritage. This is why such products merit recognition and a dignity on a footing with that of works of art. As such they should also be protected.[125]

In opposing the standardization of what we eat and drink, the revival of so-called typical products promotes an eclectic, itinerant gastronomic model in which the greatest source of gratification is that of tasting the "authenticity" of the foods shaped by material history. The cultural significance of the phenomenon is more than a mere antidote to the inferior world of supermarkets or fast food. At a deeper level, the gastronomic treasures are a way of exorcising the discomfiture of modern day views of food.

According to Claude Fischler, the worst aspect of modern food is the way comestible goods have lost their identity. Today's consumers find it increasingly hard to recognize the soundness of foods based on culturally shared and empirically controled requisites and connotations. "Food has become an adulterated mystery, a 'non identified comestible object,' an orphan with no past or origins."[126] If we really are what we eat, but we do not know precisely what we are incorporating as we ingest prefabricated, plastified, lifeless foods, then we are bound to feel uneasy about ourselves in mind and body: "modern food no longer has an identity because it cannot be identified. As the contemporary eater continues day after day to ingest foods that he is at pains to recognize, he fears he will lose control of his body and mind, and end up wondering about his own identity."[127]

Mass production, anonymity and adulteration are not the only factors that elicit fear, however. Above all people are daunted by the collapse of the prosperity and safety promised by alimentary modernity: "progress in food was supposed to defend consumers from ancestral dangers such as shortage and decay, yet with horror we discover that it conceals new threats. The cellophane wrapped foods stacked up in the refrigerated units of supermarkets or lined up on shelves as far as the eye can see increasingly seem to be unknown objects, doubtless full of mysterious poisons."[128]

Following in the wake of the Chernobyl disaster came wine containing methanol, mad cow disease, GMOs and myriad "lesser" scandals that have taken the edge off our appetites from time to time. Clearly our questions concerning what we really ingest go beyond the sphere of our inclinations and predilections, investing a wider universe that is full of hidden dangers. In the first place, the definition of what is "good to think" thus concerns ethics and health, and only later relates to gastronomic appraisal.

Indeed, the ethics of food now largely revolves around their increasingly enigmatic nature. Appearances no longer seem to tally with substance. We cannot help wondering about the real ingredients of a given product (composition, origins, processing, preservation), and yet we are seduced by the way it looks (packaging, labels, nutritional data, commercial image). As for the health aspect, consumers are so suspicious about "modern" foods that the sensation of imminent poison actually stops them making the purchase.

The rediscovery of "gastronomic treasures" is thus intimately reassuring. By returning to foods that have survived the process of industrialization, sterilization and homogenization unharmed (or so it is believed), consumers feel they can enjoy products and tastes that are authentic and uncontaminated. By contrasting soulless, adulterated foods with products that express authenticity, those who have lost their way in the slough of despondent eating habits can hope to regain the path leading to the magical land of gastronomic beatitude.

The fact that these "treasures" were unknown to most people until recently in no way diminishes their fascination: all that is needed is an act of faith to turn them into legends. As Eric Hobsbawn has pointed out, cultural traditions can be invented *ex novo*, without diminishing their "cultural yield," that is their edifying, celebratory, ritual function.[129] The same thing is true for food, where the endorsement of tradition becomes a source of faith, reassurance and consent. All this is an imaginary version of a past that is "good to think," whereby the relics of an uncontaminated tradition seem so desirable. When we relive the magical tastes of that distant world, we enjoy something akin in its effect to the Eucharist. "Nostalgic foods are thus transformed into social prostheses: they promise to placate tensions and mop up conflict. Reference to rusticity turns a meal into an imaginary remedy for real evils."[130]

The myth of genuineness thus regains all its original power of suggestion. In contemporary Italian, the word "genuine" has gradually come to be interchangeable with "natural," despite the fact they are not really synonyms. What they do reveal is growing alarm on the part of consumers regarding the adulteration of foods. Natural has come to signify genuine, meaning pure, uncontaminated, unadulterated. Yet "genuine" expresses a sense of belonging that is extraneous to "natural." The etymology of the word makes this quite clear: "Genuine" derives from Latin *genu*, meaning knee, and pertaining to the son whom the father sat on his knee as a sign of recognition. Indeed, once this rite of acknowledgment had fallen into disuse, the term survived in *genus*, meaning gender, birth, offspring. So from the etymological point of view, "genuine" suggests an act of legitimation, the revelation of origin and descent that ratifies blood ties, intimates affiliation and celebrates an ancestral communion. On the other hand "natural," as opposed to sophisticated, adulterated, counterfeit, simply expresses the least degree of corruption as brought about by human action. Thus while genuineness relates symbolically to roots and traditions, that is to material skills refined by man and handed down from one generation to another, naturalness is simply a utopia: a "non place" freed from history and geography, a salvific haven in contrast with wretched reality. In this sense, organic products are certainly natural, but only typical products are truly genuine.

The fact that the past embodied by these products does not actually belong to us and is extraneous to our own experience and traditions in no way diminishes their desirability. Indeed, the adoptive, imaginary nature of such origins makes them all the more enticing. When select products become emblems of edible desire they undergo a sort of museumization that has much in common with forms of escapism from the psycho-sociological point of view. Having somehow escaped the ravages of time and history, the so-called gastronomic treasures appear to be living relics of a lost paradise, revealing hidden treasures to be saved from oblivion. Duly traced and documented, they will thus survive for the benefit of aspiring explorers of the lands of lost delicacies.

The "gastronaut" is able to escape the pitfalls, anxieties and repulsions of alimentary modernity by taking refuge in nostalgic myths and imaginary origins. Reaching a consolatory Ithaca is the seductive mirage of the new "gastronomic archeology," replete with "real" food fairs and "authentic" tastes.

The festival of modern food mythologies would not be complete without mentioning changes that have come about in the sphere of cooking that effectively establishes what and who is "in" when it comes to gastronomy. Inventive, skilled and ostentatious, such cuisine is the polar opposite of ordinary, everyday, family cooking, "connected to local traditions and products, to seasonal availability, to inherited expertise handed down through imitation and custom."[131]

Haute cuisine shapes the "style" of appetites, defining what people should want to eat and dictating the manners appropriate for convivial dining. In other words, it defines an *ideology of taste* as a model of refinement, providing the necessary rules in an orderly, persuasive liturgy. Precisely because this is an ideological option, it takes into account the anxieties and aspirations expressed by society. Taste is never neutral: it reflects a vision of the world that defines what is and is not desirable.

The Mediterranean diet, the French paradox and the reinvention of typical foods come across as "gastronomic restoration," whereby products that explicitly refer to the real or imaginary past are invested anew with dignity and visibility. Haute cuisine, by contrast, heads in the opposite direction, exploring, experimenting and inventing in its efforts to perfect and transcend.

This is particularly apparent in the case of Nouvelle Cuisine, which in the 1970s came to the fore as heir to French haute cuisine, but in an avowedly revolutionary fashion. The new trend in cooking emphasized experimentation, taking it to unprecedented extremes as regards style of presentation, the rhetoric of recipes, new cooking techniques, new ingredients, new combinations of tastes, a wealth of new dishes—all of which were the prerogative and privilege of good taste at the table. An overview of the main stages in this evolution helps bring to light the underlying socio-cultural premises, and the appeal of novelty.

Nouvelle Cuisine was born in France in the 1970s in overt ideological contrast and commercial competition with the Grande Cuisine of nineteenth-century origins. In this it reflected new lifestyles, including greater informality, more flexibility in social relationships, the availability of a wider range of leisure pursuits, and the tendency to pay more attention to physical form.

Refined establishment cuisine involved delicacies with mysterious names that were far from describing the content of the recipes. Dedicated to sovereigns, celebrities, improbable places, the very sound of these dishes conjured up obsolete images. It was a cuisine that had become pompous and self-satisfied, suitable for the patrons of grand hotels, a crumbling, inward-looking world that was far removed from the desire for self-affirmation of a tumultuous nascent society. People were beginning to take vacations and to travel, and with very different ideas in mind. Those were the years of the first Club Méditerranées, Spartan oases of freedom in which it was finally possible to divest oneself of the conventions and hypocrisies of middleclass respectability.

Spontaneity, *joie de vivre*, the rediscovery of nature, increasing independence in consumption and behavior, physical dynamism and a certain vanity in body care were the new tendencies in French society. The good food cult was aware of this as it intercepted the budding sensibilities of a new generation of customers.

It is no coincidence that Nouvelle Cuisine was actually born in the provinces, in an area far removed from the grand hotel circuit. The great renewal came about thanks to the efforts of "owner restaurateurs," who proved to be more flexible, responsive and imaginative in their gastronomic propositions. By making dishes lighter and simpler, with an accent on fresh produce and genuine ingredients, they moved away from the so-called "alchemic" cuisine of earlier times and established the commandments of the new gastronomic faith. "The new gastronomic paradigm seems to consist in achieving the primeval truth of foods, in capturing the deep essence of victuals. The task of revealing this categorical principle was entrusted to the art of chefs, who had to identify core tastes and pleasures in their purity, rescuing them from the dross of social codes, myths and specters. It was no longer the principle of authority that characterized the job of the chef, but a modest, tenacious ability to bring forth what was latent. The culinary warlord was replaced by the Socratic cook who could nurse gastronomic truth into being."[132]

The advent of a new style was an expression of this new sensibility, one that was destined to revolutionize the vocabulary and ways of presenting recipes. First and foremost, the language of recipes changed, moving from pompous, esoteric titles to straightforward, somewhat bucolic descriptions that abounded in terms such as "small," "young," "tender," "warm" and "light," which made the potential concoction acquire a certain gentility. This was the ecological vein of Nouvelle Cuisine: the "warm *brioche* with mountain hare, new celery fondu and home-grown green tomatoes"[133] is a celebration of the idyll of nature recovered, with wild ingredients that evoke a state of grace and innocence. In the meantime, the repeated use of euphemisms suggests the equation between small and beautiful, providing in words a positive explanation of what will soon be evident on the plate.

Such changes in content were accompanied by parallel reforms in how dishes looked: they were simplified, cut back and recomposed to enhance contrasts of color that could suggest differences of taste. Moreover, food design related to individual plates, which meant that the superabundant, sculptural emphasis of classic cuisine was replaced by a more graphic, pictorial way of presenting a dish. The new sense of composition soon spread, communicating an idea of food that was cleaner and lighter, in antithesis to the monumental, baroque taste of earlier times with its triumphant apology of excess and conspicuous waste. The minimalist delicacies embodied two essential traits: they were *photogenic* (in their ineffable elegance they first delighted the eye, and then were perceived as mouth-watering); and they tended towards *miniaturization* (the arrangement on individual plates, together with the modesty of the portions, acted as an appropriate discipline for the appetites).

From the symbolic point of view, this "calligraphic cuisine" was evidently a metaphor for the body and a votive tribute to the rising tide of body worship: if we really are what we eat, even what we perceive as visually desirable reflects our desires regarding ourselves. In presenting itself as small and nice to look at, food was proclaiming the end of the binge as a morally and aesthetically acceptable event. Body care had come to figure in Nouvelle Cuisine, indicating that in the age of inexpensive overabundance the cult of slimness could achieve its own gastronomic celebration.

The message implicit in this development was that what is aesthetically attractive gratifies the eye as much as it does the palate—indeed on occasions may satisfy the eye more than the taste buds. The age of iconophagy had thus begun, and was all set to change the way people felt about good taste at the table: henceforth images and words would increasingly pave the way for desire, arousing the imagination and thereby capturing and seducing the palate.

Forty years down the line, Nouvelle Cuisine has clearly lost the right to adopt the initial adjective. While it has undeniably imposed a certain scholastic rigor on the way people talk and write about food, all that remains of the "nouvelle" claim is the tendency to experiment. In the meantime, to designate this type of cuisine other, more fitting, epithets have come to the fore: "creative," "inventive" or simply "celebrity chef," to mention but a few.

From the aesthetic point of view, how food is presented has achieved new heights of elegance and technical skill. What we considered to be remarkably modern and trendy twenty years ago now comes across as hopelessly gauche and ungainly. Yet it is clear that the contemporary style derives directly from what went before, duly updated and improved. The same basic principles remain: serving on individual plates, the taste for minimalism and "abstract" forms, the predilection for clean colors, and the tendency to juxtapose them. The only true progress regards the perfecting of compositions.

What has changed, on the other hand, is the value system central to the cult of elegant dining, expressed in visual terms by the presentation and naming of recipes.

Nouvelle Cuisine succeeded in overcoming and renewing an approach to cooking that was artificial, cumbersome and ridiculously pompous. No elegant restaurant today claims to serve classic cuisine. Yet there is one aspect of Nouvelle Cuisine's original mission that has become increasingly sterile and specious: the return to nature and the primacy of ingredients over processing.

Food and recipes today bear the indelible mark of the celebrity chef, with all focus on effect, surprise and wonderment: "today every chef is convinced that the world is anxiously awaiting a seasonal menu of his creation, stuffed with exciting new recipes, just as fashion designers come up with their spring and fall collections. In pairing foods, what really counts is the fact that the recipe should seem original and creative—in other words "good to think." It doesn't matter that much whether it is also "good to eat," that is if the ingredients seem to be well combined when it comes to tasting. The palate has been well prepared by the story told, predigesting the whole novel. It is no longer a question of taste, so there is no need to achieve real harmony. The only real customers served by high-class restaurants are the eyes and the imagination."[134]

In electing creativity as its supreme value, *haute cuisine* has thus become mannered, and the glossy world of fashion has followed fast on its heels. This explains the urge to stupefy at all costs: a tendency that occasionally spawns something truly sublime, but that usually comes down to heavy-handed imitation resulting in a hotchpotch of preposterous "creations" that sacrifice the pleasure of taste on the altar of originality as an end in itself. Yet the perpetually reinvented menu, and its sartorial equivalent in fashion shows, is served up the world over in pretty much the same terms. *Honores mutant mores*: if the specialized press flatters chefs by turning them into legendary "designers for the palate," and if glossy magazines portray their culinary creations as though they were paintings in an exhibition, then it is hardly surprising that media and figurative visibility should take absolute pride of place.

Interweaving the beautiful and the good, visual seduction and the pleasures of the palate, is evidently not a novelty of recent years, but rather a constant theme of sumptuous cuisine, indeed its very trademark. Cultivated for centuries, the art of a fine table involves techniques and expedients aimed at embellishing the presentation of dishes. The history of this particular discipline, like that of the other major arts, reveals different periods, masters, trends, borrowings and influences.[135] In the course of time, along with the different styles, the meanings and values connected with the presentation of food also change. This is likewise true for contemporary cuisine, where the mannerist leaning has upset the order of the factors involved, such that the aim of the image of food is no longer to stimulate the appetite. As a result, aesthetics comes before technique, aspect before gastronomy, the wow factor before the response of the palate. *Haute cuisine* has turned into a branch of fashion. And what is fashion if not a delight for the eyes?

The taste for refined foods has thus become the witting hostage of media enthralment, which in its turn governs the present-day definition of culinary prestige: the illusion of appearances, the tyranny of the new, the thrill of originality ordain that the experience of taste should be subordinated to its simulacrum, that the pleasures of the palate should be subservient to those of the imagination.

All this brings us back to the odyssey of taste, and what is arguably its ultimate manifestation: the pleasures of the palate. Originally indicating a physical sense, taste was the metaphorical term coined to account for the cultural nature of the sensibility that allowed for the independence of art and the refinement of customs. This figurative meaning, which once suggested a sensor of beauty and a faculty for predilection, gradually expanded to absorb banal everyday experiences. Having become effectively equivalent to consumer civilization, it then returned to its original source of inspiration: the palate, for which it established new parameters.

Just as what is unusual, eccentric and unthinkable are deemed extraordinarily attractive in the fields of the arts and fashion, so taste pertaining to the palate is currently engulfed in a fantasy world full of tantalizing tales that lead further and further away from sensorial reality.

In our culinary phantasmagoria we pursue the mirage of ourselves. The advent of alimentary modernity has failed in its promise of universal happiness, obliging the duly disillusioned and dissatisfied to fall back on alternative solutions. Taste is both the sensor and censor of desires, oscillating between the individuality of choice and the aleatory principles that are supposed to shape such preferences. The new gastronomies thus come across as fragile, temporary constructions: therapies for the soul that provide us with an improved image of ourselves and encourage the somatization of our appetites. In our consumer behavior and the corrective measures with which we try to correct them, we end up by resembling a caricature of what we would like to be, or to avoid becoming.

What different periods and civilizations have considered "good to think" has always been a conceptual construct that absorbs and rearranges myths and legend, beliefs and observance, taboos and superstition. This is still the case today in the sphere of eating habits, which differ from those of the past on account of their debatable, transitory nature.

Another aspect of contemporary taste is the tendency to project the threshold of desire beyond actuality, towards nostalgia, magic and the intangible. In this sense, taste increasingly resembles a dream world, manipulating and distorting reality with the injection of myths, archetypes and specters. Taste thus corrects and makes up for sensorial experience, subordinating it to visionary appetites and edible infatuations: fanciful, ecstatic and enraptured, it mirrors itself in the constantly changing kaleidoscope of an imaginary world overflowing with charm and short-lived chimeras.

A brief apologue of gastronomic theogony.

Taste today cannot be ensnared by the demon of bingeing and drunkenness, by lubricious appetites, orgiastic pleasures and unbridled desires. But nor can it be trapped by the despotic god of temperance, with its concomitant repression of all drive and yearning in the name of two virtuous ideals: the aesthetics of appearances and the ethics of longevity.

By taking flight into the dream world, taste can explore distant constellations, pursue elusive meteors and explore unknown planets. In so doing it necessarily adopts a new tutelary god: "Hermes is the god who leads our dreams. A small, dubious, superficial, lying god who abandons himself to toying with the imagination."[136]

The Triumph of Pleasure

Based on the reception of beauty as a contemplative activity, aesthetics has taken on the persuasive power of a revealed truth. Like every self-respecting cult, it has also imposed its own orthodoxy and the liturgy necessary to support its dogmas. Western culture has thus used its museums, schools and academies, its intellectuals and art merchants, to spread and perpetuate the paradigm of pure taste.

Because it is interiorized like an article of faith, this paradigm has had an incontestable impact, lending itself to a wide range of distortions and misuse. To justify the aesthetics of disinterestedness, Kant had recourse to ecumenical motivations based on the dichotomy between pure and contaminated, contemplation and evasion, edifying and delectable. Since then, other dichotomies have been added to the list, thereby introducing new parameters:

highbrow *versus* lowbrow, Kultur *versus* Kitsch, and sophisticated *versus* commercial.

Reformulated in these terms, instead of acting in the interests of cultural integration, as philosophers had once believed possible, the paradigm of pure taste has been adopted as a tool of cultural exclusion and discrimination. As Bourdieu has clearly shown, rather than being a pleasure of the mind, the paradigm has worked like a sense of disgust regarding whatever is seen as being easy, and as an expression of disapproval of vulgar tastes. As such, it has become a criterion of distinction and contempt that sublimates privilege as the symbol of freedom from necessity.

Kant's edict has thus ratified the *apartheid* of tastes on the basis of the cultural practices underlying their arousal and surrounding their satisfaction [Figure 1].

One ramification of this state of affairs concerns taste as disinterestedness, which takes respectful place under the aegis of the arts and knowledge that subscribe to the same cause. Central to this system is all that can be described as classical, from literature to the theater, and music to the figurative arts. By making a museum of the past, it is possible to define and delimit the sphere in which aesthetic reception can be exercised. Located far apart from this conception is the genre that revolves around what is pleasurable, tickled by the whims of fashion and the delights of the palate so dramatically stigmatized by Kant. More recently the new arts of entertainment have added to the potential range of pleasures, thereby eliciting horrified criticism on the part of the purists, from Clement Greenberg to Theodor Adorno.

Yet it is precisely this very "taste for what is pleasurable" that has fostered new expressive genres and nurtured a flourishing cultural industry, thereby redefining the aesthetic landscape of the 1900s: fashion, film, television, pop and rock music, comics, advertising and styling (as opposed to good design) have all contributed to the advent of a new popular culture based on leisure, hedonism and consumption—in other words a world that is poles apart from the sphere of traditional folklore.

In the light of current developments in cultural consumption, the hegemony of Kantian style aesthetics pertains to a particular historic period, at this point confined to a sterile limbo by socio-cultural events and dynamics. In contemporary society, lifestyles are transitory and fragmentary, such that the paradigm of pure taste can no longer exercise the decisive power of earlier times. Though it still survives within the wide range of entertainments available to the inhabitants of the Western world, it is not predominant, but on an equal footing with many other pastimes that are equally legitimate and culturally more up to date.

Many factors have contributed to the decline of the pure taste paradigm: the growing relevance of the mass media and consumer culture, a phenomenon that has attracted increasing numbers of scholars; the postmodern revolution and the progressive decline of the cultural divide between elevated and lesser tastes; the spread to various fields of the mechanisms typical of fashion and the star system (for example, to literature and cooking).

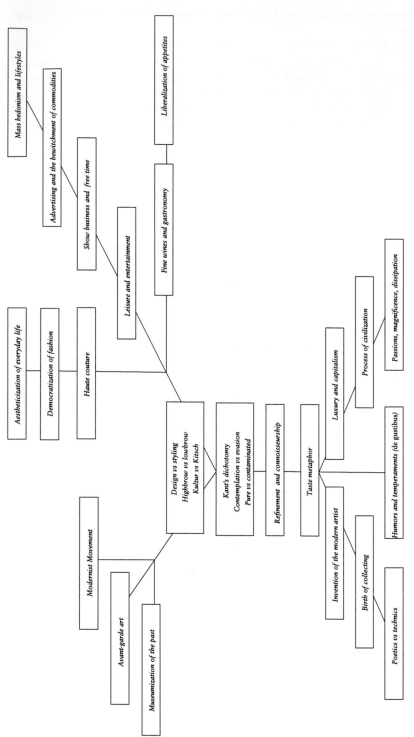

FIGURE 1 *The Tree of Tastes from its roots to the present.*

The pleasure genre has thus made headway in people's perceptions of society, easing the terms of access to the tastes of privilege. With *prêt-à-porter* and the licensing system, fashion has undergone a process of democratization, accompanied by a vast widening of choice in the field of food consumption, and thus individual appetites.

The plurality of lifestyles and the concomitant aestheticization of daily existence together decree that individual behavior is, to a certain extent, a question of personal choice. This is the culmination of a long historic and social process that began, as Sombart pointed out,[137] with the interweaving of luxury and capitalism, investing Western society as a whole, and extending its effects to increasingly widespread strata of society.

The advent of consumer society has not signified, as various moralists and old fogeys have claimed, an epidemic of bad taste and a barbarian invasion of the *hortus clausus* of symbolic and social exchange. What it has really brought about is anthropologically more interesting: the universal adoption of taste as a means for individual expression and gratification. Mass hedonism is the formula that has become part of everyday language, legitimizing the enthronement of pleasure at the top of human endeavor. The taste for what is superfluous, self-referential and ephemeral is the *forma mentis* inscribed in the collective dream of prosperity, progress and growing expectations.

Abraham Moles was right on target (albeit unwittingly, since he was a convinced imitator of the Kantian paradigm) when he used the expression "the art of happiness" as the subtitle for an essay he wrote on the psychology of kitsch,[138] which he considered a sort of pathology of the mind. If the role of taste, be it good or bad (*de gustibus*), is to investigate self-awareness by means of the emotions and pleasures that come to the fore, then the matter at stake is happiness. In the modest guise of mass hedonism, the state of inebriation, perceived by Nietzsche as the viaticum of those "strong spirits" who had freed themselves of the tame consolation of morality, amounts to a state of perpetually aroused desire: "To desire is to be happy: the satiety of happiness is simply the last instant of desire. To be full of desire with constant new desires is to be happy."[139]

Lipovetsky dealt with this subject in a recent study devoted to analyzing the mindsets and sensibilities relating to the practices of consumerism. According to the author, the myth of the *homo felix*, believed by the Enlightenment to be the supreme ideal of humankind, has found its true utopia in the profusion of material goods of consumer society. Consumer culture started to spread in the post-war period, when the accent moved from the demands of *status* to those of pleasure. Consumer culture "has decreed that hedonism should be the legitimate goal for everyone, and this has transformed the context and style of consumption, investing it with an aura of lightness and lucidity, of youthfulness and eroticism."[140]

In recent years this stage has been followed by another, which the author calls the era of hyper-consumption, characterized by the acceleration and intensification of emotional and personal gratification and experience relating to the practices of consumption: "Hyper-consumer society unfolds under the banner of happiness. The production of goods, services, media, leisure time, education, urban furnishings, everything is organized to maximize our happiness. Eating, sleeping, seducing, resting, making love, communicating with children, keeping fit: is there any sphere that still eludes the recipes for making us happy? We have passed from the closed world to the infinite universe of happiness."[141]

Clearly this is intimately connected with the individual expression of tastes in the exploration of the possible gratifications offered by the endlessly expanding world of what is pleasurable, of what can procure satisfaction.

Impure, changeable and concupiscent though it may be, taste is the true engine of consumer society, the organ of individual preferences and the tool with which people build up their personalities. Spurned by educated aesthetics, it has its revenge in ratifying an unalienable right: the search for human happiness; in other words the right to desire. To desire through taste means expressing individual aspirations, formulating a desire that shapes our daily existence: the desire that we should not be resigned to being what we are, and the hope that we may improve our lot, shape our individual personalities freely, and live life as an active project rather than suffer it as a passive fate.

NOTES

Chapter 1   The Success of a Metaphor

1 B. Croce, *Storia dell'età barocca in Italia*, Laterza, Bari, 1929.

2 F. Schümmer, *Die Entwicklung des Geschmackbegriff in der Philosophie des 17. und 18. Jahrhunderts*, "Archiv für Begriffsgeschichte," 1: 120–41, 1956.

3 U. Franckowiak, *Der gute Geschmack. Studien zur Entwicklung des Geschmackbegriff*, Fink, Munich, 1994.

4 R. Klein, *Form and Meaning. Essays on the Renaissance and Modern Art*, Princeton University Press, Princeton, 1981.

5 A. Hauser, *The Social History of Art*, Routledge, London, 1999, p. 68.

6 Hauser, see note 5, pp. 38–9.

7 Hauser, see note 5, p. 48.

8 A.K. Coomaraswamy, *Christian and Oriental Philosophy of Art*, Dover Publications, New York, 1956, p. 108.

9 A.K. Coomaraswamy, "A figure of speech or a figure of thought?," in A.K. Coomaraswamy, *Selected Papers. Traditional Art and Symbolism*, Bollingen, Dehli, 1977, p. 13.

10 Coomaraswamy, see note 8, p. 16.

11 Coomaraswamy, see note 8, pp. 64–5.

12 Coomaraswamy, see note 9, p. 14.

13 A.K. Coomaraswamy, "Ornament," in Coomaraswamy, see note 9, p. 253.

14 B. Croce, *Estetica come scienza dell'espressione linguistica generale. Teoria e storia*, Adelphi, Milan, 1990, p. 235.

15 Croce, see note 14, p. 235.

16 Croce, see note 14, p. 239.

17 B. Croce, "Iniziazione all'estetica del Settecento" (1933), in B. Croce, *Filosofia. Poesia. Storia*, Ricciardi, Milan and Naples, 1951, p. 410.

18 In the edition of 1612 and 1623, the only meaning attributed to taste is that of "pleasure, delight, appetite." In the 1691 edition, this interpretation is traced back to the Latin terms *delectatio* and *voluptas*, whereas the first meaning of taste is given as "try" (*libatio*). Moreover, the same edition ushers in the expression "good taste," restricted to the practical sense that Croce attributed to Gracián: "you can talk about having good taste in any sphere: in other words, to be intelligent." The Latin circumlocutions adopted to clarify the matter were *peritiam habere, probe callere, acri iudicio pollere*, in other words to have

practical knowledge, great skill or depth of judgment. The 1738 edition maintained the same approach, but with the additions of "*highly*" before the word "intelligent" and "intended as good."

19 Zuccolo, quoted by Croce, see note 1, p. 166, *my italics*.

20 Voltaire, "Goût," in *Encyclopédie ou dictionnaire raisonnée des sciences, des arts et des métiers*, vol. VII, Livourne, 1778, pp. 746–7. At the end of this entry, Voltaire reins in the universal extension of the metaphor: "There are many countries—he writes—as yet untouched by taste. They are those in which society has not developed, in which men and women do not resemble each other, or where certain arts such as sculpture and painting are forbidden by religion. Where there is little society, where the spirit is cramped, its stimulus is blunted: what is lacking is the matter from which taste is formed. This is why the Asians have never possessed well-made works of any sort and why taste has been the exclusive patrimony of certain peoples of Europe."

21 The term is used to refer to metaphors that are absorbed into everyday language out of necessity, without appearing to be overly manipulated: the *neck* of a bottle, the *leg* of a table, the *head* of a pin, and so on. The extended meaning of the word *taste* went one step further, however, ultimately affecting the original sense of the term.

22 "Just as the *gourmet* recognizes and immediately perceives the mixture of two liquors, so the man of taste, the *connoisseur*, will be aware at first glance of the mixing of two styles" (Voltaire, see note 20).

23 Voltaire, see note 20.

24 Montesquieu, *Essai sur le goût*, 1757.

25 Voltaire, see note 20.

26 Croce on Du Bos, in *Estetica*, see note 14, pp. 244–5.

27 Croce on Home, in *Estetica*, see note 14, p. 601.

28 A. Laurent, *De l'individualisme, enquête sur le retour de l'individu*, Presses Universitaires de France, Paris, 1985.

29 Clearly the epistemological decline of the *disputatio*, its diminishing relevance to teaching and its demise as a method for settling complex questions all contributed to the loss of validity of the medieval adage.

Chapter 2   Pleasures and Morals

1 Tacitus, *Annals*, XVI, 18. *Elegantia* is the Latin term that best sums up what we mean by taste today.

2 P. Veyne, "The Roman Empire," in P. Ariès and G. Duby (eds), *A History of Private Life: from Pagan Rome to Byzantium*, Harvard University Press, Cambridge, MA, 2003, p. 123.

3 F. Revel, *Un festin en paroles. Histoire littéraire de la sensibilité gastronomique de l'Antiquité à nos jours*, Plon, Paris, 1995, p. 53.

4 See. J. Davidson, *Courtesans and Fishcakes. The Consuming Passions of Classical Athens*, Fortuna Press, London, 1998.

5 B. Lançon, *Rome in Late Antiquity: Everyday Life and Urban Change*, Routledge, London, 2001.

6 U.E. Paoli, *Vita romana. Usi, costumi, istituzioni, tradizioni*, Mondadori, Milan, 1990, p. 96.

7 R. Flacelière, *Daily Life in Greece at the Time of Pericles*, Macmillan, New York, 1965, p. 151.

8 See C.J. Berry, *The Idea of Luxury. A Conceptual and Historical Investigation*, Cambridge University Press, Cambridge, 1994, ch. 3.

9 R. Muchembled, *L'invention de l'homme moderne. Culture et sensibilités en France du XVe au XVIIIe siècle*, Fayard, Paris, pp. 458–9, 1994.

10 See N. Elias, *The Court Society*, University College Dublin Press, Dublin, 2006; and N. Elias, *The Civilizing Process*, Blackwell, Oxford, 2000.

11 C. Casagrande and S. Vecchio, *I sette peccati capitali. Storia dei peccati nel Medioevo*, Einaudi, Turin, 2000, p. XII.

12 M. Onfray, "Sept péchés capitaux," in G. Viatte, D. Ottinger and M. Onfray, *Les Péchées capitaux*, Éditions du Centre Pompidou, Paris, 1996, p. 44.

13 Onfray, see note 12, p. 48.

14 See W. Sombart, *The Quintessence of Capitalism*, Routledge, London, 1930.

15 Elias, *The Court Society*, see note 10.

16 W. Sombart, *Luxury and Capitalism*, University of Michigan Press, Michigan, 1967.

17 Veyne, see note 2, p.179.

18 Elias, *The Court Society*, see note 10.

19 Sombart, see note 16.

20 Sombart, see note 16.

21 Sombart, see note 16.

22 Sombart, see note 16.

23 See B. de Mandeville, *The Fable of the Bees: or, Private Vices, Public Benefits* (1723).

24 Gregorius Magnus, quoted by Thomas Aquinas in *Quaestiones disputatae De malo*, q. 14, a. 1.

25 See Thomas Aquinas, *Summa theologiae* II-II, q. 148, a.6 and *Quaestiones disputatae De malo*, q. 14, a. 4

26 Thomas Aquinas, *Summa theologiae*, see note 25, q. 150, a.2.

27 Thomas Aquinas, *Summa theologiae*, see note 25, q.149. a.1.

28 Quoted in Thomas Aquinas, *Quaestiones disputatae*, see note 25, q. 148, a.4

29 Thomas Aquinas, *Quaestiones disputatae*, see note 25, q. 148, a.4.

30 Thomas Aquinas, *Quaestiones disputatae*, see note 25, q. 14, a.3.

31 Thomas Aquinas, *Quaestiones disputatae*, see note 25.

32 It is worth pointing out that in French, the term *gourmet* originally referred to wine tasters, whereas *gourmand* meant "glutton." See J.-L. Flandrin, "Distinctions through taste," in P. Ariès and G. Duby, *A History of Private Life: Passions of the Renaissance*, Harvard University Press, Cambridge, MA, 2003.

33 Thomas Aquinas, *Summa theologiae*, see note 25, q. 150, a.2.

34 *The faculties of the soul are the consequence of the temperaments of the body* is the title of a famous work by Galen.

35 Galen, *Quod animi mores corporis temperamenta sequantur*.

36 M. Jeanneret, *Des mets et des mots. Banquets et propos de table à la Renaissance*, Corti, Paris, 1987, p. 80.

37 B. Platina, *Il piacere onesto e la buona salute*, Einaudi, Turin, 1985, pp. 17–18.

38 "The civilising of appetite, if we may call it that, appears to have been partly related to the increasing security, regularity, reliability and variety of food supply. But just as the civilising of appetite was entangled with several other strands of the civilising process, including the transformation of table manners, so the improvement of food supplies was only one strand in a complex of developments within the social figuration which together exerted a compelling force over the way people behaved. The increased security of food supplies was made possible by the extension of trade, the progressive division of labour in a growing commercial economy, and also by the process of state-formation and internal pacification" (S. Mennell, *All Manners of Food. Eating and taste in England and France from Middle Ages to the Present*, University of Illinois Press, Urbana and Chicago, 1996², p. 32).

39 N. Elias, *The Civilizing Process*, see note 10.

40 M. Montanari, *La fame e l'abbondanza. Storia dell'alimentazione in Europa*, Laterza, Rome and Bari, 1993, p. 75.

41 Montanari, see note 40, pp. 106–8.

42 Mennell, see note 38, pp 33–4.

43 The very term gradually took on a different meaning: "Delicacy" initially meant the quality of being addicted to sensual pleasure and encompassed by lust and gluttony, but mostly gluttony [. . .] Delicacy was the excessive immersion in the bodily pleasure—especially that of the palate—to the exclusion of all else. But slowly the notion of delicacy got caught up in the civilization process; it got refined. Instead of referencing sin, it now referenced a delicacy of taste, a sensitivity to the elegant, to the pleasing, to refined and subtle sensation, so that from the immoral beginnings in gorging, it ends by the time Hume is writing in the first half of eighteenth century, marking feelings of modesty, and the sense of propriety, and a delicate regard for the feeling of others" (W.I. Miller, "Gluttony," in R.C. Solomon (ed.), *Wicked Pleasures*, Rowman & Littlefield, Lanham, 1999, p. 38).

44 Mennell, see note 38, p. 33.

45 Mennell, see note 38, p. 71.

46 Revel, see note 3, ch. 5.

47 P. Gillet, *Le goût et les mots. Littérature et gastronomie (XIVe–XXe siécles)*, Payot, Paris, 1993, p. 101.

48 "From the eighteenth century the belief that the quality of a food depended on the predominant humor of the eater no longer held sway. And nor did the relationship between the different national cuisines and the temperament of the nation in question. These were simply considered objectively good or bad, and that was all that mattered. And even if good taste was not evenly spread among

different nations—Voltaire discussed the matter in depth—gourmets themselves are able to appreciate good cooking wherever they happen to be. Does it not seem strange that in the seventeenth and eighteenth centuries the only good cuisines were found to be in Europe, and especially in France? No. There was no room for doubt. It became a common opinion that the French, who had learned from the Italians, had the most refined taste in the world" (J.L. Flandrin, "Dalla dietetica alla gastronomia, o la liberazione della gola," in J.-L. Flandrin and M. Montanari (eds), *Storia dell'alimentazione*, Laterza, Rome and Bari, 1997, p. 549).

49 See S. Peterson, *Acquired Taste. The French Origins of Modern Cooking*, Cornell, Ithaca and London, 1994.

50 Peterson, see note 49, p. 184.

51 Peterson, see note 49, p. 185.

52 Peterson, see note 49, p. 186.

53 Mennell, see note 38.

Chapter 3   The Birth of Aesthetics and the Bifurcation of Tastes

1 See G. Dickie, *The Century of Taste. The Philosophical Odyssey of Taste in the Eighteenth Century*, Oxford University Press, New York and Oxford, 1996.

2 Towards the end of the 1700s, Chamfort observed that "good taste and tact have more in common than many men of letters claim to believe. Tact is good taste applied to composure and conduct; and *bon ton* is good taste applied to discourse and conversation" (quoted in P. D'Angelo and S. Velotti (eds), *Il "non so che." Storia di un'idea estetica*, Aesthetica, Palermo, 1997, p. 24).

3 Voltaire, *Le Mondain*, 1736.

4 V. Bozal, *El Gusto*, Machado, Madrid, 1999.

5 W. Tatarkiewicz, *A History of Six Ideas: An Essay in Aesthetics*, Kluwer, Dordrecht, 1980, p. 139.

6 Tatarkiewicz, see note 5, p. 140.

7 See B.J. Feijóo, *Teatro crìtico universal* [1765], Tomo VI, Discurso XI, Espasa-Calpe, Madrid, 1944.

8 Feijóo, see note 7, p. 95.

9 Feijóo, see note 7, p. 100.

10 Feijóo, see note 7, p. 100.

11 Feijóo, see note 7, p. 101.

12 Feijóo, see note 7, p. 101.

13 E. Burke, *On Taste: Introductory Discourse* [1759], The Harvard Classics, Cambridge, MA, 1909–1914, p. 5.

14 Burke, see note 13, p. 6 *my italics*.

15 G. Sertoli, "Il gusto nell'Inghilterra del Settecento," in L. Russo (ed.), *Il Gusto. Storia di un'idea estetica*, cit., p. 107.

16 Sertoli, see note 15, p. 107.

17 Sertoli, see note 15, p. 106.

18 P. Bourdieu, *Les règles de l'art,* Seuil, Paris, 1992, p. 472.

19 Sertoli, see note 15, p. 102.

20 Sertoli, see note 15, p. 103.

21 S. Givone, "L'estetica del Novecento," in M. Ferraris, S. Givone and F. Vercellone, *Estetica,* Tea, Milan, 2000, p. 85.

22 D. Hume, *Of the Standard of taste* [1741], The Harvard Classics, Cambridge, MA, 1909–1914, p. 7.

23 Hume, see note 22, p. 8.

24 Hume, see note 22, p. 15.

25 Hume, see note 22, p. 9.

26 Hume, see note 22, p. 16.

27 Hume, see note 22, p. 18.

28 I. Kant, *Critique of the Power of Judgment,* Cambridge University Press, Cambridge, 2000, pp. 215–20.

29 L. Ferry, *Homo Aestheticus. The Invention of Taste in the Democratic Age,* University of Chicago Press, Chicago, 1993.

30 Ferry, see note 29, p. 58.

31 Hume, see note 22, p. 26, *my italics.*

32 See D. Summers, "Why did Kant call taste a 'common sense'?," in P. Mattick (ed.), *Eighteenth-Century Aesthetics and the Reconstruction of Art,* Cambridge University Press, Cambridge, New York and Victoria, 1993, pp. 120–51.

33 R. Schusterman, "Of the scandal of taste: social privilege as nature in the aesthetic theories of Hume and Kant," in Mattick, see note 32, p. 102.

34 Schusterman, see note 33.

35 D. Hume, "Of refinement in the arts" [1753], in D. Hume, *Political Discourses,* Part II, Essay II.

36 D. Hume, *A Treatise of Human Nature* [1739–1740], Book II, Part II, Section V.

37 D. Hume, *A Treatise of Human Nature* [1739–1740], Book III, Part III, Section I.

38 Ferry, see note 29, p. 74.

39 Tatarkiewicz, see note 5, p. 312.

40 A.G. Baumgarten, *Aesthetica,* Olms, Hildesheim, 1970.

41 C. Batteux, *Les Beaux-Arts rèduits à un même principe,* Durand, Paris, 1746.

42 See J. Barnouw, "The beginnings of 'aesthetics' and the Leibnizian Conception of sensation," in Mattick, see note 33, p. 80.

43 In his *Critique of Judgment,* see note 28, Kant used the term "aesthetic" in the etymological sense to refer to both bodily and spiritual sensitivity (in other words, the experience of beauty that was later to become its meaning).

44 J. Stolnitz, "On the origins of 'aesthetic disinterestedness' ," *Journal of Aesthetics and Art Criticism,* XX (1961), pp. 131–43.

45 I. Kant, see note 28.

46 Kant, see note 28, p. 92.

47 Kant, see note 28, p. 92.

48 Kant, see note 28, p. 93.

49 Kant, see note 28, p. 97.

50 Kant, see note 28, p. 97.

51 Kant, see note 28, p. 99.

52 Kant, see note 28, p. 106.

53 Kant, see note 28, p. 107.

54 Kant, see note 28, p. 108.

55 Kant, see note 28, p. 108.

56 Kant, see note 28, p. 94.

57 Kant, see note 28, p. 96.

58 Kant, see note 28, p. 121.

59 Kant, see note 28, pp. 165–6.

60 Summers, note 32.

61 Kant, see note 28, p. 163.

62 Kant, see note 28, p. 163.

63 Kant, see note 28, p. 165.

64 Kant, see note 28, pp. 170, 173.

65 Kant, see note 28, p. 176.

66 Kant, see note 28, p. 177.

67 Kant, see note 28, p. 185 (clearly borrowed from Batteux).

68 Kant, see note 28, p. 163.

69 Kant, see note 28, p. 163.

70 Kant, see note 28, p. 182.

71 Kant, see note 28, p. 206.

72 Kant, see note 28, p. 207.

73 Kant, see note 28, p. 211.

74 Tatarkiewicz, see note 5, p. 16.

75 Tatarkiewicz, see note 5, pp. 14, 15.

76 Tatarkiewicz, see note 5, p. 84.

77 Tatarkiewicz, see note 5, p. 84.

78 Poetry for the Ancient Greeks was always recited, never written. Moreover, there was no form of exclusively instrumental music, because the voice always played a part in it, accompanied by poetry or dance.

79 Tatarkiewicz, see note 5, p. 111.

80 Tatarkiewicz, see note 5, p. 114.

81 H.R. Jauss, *Kleine Apologie der Ästhetische Erfahrung*, Universitätsverlag, Konstanz, 1972, p. 9.

82 Jauss, see note 81, p. 10.

83 C. Korsmeyer, *Making sense of Taste. Food and Philosophy*, Cornell University Press, Ithaca and London, 1999, p. 51.

84 I. Kant, *Anthropology From a Pragmatic Point of View* [1798], Cambridge University Press, Cambridge, 2006, p. 4.

85 Kant, see note 84.

86 Kant, see note 84, my italics.

87 T. Eagleton, *The Ideology of the Aesthetic*, Oxford, Blackwell, 1990, p. 9.

88 Eagleton, see note 87, p. 23.

89 Eagleton, see note 87, pp. 93–4.

90 "There is a difficult tension within bourgeois society between the ideology of production and the ideology of consumption. Since the former realm is generally unpleasant, sanctions and disciplines are required for the subject to buckle itself in its tasks. There is no suggestion that this world of production exists *for* the subject [. . .] Like Kant's aesthetic object, the commodity would seem designed especially for our faculties, addressed to us in its very being. Viewed from the standpoint of consumption, the world is uniquely ours, shaped to nestle in our palms" (Eagleton, see note 87, p. 92).

91 Eagleton, see note 87, p. 96.

92 C. Weneger, *The Discipline of Taste and Feeling*, University of Chicago Press, Chicago and London, 1992, p. 28.

93 P. Bourdieu, *Distinction. A Social Critique of the Judgment of Taste*, Routledge, New York, 2013.

94 Bourdieu, see note 93, p. 488.

95 Bourdieu, see note 93, p. 493.

96 T. Eagleton, *The Function of Criticism*, Verso, London, 1984, p. 16.

97 N. Schneider, *Geschichte der Ästhetik von der Aufklärung bis zur Postmoderne*, Reclam, Stuttgart, 1996, p. 43.

98 Schneider, see note 97, p. 52.

99 See J.-L. Flandrin, "Distinctions through taste," in P. Ariès and G. Duby, *A History of Private Life: Passions of the Renaissance*, Harvard University Press, Cambridge, MA, 2003.

Chapter 4   The Arts of Happiness: A Journey Through Impure Tastes

1 J. de Berchoux, *La Gastronomie ou l'homme de champe à table. Poème didactique en IV chants pour servir de suite a l'Homme des champs*, Giguet et Michaud, Paris, 1801.

2 G. de la Reynière, « Itineraire nutritif ou promenade d'un gourmand dans divers quartier de Paris », 1803, reprinted in G. de la Reynière, *Ecrits gastronomiques*, 10/18, Paris, 1978, p. 233. On the same subject see also J.-P. Pitte, "Nascita e diffusione dei ristoranti," in J.-L. Flandrin and M. Montanari (eds), *Storia dell'alimentazione*, Laterza, Rome and Bari, 1997, pp. 601–9.

3 T. Zeldin, *Histoire des passions françaises 1848–1945. 3. Goût et corruption*, Seuil, Paris, 1981, p. 439.

4 J.P. Aron, *The Art of Eating in France: Manners and Menus in the Nineteenth Century*, Harper & Row, New York, 1975, p. 112.

5 J.-C. Bonnet, introduction to G. de La Reynière, *Ecrits gastronomiques*, see note 2, p. 30.

6 J.-L. Flandrin, "Gourmets, gourmands et friands," in Croniques de Platine. Pour une gastronomie historique, Jacob, Paris, 1992, pp. 93ff.

7 Bonnet, see note 5, p. 29.

8 P. Gillet, *Soyons Français à table!*, Payot, Paris, 1994, pp. 131–2.

9 J. de Berchoux would appear to have become the Baumgarten of the situation.

10 See G. Marchesi and L. Vercelloni, *La tavola imbandita. Storia estetica della cucina*, Laterza, Rome-Bari, 2001, ch. II, § 1 (*Il pasticciere architetto*).

11 Bonnet, see note 5, p. 24.

12 Gillet, see note 8, p. 133.

13 F. Portinari, "Introduction" to G. de La Reynière, *Almanacco dei buongustai seguito dal Manuale dell'Anfitrione*, Serra e Riva, Milan, 1981, p. 15.

14 Bonnet, see note 5, p. 46.

15 R. Barthes, *Physiologie du goût avec une Lecture de Roland Barthes*, Hermann, Paris, 1975, p. 8.

16 Bonnet, see note 5, p. 51.

17 J.A. Brillat-Savarin, *The Physiology of Taste*, Dover, Toronto, 2002, p. 251.

18 In Meditation XII, towards the end of an original "physiognomic analysis," Brillat-Savarin claimed the existence of a social class better suited than others to the cult of good food: "Men of finance are the heroes of *gourmandise*." To whom he added doctors, men of letters and bigots as lesser ranking priests of the new religion.

19 P.J.G. Cabanis, *Relations between the Physical and Moral Aspects of Man*, Johns Hopkins University Press, Baltimore, 1981.

20 M. Faucheux, *Fêtes de Table*, Lebaud, Paris, 1997, p. 187.

21 The complete title of Brillat-Savarin's treatise is *Physiologie du goût. Méditations de gastronomie trascendante.*

22 M. Onfray, *La raison gourmande*, Paris, Grasset, 1995, p. 114.

23 C.F. Volnay, *Tableau du climat et du sol del États Unis d'Amerique*, Courcier-Dentu, Paris, 1803.

24 See S. Moravia, "Filosofia e medicina in Francia nel XVIII secolo," in S. Moravia, *Filosofia e scienze umane nell'età dei Lumi*, Sansoni, Florence, 1982, pp. 109ff.

25 Meditation XXI of the *Physiology of Taste*, devoted to obesity, begins with a telling "If I were a trained physician" (Brillat-Savarin, see note 17, p. 172).

26 Brillat-Savarin, see note 17, Meditation XXI, p. 180.

27 Brillat-Savarin, see note 17, Meditation III, p. 33.

28 Brillat-Savarin, see note 17, Meditation XIII, pp. 126–30.

29 Brillat-Savarin, see note 17, Aphorisms, p. 4.

30 Brillat-Savarin, see note 17, Dialogue, p. 6.

31 M. Facheaux, *Fêtes de table*, Lebaud, Paris, 1997, pp. 193–4.

32 Facheaux, see note 31, p. 194.

33 Brillat-Savarin, see note 17, "Footnote of a patriotic gastronome," *Meditation* XI, p. 113.

34 This is how Brillat-Savarin liked to refer to himself, though of course no mention is made of the related seat of Academia.

35 In other words, *The Physiology of Taste* (see Brillat-Savarin, see note 17).

36 Brillat-Savarin, see note 17, p. 113.

37 H. de Balzac, *Traité de la vie élégante* [1830], Payot & Rivages, Paris, 2012.

38 See R. König, *Macht und Reiz der Mode*, Econ, Düsseldorf and Wien, 1971.

39 D. Roche, *Histoire de choses banales. Naissance de la consommation (XXVIIe–XIXe siècle)*, Fayard, Paris, 1997, p. 209.

40 The one difference lies in intensity and duration: while you can change restaurant every evening, fashion calls for devotion that lasts at least one season.

41 The period from the second half of the nineteenth century through to the early 1960s. See G. Lipovetsky, *L'empire de l'éphémère. La mode et son destin dans les sociétés modernes*, Gallimard, Paris, 1987, ch. II.

42 The "Great Sacrifice" is the historical phenomenon that marked the rejection of frivolity on the part of male elegance and the adoption in its stead of dark, drab and serious middle-class attire that stood for the new ideals of work, commitment and profit. The expression was coined by John Carl Flügel in his *Psychology of Clothes*, The Hogarth Press, London, 1930.

43 P. Perrot, *Fashioning the Bourgeoisie. A History of Clothing in the Nineteenth Century*, Princeton University Press, Princeton, 1996, p. 30.

44 See P. Sparke, *As Long as It's Pink. The Sexual Politics of Taste*, Pandora, London and San Francisco, 1995.

45 Lipovetsky, see note 41, p. 107.

46 Lipovetsky, see note 41, p. 32.

47 "Among savage peoples, clothing and decoration (like their antecedents, tattooing, painting, etc.) start anatomically at or near the genital region, and have very frequently some definite reference to a sexual occasion (puberty, marriage, etc.)" (Flügel, see note 42, p. 26).

48 Tatarkievicz, see note 5, p. 121.

49 D. Hume, *A Treatise of Human Nature*, XI (1740), Oxford University Press, Oxford, 2000.

50 G. Simmel, "Die Koketterie," in *Philosophische Kultur*, Klinkhardt, Leipzig, 1911, p. 115.

51 Voltaire, "Goût," in Encyclopédie ou dictionnaire raisonnée des sciences, des arts et des métiers, vol. VII, Livourne, 1778, p. 746.

52 I. Kant, *Anthropology from a Pragmatic Point of View* [1798], Cambridge University Press, Cambridge, 2006, pp. 142–3.

53 Kant, see note 52.

54 Kant, see note 52, p. 148.

55 See A. Schopenhauer, *Parerga and Paralipomena. A Collection of Philosophical Essays*, Cosimo, New York, 2007.

56 Schopenhauer, see note 52, p. 74.

57 Schopenhauer, see note 52, p. 75.

58 W.G. Sumner, *Folkways: A Study of the Sociological Importance of Usages, Manners, Customs, Mores, and Morals*, Ginn & Co., Boston, 1906, p. 194.

59 Lipovetsky, see note 5, p. 67.

60 Lipovetsky, see note 5, p. 68.

Chapter 5   The Economy of Taste in Consumer Society

1 É. Zola, *Au Bonheur des Dames*, Flammarion, Paris, 1999 (1883), p. 131.

2 Quoted by W. Benjamin in *The Arcades Project*, Harvard University Press, Boston, 1999, p. 31.

3 Benjamin, see note 2, p. 42.

4 Benjamin, see note 2, p. 11.

5 M.B. Miller, *The Bon Marché. Bourgeois Culture and the Department Store, 1869–1920*, Princeton University Press, Princeton, 1981, p. 183.

6 Benjamin, see note 2, p. 7.

7 O. Rühle quoted by Benjamin, see note 2, p. 181.

8 D. Harris, *Cute, Quaint, Hungry and Romantic. The Aesthetic of Consumerism*, Basic Books, New York, 2000, p. X.

9 R.H. Williams, *Dream Worlds: Mass Consumption in Late Nineteenth-Century France*, University of California Press, Berkeley and Los Angeles, 1982, p. 71.

10 P. Bourdieu, *Distinction. A Social Critique of the Judgment of Taste*, Routledge, New York, 2013, pp. 488–9.

11 Bourdieu, see note 10.

12 P. Perrot, "De l'apparat au bien-être: les avatars d'un superflu nècessaire," in J.P. Goubert (ed.), *Du luxe au confort*, Belin, Paris, 1988, p. 45.

13 See P. Sparke, *As Long as It's Pink. The Sexual Politics of Taste*, Pandora, London and San Francisco, 1995, p. 39.

14 H.P. Berlage, "Some reflections on classical architecture" (1908), in *Thoughts on Style 1886–1909*, The Getty Center Publication Program, Santa Monica, 1996, pp. 123–6.

15 A. Loos, *Ornament and Crime* (1908), Ariadne Press, Riverside, 1998, p. 167.

16 Loos, see note 15.

17 Henry Van de Velde (1863–1957) was one of the principal exponents of *Art Nouveau*.

18 Loos, see note 15, p. 155.

19 Loos, see note 15, p. 187.

20 Loos, see note 15, p. 185 (my italics).

21 S. Ewen, *All Consuming Images. The Politics of Style in Contemporary Culture*, Basic Books, New York, 1988, pp. 130–1.

22 It is no coincidence that some of the foremost names applied to this trend derived from specialized furniture stores: the *Art Nouveau* store in Paris, *Liberty's* in London, and—to a slightly lesser extent—*Tiffany* in New York. No commercial concern, however fearless in its ambition, could have volunteered to "launch" the rationalist style.

23 Le Corbusier-Saugnier, "Trois rappels à Mm. les Architectes," in *L'Esprit Nouveau*, 4 January 1921, p. 457.

24 C.G. Argan, *L'arte moderna*, Sansoni, Florence, 1988, p. 275.

25 S. Ewen, see note 21, p. 143.

26 P. Blake, *Form Follows Fiasco. Why Modern Architecture Hasn't Worked*, Atlantic and Little, Brown & Co., Boston and Toronto, 1997, p. 144.

27 Blake, see note 26, p. 138.

28 Blake, see note 26, p. 143.

29 Blake, see note 26, p. 65.

30 O. Boissière, *Streamline. Le design americain des années 30–40*, Rivage, Paris and Marseille, 1987, p. 15.

31 G. Dorfles, *Il Kitsch. Antologia del cattivo gusto*, Mazzotta, Milan, 1976[4], p. 265.

32 V. Gregotti, "Kitsch e architettura," in Dorfles, see note 31, p. 267.

33 Although it was more expressive, imaginative and colorful, the Post-Modernists did not really bring about much in the way of change regarding the received taste of the Modernist Movement. In a famous pamphlet Tom Wolfe described Post-Modernism as a form of "scholasticism" invented to "test the subtlety of other architects," in other words of orthodox Modernists (see T. Wolfe, *From Bauhaus to Our House*, Bantam Books, New York, 1999, p. 81).

34 Blake, see note 26.

35 Le Corbusier, "Eyes which do not see . . . III: Automobiles" (1921), in *Towards a New Architecture*, Dover, Mineola, NY, 1985, p. 359. The conclusion is particularly interesting: the plain "English suit" is the antithesis to the fatuity of women's fashions, while the "easel paintings" of the gentleman (as opposed to the trinkets and the naïve frescoes of the peasant) establish the proper rules of aesthetic enjoyment.

36 F. Haskell, "Enemies of Modern Art," *The New York Reviews of Books*, June 30, 1983.

37 Haskell, see note 26.

38 W. Benjamin, *The Work of Art in the Age of its Technological Reproducibility*, Belknap (Harvard University Press), Boston, 2008.

39 Much the same thing had happened five years earlier with another famous work by Duchamp, the Futuristic *Nude going down stairs n. 2*, which also met with aesthetic incomprehension, albeit of a different nature, and was rejected by the organizing committee of the Salon of Independent Artists in Paris.

40 N. Heinich, *Le triple jeu de l'art contemporain*, Les Èditions de Minuit, Paris, 1998, p. 31.

41 Heinich, see note 40, p. 34.

42 T. de Duve, *Résonances du readymade*, Chambon, Nîmes, 1989, p. 15. The snow shovel mentioned by the author refers to another famous *ready-made* by Duchamp.

43 In this regard I should like to turn to a personal memory. At the beginning of the 1970s I was fortunate enough to meet Man Ray, the artist-photographer who had been a friend and disciple of Marcel Duchamp. Man Ray told me that, greatly saddened by the latter's death, he had spent two whole days and nights of the funeral vigil photographing the artist's dead body. Although several years had gone by, he had still not found the courage to develop these photographs. One cannot help wondering what became of the films: what lost masterpieces ended up among the trash rather than being handed down to the voyeurism of posterity?

44 See J. Clair, *Sur Marcel Duchamp et la fin de l'art*, Gallimard, Paris, 2000.

45 See D. Kuspit, *Idiosyncratic Identities. Artists at the End of Avant-Garde*, Cambridge University Press, Cambridge, 1996.

46 T. de Duve, *Kant after Duchamp*, MIT Press, Cambridge, MA, 1996, p. 336.

47 O. Paz, *Marcel Duchamp: l'apparence mise à nu . . .*, Gallimard, Paris, 1977, p. 30.

48 "Taste rejects perusal and judgment, which pertain to the *gourmet*. It is torn between instinct and fashion, style and dictate. It expresses a skin-deep idea of art, something merely sensorial and social: a tickling and a sign of distinction. In the first case, taste reduces art to a sensation. In the second, it introduces a social hierarchy based on a reality that is as mysterious and arbitrary as purity or blood and color of skin. The phenomenon is more evident still in our own times: following Impressionism, painting becomes material, color, design, consistence, sensibility, sensuality. The *ready-made* is a criticism of 'retinic,' manual art" (Paz, see note 47, p. 31).

49 "The artist is not a maker; his works are not things, they are acts" (Paz, see note 47).

50 "Duchamp will have nothing to do with the idea of Beauty, and instead invents an art that is radically cerebral, conceptual and intellectual" (M. Onfray, *Antimanuel de philosophie*, Bréeal, Rosny, 2001, p. 80).

51 "If industrialization has effectively made craftsmanship pointless, then manual ability is something that an artist aware of his times must consider to be impossible. When manual skill, ability and talent are no more, all that remains is genius, or *Witz*" (de Duve, see note 42, p. 146).

52 "*Beauty flushed away.* What is the meaning of the revolution brought about by the urinal? Duchamp delivers a death sentence to Beauty, as others had to the idea of God (the French Revolution in History, or Nietzsche in philosophy). Following Duchamp, no one approaches art any more thinking of beauty, but rather of Meaning. A work of art no longer needs to be beautiful, but it is supposed to be meaningful" (Onfray, see note 50, p. 80).

53 Heinich, see note 40, p. 27.

54 See F. Guerrin and P. Montebello, *L'art. Une théologie moderne*, L'Harmattan, Paris-Montréal, 1997.

55 Heinich, see note 40, p. 313.

56 See J. Ortega y Gasset, *La deshumanización del arte*, Biblioteca de la Revista de Occidente, Madrid, 1925; A. Coomaraswamy, *Why Exhibit Works of Art?*, Luzac, London, 1943; H. Sedlmayr, *Die Revolution der modernen Kunst*, Rohwolt, Hamburg, 1955.

57 See J. Clair, *Considérations sur l'état des beaux-arts. Critique de la modernité*, Gallimard, Paris, 1983; J.-P. Domecq, *Misère de l'art. Essai sur le dernier demi-siècle de création*, Calmann-Lèvy, Paris, 1999; H. Obalk, *Andy Warhol n'est pas un grand artiste*, Flammarion, Paris, 2001.

58 B. Altshuler, *The Avant-Garde in Exhibition. New Art in the 20th Century*, University of California Press, Berkeley and Los Angeles, 1998, p. 136.

59 S. Guilbaut, *Comment New York vola l'idée d'art moderne. Expressionisme abstrait, liberté et guerre froide*, Chambon, Nîmes, 1996, p. 8.

60 "Jackson Pollock. Is he the greatest living painter in the United States?," *Life*, 8 August 1949, pp. 42–5.

61 C. Greenberg, "Avant-Garde and Kitsch," *Partisan Review*, Fall 1939, reprinted in C. Greenberg, *The Collected Essays and Criticism, 1. Perceptions and Judgments, 1939–1944*, University Chicago Press, Chicago and London, 1988, pp. 5–22.

62 C. Greenberg, see note 61, p. 14.

63 As Guilbaut has rightly observed (see note 59) he failed to appreciate that because art is the object of collective contemplation in a given historical and social context, avant-garde art is also ineluctably and eminently ideological, and indeed *a fortiori* celebrative.

64 See C. Greenberg, *Homemade Aesthetics. Observations on Art and Taste*, Oxford University Press, Oxford and New York, 1999.

65 See C. Greenberg, "Towards a newer Laocoon," *Partisan Review*, July–August 1940, reprinted in Greenberg, see note 61, pp. 23–38.

66 See A. Danto, *After the End of Art. Contemporary Art and the Pale of History*, Princeton University Press, Princeton, 1997.

67 See H. Rosenberg, *The Tradition of the New*, Horizon Press, New York, 1959, and *The De-definition of Art. Action Art from Pop to Earthworks*, Horizon Press, New York, 1972.

68 Heinich, see note 40, p. 19.

69 H. Obalk, see note 57, p. 153.

70 See H. Belting, *Das Ende des Kunstgeschichte*, Deutscher Kunstverlag, Munich, 1983; A. Danto, "The end of art," in B. Lang (ed.), *The Death of Art*, Haven, New York, 1984, pp. 3–35; R.C. Morgan, *The End of Art World*, Allworth Press, New York, 1998.

71 See J. Baudrillard, *Le complot de l'art*, Sens & Tonka, Paris, 1999.

72 See de Duve, note 42.

73 L. Ferry, *Le sens du beau. Aux origines de la culture contemporaine*, Livre de Poche, Paris, 2001, p. 16.

74 See D. Kuspit, *Psychostrategies of Avant-Garde Art*, Cambridge University Press, Cambridge, 2000.

75 G. Dorfles, *Le oscillazioni del gusto e l'arte moderna*, Lerici, Milan, 1956, p. 52.

76 Dorfles, see note 75, p. 53.

77 Ferry, see note 73, p. 21.

78 Ferry, see note 73, p. 27.

79 F. Monneyron, *De la frivolité essentielle. Du vêtement et de la mode*, Puf, Paris, 2001.

80 A fashion garment or object that carries a designer logo is thus pleonastic.

81 J. Gronow, *The Sociology of Taste*, Routledge, London and New York, 1997, p. 91.

82 See T. Agins, *The End of Fashion. How Marketing Changed the Clothing Business Forever*, Quill, New York, 2000.

83 See U. Volli, *Contro la moda*, Feltrinelli, Milan, 1988.

84 "My name has become more important than my person," as Pierre Cardin famously put it.

85 P. Bourdieu and Y. Delsaut, "Le couturier et sa griffe: contribution à une théorie de la magie," *Actes de la Recherches en Sciences Sociales*, 1: 21, January 1975.

86 Bourdieu and Delsaut, see note 85.

87 F. Lyotard, *La condition postmoderne*, Les Editions de Minuit, Paris, 1979.

88 D. Lyons, *Postmodernity*, University of Minnesota Press, Minneapolis, 1999.

89 F. Jameson, *Postmodernism, or, The Cultural Logic of Late Capitalism*, Duke University Press, Durham, 1991.

90 J. Baudrillard, *L'échange simbolique et la mort*, Gallimard, Paris, 1976.

91 M. Featherstone, *Consumer Culture and Postmodernism*, Sage, London, 1990.

92 N. Klein, *No Logo: Taking Aim at the Brand Bullies*, Picador, New York, 1999.

93 Klein, see note 92, p. 4.

94 Klein, see note 92, p. 30.

95 See L. Vercelloni, "No logo, no global, no fun. Chi è d'accordo alzi la mano," *Mark-up*, 86: 78–9, November 2001.

96 See T. Polhemus, *Street Style: from Sidewalk to Catwalk*, Thames and Hudson, London, 1994

97 F. Davis, *Fashion, Culture and Identity*, University of Chicago Press, Chicago, 1992, p. 107.

98 See M. Lee, *Fashion Victim. Our Love–Hate Relationship with Dressing, Shopping, and the Cost of Style*, Broadway Books, New York, 2003.

99 D. Richie, *The Image Factory: Fads and Fashions in Japan*, Reaktion Books, London, 2003, pp. 35–8.

100 A. Gomarasca, "Occidente estremo," in A. Gomarasca and L. Valtorta, *Sol mutante. Mode, Giovani e umori nel Giappone contemporaneo*, Costa & Nolan, Ancona-Milan, 1966, p. 30.

101 Gomarasca, see note 100, p. 39.

102 T. Miyake, "Black is beautiful. Il boom delle ganguro-gyaru," in A. Gomarasca (ed.), *La bambola e il robottone. Culture pop nel Giappone contemporaneo*, Einaudi, Turin, 2001, p. 141.

103 D. Waquet and M. Laporte, *La mode*, Puf, Paris, 1999, p. 60.

104 S. and E. Ewen, *Channels of Desire. Mass Images and the Shaping of American Consciousness*, Minnesota University Press, Minneapolis, 1992, p. 60.

105 A. Ehrenberg, *La fatigue d'être soi. Dépression et société*, Odile Jacob, Paris, 2000.

106 Ehrenberg, see note 105, p. 14.

107 Ehrenberg, see note 105, p. 277.

108 P. Bruckner, *L'euphorie perpétuelle. Essai sur le devoir de bonheur*, Grasset, Paris, 2000, p. 17.

109 Bruckner, see note 108, pp. 58–9.

110 Ehrenberg, see note 105, p. 163.

111 Ehrenberg, see note 105, p. 236.

112 C. Fischler, "Gastronomie et gastro-anomie. Sagesse du corps et crise bioculturelle de l'alimentation moderne," *Communications*, 31: 205–6, 1979.

113 C. Lévi-Strauss, *Le totémisme aujourd'hui*, Puf, Paris, 1962, p. 128.

114 See L. Vercelloni, "Big Mac 3 per cento," *Slow*, 10: 12–15, 1998.

115 A. and M. Keys, *Mangiar bene e star bene*, Piccin, Padua, 1962, p. 10.

116 L. Vercelloni, "La modernità alimentare," in *Storia d'Italia*, Annali 13, *L'alimentazione*, Einaudi, Turin, 1998, p. 973.

117 Vercelloni, see note 116, p. 978.

118 Vercelloni, see note 116, pp. 978–9. For a more detailed account of the "omnivore's paradox," see C. Fischler, *L'homnivore. Le goût, la cuisine et le corps*, Odile Jacob, Paris, 1990.

119 E. Dolnick, "Le paradoxe Français. How do the French eat all that rich food and skip the heart disease?," *Health*, 1990, pp. 41–7.

120 "*60 Minutes,*" 17 November 1991, CBS News.

121 Within a few weeks of the broadcast, a 40 percent increase on the American market, which contributed to a positive trend that continued into the following years.

122 C. Fischler, *Du Vin*, Odile Jacob, Paris, 1999, p. 183.

123 Fischler, see note 122, p. 190.

124 See G. Garrier, *Histoire sociale et culturelle du vin*, Larousse-Bordas, Paris, 1998.

125 D. Paolini, *Viaggio nei giacimenti golosi*, Mondadori, Milan, 2000, p. 7.

126 Fischler, see note 122, p. 209.

127 Fischler, see note 122, pp. 210–11.

128 Fischler, see note 112, p. 201.

129 " 'Invented tradition' is taken to mean a set of practices, normally governed by overtly or tacitly accepted rules and of a ritual or symbolic nature, which seek

to inculcate certain values and norms of behaviour by repetition, which automatically implies continuity with the past. In fact, where possible, they attempt to establish continuity with a suitable historic past" (E. Hobsbawm, "Inventing traditions," in E. Hobsbawm and T. Ranger, *The Invention of Tradition*, Cambridge University Press, Cambridge, 1983, p. 1).

130 O. Assouly, *Les nourritures nostalgiques*, Actes Sud, Arles, 2004, pp. 41–2.

131 F. Revel, *Un festin en paroles. Histoire littéraire de la sensibilité gastronomique de l'Antiquité à nos jours*, Plon, Paris, 1995, p. 36.

132 C. Fischler, "La cuisine et l'esprit de temps: quelques tendances récentes de la sensibilité alimentaire en France," in J. Labat, H. L. Nostrand and J.-C. Seigneuret, *La France en mutation depuis 1955*, Newbury House, Rowley, MA, 1979, p. 203.

133 A. Chapel, *La Cuisine c'est beaucoup plus que des recettes*, Laffont, Paris, 1980, p. 373.

134 L. Vercelloni, "Searching for lost tastes," *Slow. The International Herald of Tastes*, 5 (2002): 12.

135 See G. Marchesi and L. Vercelloni, *La tavola imbandita. Storia estetica della cucina*, Laterza, Rome-Bari, 2001, ch. II, § 1 (*Il pasticciere architetto*).

136 P. Citati, "I tiranni dell'anima," *La Repubblica*, 2 January 2004, p. 37.

137 W. Sombart, *Luxury and Capitalism*, University of Michigan Press, Michigan, 1967.

138 A. Moles, *Psychologie du Kitsch. L'art du bonheur*, Mame, Paris, 1971.

139 F. Nietzsche, *Nachgelassene Fragmente, 1882–84*, 5(1): 209.

140 G. Lipovetsky, *Le bonheur paradoxal. Essai sur la société d'hyperconsummation*, Gallimard, Paris, 2006, p. 37.

141 Lipovetsky, see note 140, p. 306.

BIBLIOGRAPHIES

Histories and Theories of Taste

Agamben, G., "Gusto," in *Enciclopedia*, vol. 6, Einaudi, Turin, 1979, pp. 1019–38.

Barrère, J.-B., *L'idée de goût de Pascal à Valery*, Klincksieck, Paris, 1972.

Baumgarten, G., *Aesthetica* [1750], Olms, Hildesheim, 1970.

Becker, G.S., *Accounting for Tastes*, Harvard University Press, Cambridge MA and London, 1996.

Bolles, R.C., *The Hedonics of Taste*, Lawrence Erlbaum Associates, Hilldale, 1991.

Bourdieu, P., *Distinction. A Social Critique of the Judgment of Taste*, Routledge, New York, 2013.

Bozal, V., *El Gusto*, Machado, Madrid, 1999.

Boyer, G., *Relativisme et Esthétique: Des goûts et des couleurs peut-on discuter?*, Éditions universitaires européennes, Sarrenbruck, 2014.

Brugère, F., *Le goût. Art, passion et société*, Puf, Paris, 2000.

Burke, E., *A Philosophical Enquiry into the Origin of our Ideas of the Sublime and Beautiful*, Oxford University Press, Oxford, 2008.

—— *On Taste: Introductory Discourse* [1759], The Harvard Classics, Cambridge, MA, 1909–14.

Cornerhouse Gallery, *The Ministry of Taste*, Manchester, 1999.

—— *Taste: The New Religion*, Manchester, 2000.

Cottom, D., "Taste and the civilized imagination," *Journal of Aesthetics and Art Criticism*, 39: 367–80, 1981.

Croce, B., *Storia dell'età barocca in Italia*, Laterza, Bari, 1929.

—— *Filosofia. Poesia. Storia*, Ricciardi, Milan and Naples, 1951.

—— *Estetica come scienza dell'espressione e linguistica generale. Teoria e storia* [1941], Adelphi, Milan, 1990.

D'Angelo P., and S. Velotti (eds), *Il "non so che." Storia di un'idea estetica*, Aesthetica, Palermo, 1997.

De Robertis, D., "'Buon Gusto' quattrocentesco," *Lingua Nostra*, V(3): 65–7, September 1974.

Descuret, G.B.F., *Théorie morale du goût, ou le goût considéré dans ses rapports avec la nature, les beaux-arts, les belles-lettres et les bonnes mœurs*, Périsse frères, Paris and Lyon, 1847.

Dickie, G., *The Century of Taste. The Philosophical Odyssey of Taste in the Eighteenth Century*, Oxford University Press, New York and Oxford, 1996.

Diderot, D., *Traité du Beau* [1751], La Republique des Lettres, Paris, 2012.

Dumayet, P., *Des goûts et des dégoûts*, L'échoppe, Paris, 1996.

Ferraris, M., S. Givone and F. Vercellone, *Estetica*, Tea, Milan, 2000.

Feijóo, B.J., *Teatro crìtico universal* [1765], Tomo VI, Discurso XI, Espasa-Calpe, Madrid, 1944.

Ferry, L., *Homo Aestheticus. The Invention of Taste in the Democratic Age*, University of Chicago Press, Chicago, 1993.

—— *Le sens du beau. Aux origines de la culture contemporaine*, Le livre de poche, Paris, 2001.

Frackowiack, U., *Der gute Geschmack. Studien zur Entwicklung des Geschmackbegriff*, Fink, Monaco, 1994.

Gang, G. and P. Ariès, *Le Goût*, Desclée de Brouwer, Paris, 1999.

Gans, H.J., *Popular Culture and High Culture. An Analysis and Evaluation of Taste*, Basic Books, New York, 1999.

Gerard, A., *An Essay on Taste*, London, 1759.

Gracián, B., *Agudeza y arte de ingenio*, Nogues, Huesca, 1648.

Gronow, J., *The Sociology of Taste*, Routledge, London and New York, 1997.

Gruyer, P., *Kant and the Claim of Taste*, Cambridge University Press, Cambridge, 1997.

—— *Knowledge, Reason, and Taste: Kant's Response to Hume*, Princeton University Press, Princeton, NJ, 2008.

Hillman, J., "Politics of beauty," in *City and Soul*, Spring, Glasgow, 2006.

Hogarth, W., *The Analysis of Beauty* [1753], Clarendon Press, Oxford, 1955.

von Hoffman, V., *Goûter le monde: une histoire culturelle du goût à l'époque moderne*, Peter Lang, Pieterlen, 2013.

Howes, D. and M. Lalonde, "the history of sensibilities: of the standard of taste in eighteenth-century England and the circulation of smells in post-revolutionary France," *Dialectical Anthropology*, 16: 125–35, 1991.

Hume, D., *A Treatise of Human Nature* [1739–1740], Book II, Part II, Section V.

—— *Of the Standard of taste* [1741], The Harvard Classics, Cambridge, MA, 1909–1914.

—— *Of Refinement in the Arts* [1753], in D. Hume, *Political Discourses*, Part II, Essay II.

Hutcheson, F., *An Inquiry into the Original of our Ideas of Beauty and Virtue* [1726], Liberty Fund, Indianapolis 2004.

Kant, I., *Critique of the Power of Judgment* [1790], Cambridge University Press, Cambridge, 2000.

—— *Anthropology from a Pragmatic Point of View* [1798], Cambridge University Press, Cambridge, 2006.

Klein, R., *Form and Meaning: Essays on the Renaissance and Modern Art* [1970], Princeton University Press, Princeton, 1980.

Korsmeyer, C., "Taste as sense and sensibility," *Philosophical Topics*, 25(1): 201–30, 1997.

—— *Making Sense of Taste. Food and Philosophy*, Cornell University Press, Ithaca and London, 1999.

Levine, L.W., *Highbrow Lowbrow. The Emergence of Cultural Hierarchy in America*, Harvard University Press, Cambridge, MA and London, 1998.

Lynes, R., *The Taste Makers*, Harper and Bros, New York, 1955.

McCracken, J., *Taste and the Household. The Domestic Aesthetic and Moral Reasoning*, State University of New York Press, Albany, 2001.

Macdonald, D., "Masscult e midcult," *Partisan review*, 27: 203–33, 1960.

Miller, W.I., *The Anatomy of Disgust*, Harvard University Press, Cambridge, MA, and London, 1997.

Montesquieu, *Essai sur le goût* [1757], Gallimard, Paris, 2010.

Muratori, L., *Riflessioni sopra il buon gusto nelle scienze e nelle arti*, Venice, 1723.

Pietra R. (ed.), *Esthétique: des goûts et des couleurs . . .*, Recherches sur la philosophie et le langage, Grenoble, 1998.

Rosenkranz, K., *Ästhetik der Häßlichen* [1853], Reclam, Dizingen, 2007.

Russo L. (ed.), *Il Gusto. Storia di un'idea estetica*, Aesthetica, Palermo, 2000.

Schümmer, F., "Die Entwicklung des Geschmackbegriff in der Philosophie des 17. und 18. Jahrhunderts," *Archiv für Begriffsgaschichte*, 1: 120–41, 1956.

Sparke, P., *As Long as It's Pink. The Sexual Politics of Taste*, Pandora, London and San Francisco, 1995.

Strube, V.W., "Zur Geschichte des Sprichworts, Über den Geschmack läßt sich nicht streiten'," *Zeitschrift für Ästhetik und Allgemeine Kunst-Wissenschaft*, XXX(1): 158–85, 1985.

Tacitus, *Annals*, XVI.

Thomas Aquinas in *Quaestiones disputatae De malo*.

Vercelloni, L., "La dichotomie chez Kant et le destin de l'agréable," in O. Assouly (ed.), *Goûts à vendre : Essais sur la captation esthétique*, IFM, Paris, 2008 pp. 75–91.

Veronese, P., *Ipotesi per una filosofia del "gusto,"* Marsilio, Venice, 1972.

Voltaire, "Goût," in *Encyclopédie ou dictionnaire raisonnée des sciences, des arts et des métiers*, tomo VII, Livourne, 1778, pp. 746–7.

Weneger, C., *The Discipline of Taste and Feeling*, University of Chicago Press, Chicago and London, 1992.

Histories of Customs, Morals, Mindsets and Sensibilities

d'Aquino, T., *Quaestiones disputatae De malo*, 1269.

—— *Summa theologiae*, 1259–1273.

de Balzac, H., *Traité de la vie élégante* [1830], Payot & Rivages, Paris, 2012.

Baudrillard, J., *L'échange simbolique et la mort*, Gallimard, Paris, 1976.

Berg, M. and H. Clifford (eds), *Consumers and luxury. Consumer culture in Europe 1650–1850*, Manchester University Press, Manchester and New York, 1999.

Berry, C.J., *The Idea of Luxury. A Conceptual and Historical Investigation*, Cambridge University Press, Cambridge, 1994.

Borghero, C. (ed.), *La polemica sul lusso nel Settecento francese*, Einaudi, Turin, 1974.

Braudel, F., *Civilisation matérielle, économie et capitalisme. XVe au XVIIIe siècle 2. Les jeux de l'échange*, Colin, Paris, 1979.

Bruckner, P., *L'euphorie perpétuelle. Essai sur le devoir de bonheur*, Grasset, Paris, 2000.

Cabanis, P.J.G., *Rapports du physique et du moral de l'homme*, Paris, 1796–1808.

Campbell, C., *The Romantic Ethic and the Spirit of Modern Consumerism*, Blackwell, Oxford, 1981.

Canévet, M., P. Adnès, W. Yeomans and A. Derville, *Les sens spirituels*, Beauchesne, Paris, 1993.

Casagrande, C. and S. Vecchio, *I sette peccati capitali. Storia dei peccati nel Medioevo*, Einaudi, Turin, 2000.

De Jean, J., *The Essence of Style. How the French Invented High Fashion, Fine Food, Chic Cafés, Style, Sophistication, and Glamour*, Free Press, New York, 2005.

Delon, M., *Le savoir-vivre libertin*, Hachette, Paris, 2000.

Ehrenberg, A., *La fatigue d'être soi. Dépression et société*, Jacob, Paris, 2000.

Elias, N., *The Court Society* [1965], University College Dublin Press, Dublin, 2006;.

—— *The Civilizing Process* [1969], Blackwell, Oxford, 2000.

Galimberti, U., *I vizi capitali e i nuovi vizi*, Feltrinelli, Milan, 2003.

Géné J.P. and M. Ndiaye, *La Gourmandise. Les Péchées capitaux.*, Éditions du Centre Pompidou, Paris, 1996.

Goubert J.P. (ed.), *Du luxe au confort*, Belin, Paris, 1988.

Jameson, F., *Postmodernism, or, The Cultural Logic of Late Capitalism*, Duke University Press, Durham, 1991.

Laurent, A., *De l'individualisme, enquête sur le retour de l'individu*, Presses Universitaires de France, Paris, 1985.

Lyons, D., *Postmodernity*, University of Minnesota Press, Minneapolis, 1999.

Lyotard, F., *La condition postmoderne*, Les Éditions de Minuit, Paris, 1979.

—— *The Postmodern Explained: Correspondence, 1982–1985*, University of Minnesota Press, Minneapolis 1993.

de Mandeville, B., *The Fable of the Bees: or, Private Vices, Public Benefits* [1723], Penguin, New York, 1989.

Marwick, A., *Beauty in History: Society, Politics and Personal Appearance c. 1500 to the Present*, Thames and Hudson, London, 1988.

Muchembled, R., *L'invention de l'homme moderne. Culture et sensibilités en France du XVe au XVIIIe siècle*, Fayard, Paris, 1988.

Perrot, P., *Le Luxe. Une richesse entre faste et confort. XVIIIe-XIXe siècles*, Du Seuil, Paris, 1995.

Robert, J.-N., *Les plaisir à Rome*, Les belles lettres, Paris, 1983.

Schimmel, S., *The Seven Deadly Sins. Jewish, Christian, and Classical Reflections on Human Psychology*, Oxford University Press, Oxford and New York, 1997.

Scruton, R., *Modern Culture*, Continuum, London, 2000^2.

Solomon R.C. (ed.), *Wicked Pleasures. Meditations on the Seven "Deadly" Sins*, Rowman & Littlefield, Lanham, 1999.

Sombart, W., *Luxury and Capitalism*, University of Michigan Press, Michigan, 1967.

—— *The Quintessence of Capitalism*, Routledge, London, 1930.

—— *Der Bourgeois. Zur Geistesgeschichte des modernen Wirtschaftsmenschen*, Duncker & Humblot, Berlin, 1913.

Sumner, W.G., *Folkways: A Study of the Sociological Importance of Usages, Manners, Customs, Mores, and Morals*, Ginn & Co., Boston, 1906.

Tseëlon, E., *The Masque of Femininity. The Presentation of Woman in Everyday Life*, Sage, London, 1995.

Verdon, J., *Le Plaisir au Moyen-âge*, Tempus, Paris, 2010.

Viatte, G., D. Ottinger and M. Onfray, *Les Péchées capitaux.*, Éditions du Centre Pompidou, Paris, 1996.

Weber, C.W., *Panem et circenses. Massenunterhaltung als Politik im antiken Rom*, Econ, Düsseldorf/Wien, 1983.

Welch, E., *Shopping in the Renaissance. Consumer Cultures in Italy 1400–1600*, Yale University Press, New Haven and London, 2005.

Zeldin, T., *Histoire des passions françaises 1848–1945. 3. Goût et corruption*, Seuil, Paris, 1981.

—— *Les françaises et l'histoire intime de l'humanite*, Fayard, Paris, 1994.

Art Criticism and History

Altshuler, B., *The Avant-Garde in Exhibition. New Art in the Twentieth Century*, University of California Press, Berkeley and Los Angeles, 1998.

Batteaux, C., *Les beaux arts reduits à un même princip*, Durand, Paris, 1746.

Baudrillard, J., *Le complot de l'art*, Sens & Tonka, Paris, 1999.

Belting, H., *Das Ende des Kunstgeschicthe?*, Deutscher Kunstverlag, Monaco, 1983.

—— *Das Bild und sein Publikum im Mittelalter: Form und Funktion früher Bildtaf. der Passion*, Mann Verlag, Berlin, 1981.

Benhamou-Huet, J., *Art Business. Le marché de l'art ou l'art de marchè*, Assouline, Paris, 2001.

Benjamin, W., *The Work of Art in the Age of its Technological Reproducibility* [1955], Harvard University Press, Boston, 2008.

Bourdieu, P., *Le règles de l'art. Genèse et structure du champ littéraire*, Seuil, Paris, 1992.

Broch, H., "Der Kitsch," in *Dichten und Erkennen*, Bd. 1, Rhein-Verlag, Zürich 1955.

Chambers, F.P., *The History of Taste. An Account of the Revolutions of Art Criticism and Theory in Europe*, Columbia University Press, New York, 1932.

Changeux, J.-P., *Raison et Plaisir*, Jacob, Paris, 1994.

Clair, J., *Considérations sur l'état des beaux-arts. Critique de la modernité*, Gallimard, Paris, 1983.

—— *Sur Marcel Duchamp et la fin de l'art*, Gallimard, Paris, 2000.

—— *De Immundo*, Galilée, Paris, 2004.

Coomaraswamy, A.K., *1: Selected Papers. Traditional Art and Symbolism* [1943], Bollingen, Dehli, 1977.

—— *Christian and Oriental Philosophy of Art*, Dover Publications, New York, 1956.

—— "A figure of speech or a figure of thought?," in *Selected Papers. Traditional Art and Symbolism*, Bollingen, Dehli, 1977.

—— "Ornament," in *Selected Papers. Traditional Art and Symbolism*, Bollingen, Dehli, 1977.

—— *Why Exhibit Works of Art?*, Luzac, London, 1943.

Crow, T., *Modern Art in Common Culture*, Yale University Press, New Haven and London, 1996.

Danto, A., *The Transfiguration of the Commonplace. A Philosophy of Art*, Harvard University Press, Cambridge, MA, 1981.

—— *After the End of Art. Contemporary Art and the Pale of History*, Princeton University Press, Princeton, 1997.

Della Volpe, G., *Storia del gusto*, Editori Riuniti, Rome, 1971.

de Duve, T., *Résonances du readymade. Duchamp entre avant-garde et tradition*, Chambon, Nîmes, 1989.

—— *Kant after Duchamp*, MIT Press, Cambridge, MA, 1996.

Dickie, G., *Art and Value*, Blackwell, Malden and Oxford, 2001.

Domecq, J.-P., *Misère de l'art. Essai sur le dernier demi-siècle de création*, Calmann-Lèvy, Paris, 1999.

Dorfles, G., *Le oscillazioni del gusto e l'arte moderna*, Lerici, Milan, 1956.

—— and J. McHale (eds), *Kitsch: The World of Bad Taste*, Bell Publishing, New York, 1969.

—— *Ultime tendenze nell'arte d'oggi*, Feltrinelli, 1999[16].

Eagleton, T., *The Function of Criticism*, Verso, London, 1984.

—— *The Ideology of the Aesthetic*, Blackwell, Oxford, 1990.

Eco, U., *History of Beauty*, Rizzoli, Milan, 2010.

Ferniot, J., *Le gout, la sentè et l'argent*, Sand, Paris, 1999.

Gilbert-Rolfe, J., *Beauty and the Contemporary Sublime*, Allworth Press, New York, 1999.

Gimpel, J., *Against Art and Artists* [1968], Polygon, Edinburgh, 1991.

Greenberg, C., *The Collected Essays and Criticism, 1. Perceptions and Judgments, 1939–1944*, University of Chicago Press, Chicago and London, 1988.

—— *Homemade Aesthetics. Observations on Art and Taste*, Oxford University Press, Oxford and New York, 1999.

Groys, B., *Du Nouveau. Essai d'économie culturelle*, Chambon, Nîmes, 1995.

Guerrin, F. and P. Montebello, *L'art. Une théologie moderne*, L'Harmattan, Paris and Montréal, 1997.

Guilbaut, S., *Comment New York vola l'idée d'art moderne. Expressionisme abstrait, liberté et guerre froide*, Chambon, Nîmes, 1996.

Hauser, A., *The Social History of Art* [1955], Routledge, London, 1999.

Haskell, F., "Enemies of modern art," *The New York Reviews of Books*, 30, 1983.

Heinich, N., *L'art contemporain exposé aux rejets*, Chambon, Nîmes, 1997.

—— *Le triple jeu de l'art contemporain*, Les Èditions de Minuit, Paris, 1998.

—— *Pour en finir avec la querelle de l'art contemporain*, L'Echoppe, Paris, 1999.

Hobsbawm, E.J., *Behind the Times: The Decline and Fall of the Twentieth-Century Avant-Gardes*, Thames and Hudson, London, 1998.

Hopkins, D., *After Modern Art. 1945–2000*, Oxford University Press, Oxford, 2000.

Jauss, H.R., *Kleine Apologie der Ästhetische Erfahrung*, Universitätsverlag, Konstanz, 1972.

Kuspit, D., *Idiosyncratic Identities. Artists at the End of Avant-Garde*, Cambridge University Press, Cambridge, 1996.

—— *Psychostrategies of Avant-Garde Art*, Cambridge University Press, Cambridge, 2000.

Lang B. (ed.), *The Death of Art*, Haven, New York, 1984.

McEvilley, T., *Art and Discontent. Theory at the Millennium*, McPherson, New York, 1991.

Mattick P. (ed.), *Eighteenth-Century Aesthetics and the Reconstruction of Art*, Cambridge University Press, Cambridge, New York and Victoria, 1993.

Messadié, G., *La messe de Saint Picasso*, Laffont, Paris, 1989.

Michaud, Y., *Critères esthétiques et jugement du goût*, Chambon, Nîmes, 1999.

Morgan, R.C., *The End of Art World*, Allworth Press, New York, 1998.

Obalk, H., *Andy Warhol n'est pas un grand artiste*, Flammarion, Paris, 2001.

Onfray, M., *Antimanuel de philosophie*, Bréal, Rosny, 2001.

Ortega, J. and Gasset, *La deshumanización del arte*, Biblioteca de la Revista de Occidente, Madrid, 1925.

Paz, O., *Marcel Duchamp: l'apparence mise à nu . . .*, Gallimard, Paris, 1977.

Perniola, M., *L'estetica del Novecento*, Il Mulino, Bologne, 1997.

—— *Disgusti. Le nuove tendenze estetiche*, Costa & Nolan, Genoa and Milan, 1998.

Rosenberg, H., *The Tradition of the New*, Horizon Press, New York, 1959.

—— *The De-definition of Art. Action Art from Pop to Earthworks*, Horizon Press, New York, 1972.

Schneider, N., *Geschichte der Ästhetik von der Aufklärung bis zur Postmoderne*, Reclam, Stuttgart, 1996.

Sedlmayr, H., *Die Revolution der modernen Kunst*, Rohwolt, Hamburg, 1955.

—— *Verlust der Mitte. Die bildende Kunst des 19. und 20. Jahrhunderts als Symptom und Symbol der Zeit*, Otto Müller Verlag, Salzburg and Wien, 1948.

Schopenhauer, A., *Parerga and Paralipomena. A Collection of Philosophical Essays*, Cosimo, New York, 2007.

Sollers, P., *La guerre du Goût*, Gallimard, Paris, 1996.

Stolnitz, J., "On the origins of 'aesthetic disinterestedness'," *Journal of Aesthetics and Art Criticism*, XX, 131–44, 1961.

Talon-Hugon, C., *Goût et degoût. L'art peut-il tout montrer?*, Chambon, Nîmes, 2003.

Tatarkiewicz, W., *A History of Six Ideas: An Essay in Aesthetics* [1976], Kluwer, Dordrecht, 1980.

Ward, P., *Kitsch in Sync. A consumer's Guide to Bad Taste*, Plexus, London, 1991.

Wolfe, T., *The Painted Word* [1975], Bantam Books, New York, 1999.

Architecture and Design

Bel Geddes, N., *Horizons* [1932], Dover, New York, 1977.

Berlage, H.P., "Some reflections on classical architecture" [1908], in *Thoughts on Style 1886–1909*, The Getty Center Publication Program, Santa Monica, 1996.

Blake, P., *Form Follows Fiasco. Why Modern Architecture Hasn't Worked* [1974], Atlantic and Little, Brown & Co., Boston and Toronto, 1997.

Boissière, O., *Streamline. Le design americain des années 30–40*, Rivage, Paris and Marseille, 1987.

Hitchcock, H.R. and P. Johnson, *The International Style* [1932], Norton, New York, 1966.

Hoffenberg, A. and A. Lapidus, *La société du design*, Puf, Paris, 1977.

Jenks, C., *The Prince, the Architects and New Wave Monarchy*, Academy Editions, London, 1988.

Le Corbusier, "Eyes which do not see . . . III: Automobiles" [1921], in *Towards a New Architecture*, Dover, Mineola, NY, 1985.

—— and J. Saugnier, "Trois rappels à Mm. les Architects" [1920], in *Towards a New Architecture*, Dover, Mineola, NY, 1985.

Loos, A., *Ornament and Crime* [1908], Ariadne Press, Riverside, 1998.

Pevsner, N., *The Sources of Modern Architecture and Design*, Thames and Hudson, London, 1968.

—— *Pioneers of Modern Design* [1943], Palazzo, Bath, 2011.

H.R.H. The Prince of Wales, *A Vision of Britain. A Personal View of Architecture*, Doubleday, London, 1989.

Ryan, D.S., *The Ideal Home through the Twentieth Century*, Hazar, London, 1977.

Wolfe, T., *From Bauhaus to Our House* [1981], Bantam Books, New York, 1999.

Food, Gastronomy and Wine

Aron, J.P., *The Art of Eating in France: Manners and Menus in the Nineteenth Century*, Harper & Row, New York, 1975.

Assouly, O., *Les nourritures nostalgiques*, Actes Sud, Arles, 2004.
—— *Le capitalisme esthétique: Essai sur l'industrialisation du goût*, Cerf, Paris, 2008.
—— (ed.), *Goûts à vendre : Essais sur la captation esthétique*, IFM, Paris, 2008.
Bancquart, M.-C., *Fin de siècle gourmande. 1880–1900*, Puf, Paris, 2001.
Barthes, R., *Physiologie du goût avec une Lecture de Roland Barthes*, Hermann, Paris, 1975.
Beardsworth, A. and T. Keil, *Sociology on the Menu. An Invitation to the Study of Food and Society*, Routledge, London and New York, 1997.
Beaugé, B., *Aventures de la cuisine française. Cinquante ans d'histoire du goût*, Nil, Paris, 1999.
—— and S. Demorand, *Les cuisines de la critique gastronomique*, Seuil, Paris, 2009.
Belasco, W.J. and P. Scranton (eds), *Food Nations: Selling Taste in Consumer Societies*, Routledge, New York, 2001.
Bell, D. and G. Valentine, *Consuming Geographies. We Are Where We Eat*, Routledge, London and New York, 1997.
de Berchoux, J., *La Gastronomie ou l'homme de champe à table. Poème didactique en IV chants pour servir de suite a l'Homme des champs*, Giguet and Michaud, Paris, 1801.
Brillat Savarin, A., *Physiologie du goût. Méditations de gastronomie trascendante*, Paris, 1826.
Bonnet, J.C., "Introduzione a Grimod de La Reynière," *Écrits gastronomiques*, 10(18): 7–92, 1978.
Boudan, C., *Géopolitique du goût. La guerre culinaire*, Puf, Paris, 2004.
Burnham, D. and O.M. Skilleas, *The Aesthetics of Wine*, Blackwell, Oxford, 2012.
Capatti, A., *Le goût du nouveau. Origines de la modernité alimentaire*, Albin Michel, Paris, 1999.
—— and M. Montanari, *Italian Cuisine. A Cultural History*, Columbia University Press, New York, 2003.
Courbeau, J.P. and J.P. Poulain, *Penser l'alimentation. Entre imaginaire et rationalité*, Privat, Toulouse, 2002.
Counihan, C., *The Anthropology of Food and Body: Gender, Meaning and Power*, Routledge, New York, 1999.
Davidson, J., *Courtesans and Fishcakes. The Consuming Passions of Classical Athens*, Fortuna Press, London, 1998.
Dermorand, N., L. Dubanchet and J.P. Géné, "La bataille du gout," *GaultMillau*, 339: 20–34, 2000.
Dolnick, E., "Le paradoxe Français. How do the French eat all that rich food and skip the heartdisease?," *In Health*, 3/4, 41–7, 1990.
—— "Beyond the French paradox," *Health*, 6/6, 40–9, 1992.
Douglas, M., "Food as an art form" [1982], in *In the Active Voice*, Routledge, London and New York, 2012.
Faucheux, M., *Fêtes de table*, Lebaud, Paris, 1997.
Fischler, C., "La cuisine et l'esprit de temps: quelques tendances récentes de la sensibilité alimentaire en France," in J. Labat, H.L. Nostrand and J.-C. Seigneuret, *La France en mutations depuis 1955*, Newbury House, Rowley, MA, 1979, pp. 191–207.
—— "Gastronomie et gastro-anomie. Sagesse du corps et crise bioculturelle de l'alimentation modern," *Communications*, 31: 189–208, 1979.

—— *L'homnivore. Le goût, la cuisine et le corps*, Odile Jacob, Paris, 1990.

—— (ed.), *Manger magique. Aliments sorciers, croyance comestibles*, Autrement, Paris, 1994.

—— *Du Vin*, Odile Jacob, Paris, 1999.

Flammang, J.A., *The Taste for Civilization: Food, Politics, and Civil Society*, University of Illinois Press, Champaign, 2009.

Flandrin, J.L., *Croniques de Platine. Pour une gastronomie historique*, Jacob, Paris, 1992.

—— "Distinctions through taste," in P. Ariès and G. Duby (eds), *A History of Private Life: Passions of the Renaissance*, Vol. 3, Harvard University Press, Cambridge, MA, 2003.

—— and M. Montanari (eds), *Storia dell'alimentazione*, Laterza, Rome and Bari, 1997.

Garrier, G., *Histoire sociale et culturelle di vin*, Larousse-Bordas, Paris.

Gault, H. and C. Millau, *Gault et Millau se mettent à table*, Stock, Paris, 1975.

Gautier, J.-F., *Le vin de la mythologie à l'œnologie. L'esprit d'une civilisation*, Féret, Bordeaux, 2003.

Giachetti, I. (ed.), *Plaisir et préferences alimentaires*, Polytechnica, Paris, 1992.

—— *Identités des mangeurs, images des aliments*, Polytechnica, Paris, 1996.

Gillet, P., *Le goût et les mots. Littérature et gastronomie (XIVe–XXe siècles)*, Payot, Paris, 1993.

—— *Soyons Français à table!*, Payot, Paris, 1994.

Grimod de La Reynière, *Écrits gastronomiques* [1804–1808], 10/18, Paris, 1978.

Guy, C., *La vie quotidienne de la société gourmande en France au XIXe siècle*, Hachette, Paris, 1971.

Jeanneret, M., *Des mets e des mots. Banquets et propos de table à la Renaissance*, Librairie José Corti, Paris, 1987.

Ketcham Wheaton, B., *L'office et la bouche, Historie des moeurs de la table en France 1300–1789* [1983], Calman-Lévy, Paris, 1984.

Lahlou, S., *Penser manger. Alimentations et représentations sociales*, Puf, Paris, 1998.

Lane, C., *The Cultivation of Taste: Chefs and the Organization of Fine Dining*, Oxford University Press, Oxford, 2014.

Lévi-Strauss, C., *Le totémisme aujourd'hui*, Puf, Paris, 1962.

Lile, P.C., *Histoire médicale du vin*, Oenoplurimedia, Chaintré, 2002.

Macbeth, H. (ed.), *Food Preference and Taste. Continuity and Change*, Berghahn Books, Providence and Oxford, 1997.

Mennell, S., *All Manners of Food. Eating and taste in England and France from Middle Ages to the Present*, University of Illinois Press, Urbana and Chicago, 1996[2].

Morton, T. (ed.), *Cultures of Taste/Theories of Appetites. Eating Romanticism*, Palgrave Macmillan, New York, 2004.

N'Diaye, C., *La gourmandise. Délices d'un péché*, Autrement, Paris, 1993.

Onfray, M., *La raison gourmande*, Grasset, Paris, 1995.

Ory, P., *Les discours gastronomique français des origines à nos jours*, Gallimard-Julliard, Paris, 1998.

Paolini, D., *Viaggio nei giacimenti golosi*, Mondadori, Milan, 2000.

—— *Il mestiere del gastronauta*, Sperling & Kupfer, Milan, 2005.

Petrini, C., *Slow Food: The Case for Taste*, Columbia University Press, New York, 2004.

——— and G. Padovani, *Slow Food Revolution*, Rizzoli, Milan, 2005.

Perdue, L., *The French Paradox and Beyond. Live Longer with Wine and the Mediterranean Lifestyle*, Renaissance Publishing, Sonoma, 1992.

Peterson, S., *Acquired Taste. The French Origins of Modern Cooking*, Cornell, Ithaca and London, 1994.

Pfirsch, J.-V., *Le saveur des sociétés*, Presses Universitaires de Rennes, Rennes, 1997.

Piault, F. (ed.), *Le mangeur. Menus, mots et maux*, Autrement, Paris, 1993.

Pinkard, S., *A Revolution in Taste: The Rise of French Cuisine, 1650–1800*, Cambridge University Press, New York, 2010.

Pitte, J.-P., *Gastronomie française. Histoire et géographie d'une passion*, Fayard, Paris, 1991.

Portinari, F., *Introduzione a Grimod de La Reynière, Almanacco dei Buongustai seguito dal Manuale dell'Anfitrione*, Serra e Riva, Milan, 1981, pp. 11–16.

Poulain, J.-P., *Sociologies de l'alimentations. Les mangeurs et l'espace social alimentaire*, Puf, Paris, 2002.

Revel, F., *Un festin en paroles. Histoire littéraire de la sensibilité gastronomique de l'Antiquité à nos jours*, Plon, Paris, 1995.

Safran, S., *L'amour gourmand. Libertinage gastronomique au XVIIIe siècle*, La Musardine, Paris, 2000.

Schivelbusch, W., *Storia dei generi voluttuari* [1980], Bruno Mondadori, Milan, 1999.

Spang, R., *The Invention of the Restaurant. Paris and Modern Gastronomic Culture*, Harvard University Press, Cambridge, MA, 2001.

Strong, J., *Educated Tastes: Food, Drink, and Connoisseur Culture*, University of Nebraska Press, Lincoln, 2011.

Telfer, E., *Food for Thought. Philosophy and Food*, Routledge, London and New York, 1996.

Vercelloni, L., "La modernità alimentare," in *Storia d'Italia, Annali 13, L'alimentazione*, Einaudi, Turin, 1998, pp. 949–1005.

——— and G. Marchesi, *La tavola imbandita. Storia estetica della cucina*, Laterza, Rome, 2001.

——— "Searching for lost tastes," *Slow. The International Herald of Tastes*, 5: 6–15, 2002.

——— "A branch of fashion," *Slow. The International Herald of Tastes*, 46: 82–5, 2004.

——— "L'esthétisation de l'appétit ou le développement de la cuisine par la mode," *Mode de recherche*, 13: 1214, 2010.

——— *Il nuovo esperanto culinario inquina le radici del gusto*, www.gastronauta.it, August 2014.

——— *Contro gli Chef*, www.gastronauta.it, August 2014.

Visser, M., *The Rituals of Dinner. The Origins, Evolutions, Eccentricities, and Meaning of Table Manners*, Penguin, New York, 1991.

Warde, A., *Consumption, Food and Taste. Culinary Antinomies and Commodity Culture*, Sage, London, 1997.

Wood, R.C., *The Sociology of Meal*, Edinburgh University Press, Edinburgh, 1995.

Consumption and Fashion

Agins, T., *The End of Fashion. How Marketing Changed the Clothing Business Forever*, Quill, New York, 2000.

Appadurai, A. (ed.), *The Social Life of Things. Commodities in Cultural Perspective*, Cambridge University Press, Cambridge, 1986.

Bauman, Z., *Consuming Life*, Polity Press, Cambridge, 2007.

Bell, D. and J. Hollows (eds), *Ordinary Lifestyles. Popular Media, Consumption and Taste*, Open University Press, New York, 2005.

Bell, Q., *On Human Finery*, The Hogarth Press, London, 1976.

Ben Ytzhak, L., *Petite histoire du maquillage*, Stock, Paris, 2000.

Benjamin, W., *The Arcades Project*, Harvard University Press, Boston, 1999.

Bourdieu, P. and Y. Delsaut, "Le couturier et sa griffe: contribution à une théorie de la mgie," *Actes de la Recherches en Sciences Sociales*, 1: 7–36, 1975.

Corrigan, P., *The Sociology of Consumption*, Sage, London, 1997.

Csikszentmihalyi, M. and E. Rochber-Halton, *The Meaning of Things. Domestic Symbols and the Self*, Cambridge University Press, Cambridge, 1981.

Davis, F., *Fashion, Culture and Identity*, University of Chicago Press, Chicago, 1992.

De Grazia, V., *Irresistibile Empire. America's Advantage through Twentieth-Century Europe*, Belknap Press, Cambridge, MA, 2006.

DeJean, J., *The Essence of Style. How the French Invented High Fashion, Fine Food, Chic Cafés, Style, Sophistication, and Glamour*, Free Press, New York, 2005.

Dorfles, G., *Mode & Modi*, Mazzotta, Milan, 1990.

—— *La moda della moda*, Costa & Nolan, Milan, 1993.

Douglas, M., *Thought Styles*, Thousand Oaks, London and New Dehli, 1996.

Ewen, S., *All Consuming Images. The Politics of Style in Contemporary Culture*, Basic Books, New York, 1988.

—— and E. Ewen, *Channels of Desire. Mass Images and the Shaping of American Consciousness*, Minnesota University Press, Minneapolis, 2000[2].

Falk, P., *The Consuming Body*, Sage, London 1994.

Featherstone, M., *Consumer Culture and Postmodernism*, Sage, London, 1990.

Flügel, J.C., *Psychology of Clothes*, Hogarth Press, London, 1930.

Forty, A., *Objects of Desire. Design and Society from Wengwood to IBM*, Pantheon Books, New York, 1986.

Gans, H.J., *Popular Culture and High Culture: An Analysis and Evaluation of Taste*, Basic Books, New York, 1999.

Gomarasca, A. (ed.), *La bambola e il robottone. Culture pop nel Giappone contemporaneo*, Einaudi, Turin, 2001.

—— and L. Valtorta, *Sol mutante. Mode, Giovani e umori nel Giappone contemporaneo*, Costa & Nolan, Ancona and Milan, 1966.

Harris, D., *Cute, Quaint, Hungry and Romantic. The Aesthetic of Consumerism*, Basic Books, New York, 2000.

Haug, W.F., *Critique of Commodity Aesthetics. Appearance, Sexuality and Advertising in Capitalist Society* [1971], University of Minnesota Press, Minneapolis, 1986.

Hebdige, D., *Hiding in the Light. On Images and Things*, Routledge, London and New York, 1988.

Hine, T., *I Want That! How We All Became Shoppers*, HarperCollins, New York, 2002.

Kammen, M.G., *American Culture, American Tastes: Social Change and the Twentieth Century*, Basic Books, New York, 2000.

Klein, N., *No Logo: Taking Aim at the Brand Bullies*, Picador, New York, 1999.

König, R., *Macht und Reiz der Mode*, Econ, Düsseldorf and Wien, 1971.

—— *Menschheit auf dem Laufsteg. Die Mode im Zivilisationsprozeß*, Carl Hanser Verlag, München, 1985.

Lafosse Dauvergne, G., *Mode & Fétichisme*, Éditions Alternatives, Paris, 2002.

Lanneglongue, M.-P., *La mode racontée à ceux qui la portent*, Hachette, Paris, 2004.

Laver, J., *Costume & Fashion*, Thames and Hudson, London, 1996.

Lemoine-Luccioni, E., *Psicoanalisi della moda* [1982], Bruno Mondadori, Milan, 2002.

Lee, M., Fashion Victim. *Our Love–Hate Relationship with Dressing, Shopping, and the Cost of Style*, Broadway Books, New York, 2003.

Lipovetsky, G., *L'empire de l'éphémère. La mode et son destin dans les sociétés modernes*, Gallimard, Paris, 1987.

Lurie, A., *The Language of Clothes*, Owl Book, New York, 2000.

Mendes, V. and A. de la Haye, *La mode au XXe siècle*, Thames and Hudson, London, 2000.

Miller, M.B., *The Bon Marché. Bourgeois Culture and the Department Store, 1869–1920*, Princeton University Press, Princeton, 1981.

Miles, S., *Consumerism as a Way of Life*, Sage, London, 1998.

Monneyron, F., *De la frivolité essentielle. Du vêtement et de la mode*, Puf, Paris, 2001.

Morton, P., *Pop Culture and Postwar American Taste*, Blackwell, Oxford, 2008.

Obalk, H., A. Soral and A. Pasche, *Le mouvements de mode expliqués aux parents*, Laffont, Paris, 1984.

Perrot, P., *Fashioning the Bourgeoisie. A History of Clothing in the Nineteenth Century* [1981], Princeton University Press, Princeton, 1996.

—— "De l'apparat au bien-être: les avatars d'un superflu necessaire," in J.P. Goubert (ed.), *Du luxe au confort*, Belin, Paris, 1988.

Polhemus, T., *Street Style: From Sidewalk to Catwalk*, Thames and Hudson, London, 1994.

—— *Style Surfing. What to wear in the 3rd Millennium*, Thames and Hudson, London, 1996.

Postrell, V., *The Substance of Style. How the Rise of Aesthetic Value is Remaking Commerce, Culture, and Consciousness*, HarperCollins, New York, 2003.

Richie, D., *The Image Factory: Fads and Fashions in Japan*, Reaktion Books, London, 2003.

Ritzer, G., *Enchanting a Disenchanted World: Revolutionizing the Means of Consumption*, Thousand Oaks, London and New Dehli, 1999.

Roche, D., *La culture des apparences. Essai sur l'Histoire du vêtement aux XVIIe et XVIIIe siècles*, Fayard, Paris, 1989.

—— *Histoire des choses banales. Naissance de la consommation (XXVIIe–XIXe siècle)*, Fayard, Paris, 1997.

Seabrook, J., *Nobrow*, Vintage Books, New York, 2000.

Simmel, G., "Die Koketterie," in *Philosophische Kultur*, Klinkhardt, Leipzig, 1911.

Stewart, S., *A Sociology of Culture, Taste and Value*, Palgrave Macmillan, London, 2013.

Tomlinson, A., *Consumption, Identity and Style. Marketing, Meanings, and the Packaging of Pleasure*, Routledge, London and New York, 1990.

Trifonas, P. and E. Balomenos, *Good Taste. How What You Choose Defines Who You Are*, Icon Books, London, 2003.

Vercelloni, L., "No logo, no global, no fun. Chi è d'accordo alzi la mano," *Mark-up*, 86: 78–9, 2001.

Volli, U., *Contro la moda*, Feltrinelli, Milan, 1988.

Waquet, D. and M. Laporte, *La mode*, Puf, Paris, 1999.

Williams, R.H., *Dream Worlds: Mass Consumption in Late Nineteenth-Century France*, University of California Press, Berkeley and Los Angeles, 1982.

Wilson, E., *Adorned in Dreams. Fashion and Modernity*, Tauris, New York, 2003.

INDEX